Divided Unions

AMERICAN GOVERNANCE: POLITICS, POLICY, AND PUBLIC LAW

Series editors:
Richard Valelly, Pamela Brandwein, Marie Gottschalk, Christopher Howard

A complete list of books in the series is available from the publisher.

Divided Unions

The Wagner Act, Federalism, and Organized Labor

Alexis N. Walker

PENN

UNIVERSITY OF PENNSYLVANIA PRESS

PHILADELPHIA

Copyright © 2020 University of Pennsylvania Press

All rights reserved. Except for brief quotations used for purposes of review or scholarly citation, none of this book may be reproduced in any form by any means without written permission from the publisher.

Published by
University of Pennsylvania Press
Philadelphia, Pennsylvania 19104-4112
www.upenn.edu/pennpress

Printed in the United States of America
on acid-free paper

10 9 8 7 6 5 4 3 2 1

Library of Congress Cataloging-in-Publication Data

Names: Walker, Alexis N., author.
Title: Divided unions : the Wagner Act, federalism, and organized labor / Alexis N. Walker.
Other titles: American governance.
Description: 1st edition. | Philadelphia : University of Pennsylvania Press, [2020] | Series: American governance: politics, policy, and public law | Includes bibliographical references and index.
Identifiers: LCCN 2019030193 | ISBN 9780812251821 (hardcover)
Subjects: LCSH: United States. National Labor Relations Act. | Labor unions—United States. | Labor unions—Law and legislation—United States. | Government employee unions—United States. | Collective bargaining—Government employees—United States. | Collective bargaining—Law and legislation—United States. | Labor unions—Political activity—United States.
Classification: LCC HD6508 .W256 2020 | DDC 331.88/1135173—dc23
LC record available at https://lccn.loc.gov/2019030193

For Casey and Rory

Contents

Chapter 1. Introduction 1

Chapter 2. The Wagner Act: A Critical Exclusion 17

Chapter 3. After Wagner (1936–1960):
   Life Without Collective Bargaining Rights 31

Chapter 4. 1961: The Public Sector's Watershed Moment 53

Chapter 5. The 1970s: Labor Out of Alignment 65

Chapter 6. The Late 1970s to the 2010s: Labor on the Decline 95

Chapter 7. The 2010s: The Modern Assault
   Against Public Sector Unions 114

Chapter 8. Conclusion: The Consequences
   of Labor's Enduring Divide 130

Appendix: Interview Method Description 147

Notes 151

Bibliography 157

Index 175

Acknowledgments 183

Chapter 1

Introduction

On February 14, 2011, Governor Scott Walker introduced his self-proclaimed "budget repair" bill in the Wisconsin state legislature that would strip most public sector employees of their collective bargaining rights. Opposition to the bill represented one of the largest, most sustained protests since the Vietnam War. For more than three weeks from February to March 2011, protestors peacefully occupied the Wisconsin State Capitol, sleeping on the hard marble floors for days on end to oppose the bill. The statehouse occupiers had traveled from across the country, and supporters nationwide called local Madison restaurants to arrange for pizza and takeout food to be delivered to those filling the capitol. Fourteen state senators camped across the border in Illinois to prevent a quorum that would allow a vote. Mass rallies were held in downtown Madison and across Wisconsin excoriating the legislation. School districts were shut down as masses of teachers called in sick and students walked out of class to attend the protests. Why did a bill dealing with the collective bargaining rights of a minority of workers in a single state galvanize Americans, liberals and conservatives alike, during those chilly weeks in February and March 2011?

Just weeks into his first term and days before introducing the bill, Governor Walker stood up at a dinner with his cabinet, held up a picture of Ronald Reagan, and said, "This may seem a little melodramatic, but 30 years ago Ronald Reagan ... had one of the most defining moments of his political career, not just his presidency, when he fired the air traffic controllers ... this may not have as broad of world applications, but in Wisconsin's history ... this is our moment. This is our time to change the course of history" (Schultze 2011).[1] Walker saw his actions through the lens of Ronald Reagan's crushing blow to organized labor. Reagan's firing of striking air traffic controllers broke the strike and the union and, for supporters, was seen as a decisive moment of presidential leadership. In the governor's mind, this would be his own crushing blow to organized labor that would recast Wisconsin politics and, with his eyes on the 2016 presidential election, further Walker's own political career.

Union leaders, union members, and their allies who opposed the bill were in agreement with Walker that the moment had significance beyond both the bill itself and Wisconsin's borders. Seven thousand protesters packed outside the Senate chamber chanted, "The whole world is watching!" as the Senate acted on the bill (NBC News 2011). But the bill's opponents interpreted the significance of the bill quite differently from the way Walker did. The battle to oppose the bill was seen as "labor's last stand" and "the death knell for Big Labor" (McAlevey 2011; Samuelson 2011). Supporters feared that organized labor, which had already become "little labor," would become "mini labor" if the bill passed (Samuelson 2011). The assault on government unions was viewed as a point of no return for organized labor in the eyes of pro-union supporters, embodying a threat to the last bastion of union power in the United States, the public sector.

On March 9, after nearly a month of protests, Republicans hastily called together a Senate-Assembly conference committee, giving the sole Democrat present, Assembly Minority Leader Peter Barca, only a few minutes to review the 138-page bill. The bill was then stripped of its fiscal provisions in a procedural maneuver, enabling the Senate to avoid the usual quorum that would require the absent fourteen senators to be present in order to pass the bill. Having bypassed the quorum, the Senate approved the bill with no Democrats present late that afternoon. The next morning, Republican lawmakers in the Assembly passed the legislation over the protests and screams of "Shame!" from Democrats (Spicuzza and Barbour 2011).

Barca described the maneuvers used to pass the bill as "trampling on democracy." His fellow Democratic assemblyman, Bob Jauch, called the methods "an act of legislative thuggery." Senate Minority Leader Mark Miller, across the border in Illinois watching the proceedings online with his fellow Democrats, said, "We saw the complete stripping of long-held rights before our eyes.... It was stunning" (Spicuzza and Barbour 2011). On March 12, an estimated 100,000–125,000 protestors surrounded the capitol to protest passage of the bill, now formally known as Act 10, after receiving Governor Walker's signature, to no avail (Stein and Marley 2013). Walker's "budget repair" bill had become law.

Act 10 dealt a crippling blow to public sector workers' collective bargaining rights and to public sector unions in Wisconsin. The legislation limited what services unions could provide their members by allowing employees to bargain only on wage increases at or below inflation while prohibiting negotiations on issues like working conditions and pensions; the Act also stipulated that any state employee who participated in a strike or other disruptive tactic like a sick-out would be fired. The law further threatened the viability of unions by requiring annual union certification elections of a majority of all workers, not just those voting in the election, and prohibiting automatic payroll deductions of union dues (Freeman and Han 2012a, 391). Certification elections and collecting union dues require significant amount of time and resources that detract from other union activities like contract negotiation and political action.

The Act has undeniably harmed public sector union viability in Wisconsin. After the Act's passage, public sector unions had to convince their membership each year that they were worth the effort of voting in the certification election, and, in turn, the union had to decide every year whether the effort of certification elections was worth the limited bargaining role now granted to them by the law. Many unions, faced with diminished options and resources, chose not to pursue recertification. As a result, public sector union density in Wisconsin dropped from 50.3 percent in 2011 to 22.7 percent in 2016. This represents a loss of over 95,000 public sector members in just five years—in a state with only approximately 350,000 union members total in 2011 (Hirsch and Macpherson 2017).[2] Wisconsin was the first state to grant public sector employees collective bargaining rights in 1959. How was Act 10 possible in a state that had been at the forefront of government unionism for over half a century?

Although Wisconsin has been the most high-profile example of attacks on public sector employees, the state is certainly not alone. Indiana governor Mitch Daniels had ended public sector collective bargaining rights in his state six years earlier in 2005, and in 2017 Iowa passed a law that is very similar to Act 10 in Wisconsin. Other states have targeted specific parts of union organizing. For instance, on February 9, 2015, newly elected Illinois governor Bruce Rauner issued an executive order dismantling compulsory union dues for state workers. These examples are just a few of the myriad pieces of legislation concerning government employee collective bargaining rights that have made their way through statehouses across the country. For example, a total of 2,355 bills concerning public sector collective bargaining were introduced in the United States from 2011 to 2015; 36 of these bills were enacted into law (NCSL

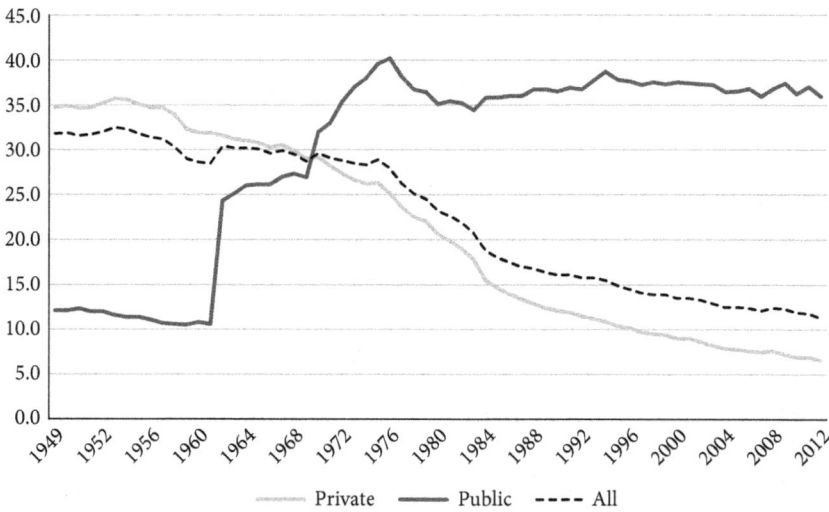

Figure 1. Public, private, and total union density as a percentage of the total workforce, 1949–2012. Jamieson 2013.

2017).[3] Only a fraction of these bills curtailed public sector collective bargaining, but the sheer number of bills and enacted laws illustrate the volatility of government employee collective bargaining rights. Of late, the fluctuation in collective bargaining rights has included the elimination of these rights for government workers in states like Wisconsin and Indiana.

Why have public sector unions been the target of conservative attacks? Moreover, why have these attacks been largely successful? To answer these questions and understand organized labor's current political weakness, it is important to explore the historical underpinnings of today's events. Conservative politicians have set their sights on scaling back public sector unions because they represent an increasingly larger share of the union movement. Over the last half century, organized labor has undergone a dramatic transformation. Public sector union members, less than 5 percent of labor's membership in the 1950s, outnumbered private sector union members for the first time in American history in 2010 (Jamieson 2013; Greenhouse 2010). As Figure 1 illustrates, private sector union density—the percentage of the private sector workforce that belongs to a union—reached its peak in the mid-1950s and has been steadily declining ever since. In contrast, public sector union density rose dramatically in the 1960s and 1970s and then plateaued at a relatively high rate of over 35 percent.[4]

Thus, because public sector union members now make up around half of the labor movement, to hobble government unions today is to hobble the labor movement as a whole. Government unions have become a target because of their growing prominence in the labor movement combined with their legal vulnerability. Public sector collective bargaining rights have a separate legal foundation from those of their private sector counterparts, which has enabled these legislative attacks. Indeed, as a result of this weaker legal foundation, government unions have faced such attacks on their collective bargaining rights for decades. The source of this legal weakness and the growth in the public sector within the labor movement have deep historical roots.

To understand today's attacks and the weakness of the contemporary labor movement, we must look back to a crucial moment in the history of American labor: the exclusion of public sector employees from the foundation of private sector labor law, the 1935 National Labor Relations Act, more informally known as the Wagner Act. The decision by the drafters of the Wagner Act to exclude government employees in 1934–1935 created separate legal and institutional jurisdictions within which private and public sector labor laws operate, which have had lasting consequences for organized labor's development.

The Wagner Act formally established private sector collective bargaining rights at the national level. This national floor of protection served as an organizing catalyst, enabling the private sector labor movement to grow by leaps and bounds in the years after passage. More recently, the failure to update the Wagner Act due to obstruction in the Senate has hobbled private sector labor's ability to organize and adapt to modern-day realities.

In contrast, the exclusion of public sector employees from the centerpiece of private sector American labor law, the Wagner Act, left the question of public sector collective bargaining rights unanswered at the federal level; this meant that individual states and localities were left to negotiate with public sector unions on their own. Public sector collective bargaining rights were slow to develop as government employees struggled to overcome public fears of their organizing and gain enough legislative momentum. Unable to ride on the coattails of private sector union growth at the national level thanks to the Wagner Act, public sector employees had to fight for legal recognition in every state and locality, which progressed slowly. Federalized, divided labor law consequently "artificially repressed" government union expansion as the absence of a national law for public sector employees dampened union organizing at the very time public sector employment began to grow (Slater 2004, 199).

When demand for public sector collective bargaining rights reached a critical mass in the 1960s, it was at the state and local levels, which had important ramifications for the quality and durability of government employees' collective bargaining rights. Having to pursue their collective bargaining rights in the states and localities not only delayed public sector union expansion but meant the fruits of public employees' struggles could not compare to those of their private sector counterparts. In contrast to the firm, standardized private sector collective bargaining rights situated at the national level—including over eighty years of case law reinforcing placement at the federal level—public sector collective bargaining rights remained an open question with passage of the Wagner Act in 1935. States and localities have had the freedom to address this question in a variety of ways and face little pressure to adhere to national standards and equal treatment within their individual jurisdictions. Instead, federalism welcomes and encourages variation and experimentation in the United States. Targeting their demand-making at the state and local levels meant government employees had some success after being shut out at the national level, but the rights they have obtained have been limited to a set number of union-friendly states—reinforcing the geographic concentration of labor—and have been erratic and subject to revision. Public sector collective bargaining rights have proven inherently more unequal and vulnerable to retrenchment as a result of the federalized nature of U.S. labor law.

Further, in the absence of a national legal provision for public sector workers, government employees' collective bargaining rights continue to be contested because they lack the national-level floor of protection that private sector employees possess thanks to the Wagner Act and decades of federal case law. At the time, the decision to exclude public sector employees from the Wagner Act was little discussed or noticed, but the exclusion put public and private sector unions on separate developmental trajectories with lasting ramifications for the strength of organized labor and the vulnerability of government unions.

American Labor's Comparative Weakness: An Enduring Puzzle

Understanding why the American labor movement is relatively weak has been an enduring puzzle; it began in 1906 when Werner Sombart famously asked, "Why is there no socialism in the United States?" The question has been expanded to ask why the United States never developed a labor party, and why total union density, even at its peak, remains much lower in the United States than in other advanced industrialized countries. To this day, we struggle to understand organized labor's weakness in the United States when viewed against labor movements in other advanced industrialized nations. This research offers a crucial missing component to help figure out this lasting puzzle: the public sector. In general, studies of organized labor pay scant attention to the public sector.[5] There is little research that explores the history of public sector unions, can shed light on the recent public sector attacks, or, on a very basic level, actually talks about the labor movement as comprised of two sectors, private and public.[6] Understanding the history and trajectory of public sector unionism can help explain labor's comparative weakness.

When we look at both the public and private sector labor movements, the traditional explanations for the private sector's comparative weakness cannot also account for the public sector. First, proponents of economic explanations for union decline see decreasing unionization in the United States as a result of deindustrialization, changing occupations, and reduced employee demand (e.g., Farber and Western 2002; Sloane and Witney 2007, 3). However, public sector union density trends do not fit these explanations: the public sector grew in a brief, sharp bout that does not track the overall steady growth of government employment, which began much earlier and continued beyond the 1960s–1970s. Further, public sector union density spread unevenly across states despite growing public sector employment across the country and remains geographically concentrated. Thus, public sector union growth does not seem to track easily with overall trends in the expansion of government employment.

Second, proponents of cultural explanations argue that the United States is exceptional in its individual, anti-statist, anti-union attitudes that have always been antithetical to union organizing (Lipset 1987, 1995, 1996; Lipset and Marks 2000; Lipset and Meltz 2004). For cultural scholars, the real question is: Why was there a spike in private sector union density during the Great Depression and World War II given the United States' cultural antipathy to unions? Their response is that this period is the great exception to Americans' traditional anti-union sentiment, and thus the decline in private sector union density since that time is just union density returning to the American cultural mean (Lipset and Meltz 2004, 174). However, the cultural explanation cannot account for the dramatic growth in the public sector. This increase occurred after the exceptional period of the 1930s and 1940s, and public sector union density has remained relatively steady. Government union expansion occurred without the unique events of war or depression to explain the rise, and it has yet to revert to an American cultural mean.

When we consider the public sector alongside the private sector, our traditional explanations for the comparative weakness of the American labor movement come up short. How can we thus explain the overall weakness of the U.S. labor movement compared to that of other nations, including both the steady decline of the private sector and the brief rise and then plateauing of public sector union density? Because economic and cultural explanations cannot answer this question for both private and public sector union development, looking at political institutions, particularly American federalism, is enlightening.

When comparing the United States to similarly advanced industrialized nations,[7] American labor law is distinct in two relevant respects. First, while these countries all have national legislation that addresses private sector labor relations, none have left their original laws largely untouched since their inception. For example, substantial amendments to private sector labor law were passed in Canada in 1995, Finland in 2001, France in 1971 and 1982, Germany in 1972, 1976, and 2004, and the United Kingdom in 1999 (Casale and Tenkorang 2008). In contrast, the foundation of American private sector labor relations, the Wagner Act (1935) and Taft-Hartley Act (1947), has remained largely intact since the passage of these two acts. The second important way in which the United States differs from other nations is with respect to the rights of public sector workers. In other industrialized nations, with very few exceptions, public sector workers possess the right to collectively bargain and "a single, national collective bargaining law prevails for all public workers" (Kearney and Mareschal 2014, 49; Casale and Tenkorang 2008; Public Services International 1985). As Chris Brewster et al. note, "In most industrialized countries, public sector employment is synonymous with unionized employment; union membership . . . has been just as much a feature of public service as employment security" (2001, 136). In contrast, there is no national-level law governing public sector workers in the United States, and various courts have held that public sector employees have no constitutional right to bargain collectively (Kearney and Mareschal 2014, 51).

Most advanced industrialized countries have seen more robust public sector union density rates compared to those in the private sector over the last half century. U.S. union density rates, however, reveal the delayed growth of the public sector compared to the private sector, as well as the very sharp rise of public sector union density and then plateauing at a relatively lower rate than in other advanced industrialized countries (Visser 2012). Whereas the rate of public sector workers' union density peaked at nearly three-fourths of all workers or more in other advanced industrialized societies, in the United States the rate has never exceeded 40 percent (Visser 2012). Across countries, economic pressures have led to decreasing private sector union density and, in general, the public sector has been more protected from these challenges. However, economic explanations cannot account for the distinct features of U.S. public sector union development. A variety of forces—economic, political, and social—shape and constrain labor unions in most advanced industrial countries, but to understand the distinct features of labor's dual trajectories in the United States requires an institutional explanation attuned to the divided nature of American labor law.

Canada is a particularly useful comparison for grasping the distinctiveness of U.S. labor law because it also has a federalized system with much of collective bargaining law set at the provincial level. However, while provinces play an important role in labor law just like the states do in the United States, since the 1960s, public sector workers in Canada have been guaranteed collective bargaining rights across the provinces and in the federal service (Farrell 2008). In Canada, public sector union density is nearly double that of the United States, and we do not see the same brief rise and then plateauing of government union density that we do in the United States. Instead, after Canada extended collective bargaining rights to government employees, public sector union density rose and kept on growing; nearly three-fourths of the sector is currently unionized (Visser 2012). The lack of a basic floor of protection and the distinct development of the public sector labor movement that followed set the United States apart, even from other federalized systems like Canada. Thus, two aspects of American labor law—the lack of private sector labor law reform and the absence of national collective bargaining rights for public sector workers—distinguish the United States from other nations. It is these institutional arrangements, more than economic or cultural forces, that have been fundamental in shaping labor's development in the United States and help explain labor's comparative weakness.

Is the Public Sector Part of the Weak Labor Movement?

It is important to pause for a moment and consider a counterclaim: some might argue that public sector unions are tangential to understanding America's weak labor movement because government unions are actually quite dominant and powerful. For instance, Terry Moe argues that teachers unions are at "the heart" of education problems in the United States as these unions, acting as special interests, have "reigned supreme," dominating education politics and collective bargaining to steer school districts in the direction of their interests rather than those of the children they are supposed to serve (2011, 6–7). Moe's portrayal overstates the dominance and power of teachers unions, and this critique can be expanded to the broader public sector union movement.

Moe portrays the power of teachers unions within school districts and education politics as in "equilibrium"; their steady membership levels and dominance have solidified over the last thirty years (2011, 48). When we examine this equilibrium in detail, however, it stands on less solid ground. First, the timing of this stable system is important for understanding labor's current weakness. Moe rightly notes that the equilibrium has only been in place for the last thirty years or so. As this book makes clear, the delayed emergence of public sector unions, including those of teachers, is consequential. Government union growth was artificially repressed, and its delayed growth during the peak of private sector union ascendance was a key missed opportunity. Thus, whatever gains have been made in the last thirty years came only after a decisive missed opportunity for the labor movement as a whole to have both the private and public sector union movements at the peak of their power.

Second, Moe's claims about the dominance of teachers unions overstate the size and scope of these unions. Moe contends that across the states, the majority of teachers are members of unions. He reports that the lowest density of union members is 35 percent in Mississippi, that only five states have membership under 50 percent, and that in half the states over 80 percent of teachers are unionized (2011, 54–55). When we look at the Current Population Survey (CPS) union membership data, however, the percentage of union members among teachers is much lower. Over the same period Moe examines, the CPS data count 52 percent of elementary, middle school, and secondary school teachers in a union (Hirsch and Macpherson 2017). These revised numbers reflect the public sector union movement more broadly, which is more robust than the private sector union movement but by no means as omnipresent as Moe suggests. Although it is true that public sector union density has remained relatively steady since the 1970s, union density in the government sector stands at just over a third of the public sector workforce.[8] This is a far cry from the high levels of public sector union membership in other advanced industrialized societies, which remain at over 50 percent in the United Kingdom, Australia, and Germany, and over 70 percent in Canada, Denmark, Finland, Norway, and Sweden (Visser 2012).

Finally, Moe's concept of equilibrium implies consistency and stability rather than change in government unionism. However, public sector labor law is neither consistent nor stable. Moe acknowledges that there is tremendous variation in collective bargaining rights for teachers across the states (2011, 56–59). When we look at all types of government employment, the variation in collective bargaining rights is even more extreme. As this book will illustrate, the reason for this variation (divided labor law) and the continued presence of variable law have limited public sector union expansion and continue to create unequal protections for government employees. Moreover, public sector collective bargaining rights remain an open question and open to contestation. For instance, since 2011, sixty-nine bills have been introduced in state legislatures across the country to eliminate automatic dues checkoff, an important tool that allows public sector unions to collect dues from the paychecks of their members (NCSL 2017).[9] Only a small fraction of these bills were successful, but they illustrate the continued volatility surrounding government unions. The level and durability of these rights have been subject to expansion and retrenchment that challenge the idea of equilibrium.

Government unions, including teachers unions, have had success and gained ground in union-friendly areas where statutes protect their collective bargaining rights. But these unions stand on shifting sands because their collective bargaining rights lack a national floor of protection. Set at the state level, government employee collective bargaining rights are open to attack. As a consequence of the most recent assaults (2009–2016), public sector union density declined from just over 37 percent to just over 34 percent (Hirsch and Macpherson 2017). This represents a decline of nearly eight hundred thousand union members in a labor movement of around fifteen million union members, a decline of just over 5 percent.[10] Thus, when it comes to total membership levels and legal protections, the public sector union movement is not necessarily as stable as we might first assume. As a result of divided labor law, the power government unions have gained in the last thirty years came late, was geographically limited, was unequal to that of their private sector counterparts, and was subject to attack and retrenchment.

Labor Law and Federalism

The federalized nature of American labor law has had important consequences for the development of organized labor in the United States. In particular, the exclusion of public sector employees from the Wagner Act created a durable divide between public and private sector labor law. Private sector labor law was placed firmly at the national level with a growing body of case law to reinforce this position. In contrast, public sector collective bargaining was an open question. Barring public sector employees from the cornerstone of private sector labor law delayed public sector union expansion as government employees struggled to gain legal recognition at the state and local levels—sites where the fruits of their struggle would never compare to those of their private sector counterparts.

Federalism has played a crucial role in constraining and shaping the development of organized labor in the United States. There is a tendency to assume that federal arrangements that empower states and localities are either positive, enabling innovation at the local level (Skocpol 1992; Freeman and Rogers 2007), or negative, enabling bastions of prejudice to be formalized into law (Mettler 1998). As the following analysis will demonstrate, both assessments of federalism are accurate when looking at organized labor. However, previous research has underemphasized a central feature of American federalism that is clearly illustrated by the distinct paths of public and private sector labor in the United States: federalism's results are inconsistent not just because states and localities have been laboratories for both liberal and conservative causes but also because laws made at the state level lack the protections and egalitarianism of those set at the national level.

Rights and privileges granted at the state and local levels are not only unequal but also inherently more tenuous compared to national-level rights because: (a) at any time, a state or locality has abundant examples of policy alternatives in action; (b) groups engaged in political conflicts that have become intractable at the national level can find more success capturing politics at lower levels of government; (c) national-level rights become reinforcing as case law over time creates path-dependent pressures to maintain existing law; (d) federalism as a governing structure welcomes and even encourages variation and innovation at the local level; and (e) most fundamentally, states and localities lack the expectations of national standards and equality—in other words, a floor of protection—that have been central to rights protections at the national level. A floor of protection is a crucial foundation for union growth. Thus, dividing public and private sector labor law not only set labor on two different paths but also made them inherently unequal: public sector labor law has had more room for innovation, but the rights and standards established have been more vulnerable to outright retrenchment of collective bargaining rights. The gains they have been able to achieve at the state and local levels have been mixed, unequal, and tenuous in comparison to the Wagner Act's unswerving commitment to all private sector workers. In order to understand the development of organized labor, a seemingly private organization, over the last half century, we must be attentive to the ways government policy has patterned labor relations. Labor's enduring divide began with an ostensibly minor decision within one clause of the Wagner Act that has had far-reaching ramifications.

Economic Inequality: Labor's Continued Relevance and Importance

Tracing organized labor's development over the last half century can seem distant and removed from modern-day politics. But exploring how federalized labor law has shaped the size, composition, organizational cohesion, and, ultimately, success of organized labor is of crucial importance because organized labor has a unique role in American politics. Terry Moe, writing about teachers unions, argues that "union leaders are special interest advocates" and their unions are "special interest organizations" (2011, 21). While labor unions undoubtedly focus on their members' and their organizations' interests, it is a mistake to classify unions as purely self-interested. Labor is not simply one among many interest groups in the United States. Despite declining union density, there are over 14 million union members in the United States (Hirsch and Macpherson 2017). Union density may have been cut more than in half since the peak in 1953, but the number of union members has declined by less than 3.5 million from the 1953 level (Jamieson 2013). Today's 14 million members and their labor unions represent a highly active, organizationally sophisticated group working on behalf of not only their members but also the larger cause of working America.

Labor's unique position in American politics is quantifiable. American labor unions continue to act mutually as a fundamental financial and an organizational arm of the Democratic Party. They are consistently among the top contributors to federal elections and spenders of independent expenditures through PACs, and this money is overwhelmingly directed to Democratic candidates (Francia 2010, 294). This leads Dorian Warren to conclude that "measured by both members and money, the labor movement is the most powerful and resourceful political constituency on the political left in American politics" (2010, 848). Labor's power lies largely in their get out the vote (GOTV) efforts during elections. During the 2008 presidential election, the

AFL-CIO's GOTV efforts "included knocking on 10 million doors, distributing 27 million flyers at worksites, sending 57 million political mailers, and making 70 million phone calls to encourage union voters to go to the polls." Likewise, Change to Win, a coalition of labor unions, "dedicated 1,500 organizers to their member-to-member voter canvass, made 20 million phone calls, sent 10 million pieces of direct mail, and enlisted the help of 50,000 volunteers on Election Day" (Orr and Francia 2012). Unions continue to field an impressive ground game in American elections.

Labor's influence in American politics is most evident in the grassroots mobilization of their membership; union members compose a disproportionate share of the voting population. Peter Francia estimates that "union households accounted for more than one of every five voters in the 2004, 2006, and 2008 elections" (2012, 4). Broken down by region, "three of every ten voters in the Northeast came from union households in both the 2004 and 2008 elections" (4). In the Midwest, 25–30 percent of the electorate in the 2004, 2006, and 2008 elections were union members. In the West, more than 20 percent of the electorate in the 2004 and 2008 elections were union households. Few other organizations can claim the membership size, political influence, grassroots mobilization, and ideological commitment of organized labor.

Organized labor is a unique force of singular importance on the American left in U.S. politics. Thus the vulnerability of organized labor is of concern because of the central role the labor movement plays in American politics and, further, because of the growth in economic inequality and insecurity in the United States. The United States "now possesses a small class of very rich Americans who are much richer than other Americans, than the affluent of other nations, and than American elites in historical perspective" while at the very same time the majority of Americans are working more hours but experiencing greater income volatility and lack the economic security they had in the mid-twentieth century (Hacker, Mettler, and Soss 2007, 7). These economic trends are neither natural nor inevitable, and organized labor's declining density has "abetted rising inequality" (Hacker and Pierson 2010, 57). Organized labor boosts wages and benefits and, more significantly, has "had a much broader and less appreciated effect on the distribution of American economic rewards" by offering "an organizational counterweight to the power of those at the top" (57). Thus, with the decline of union density, "middle- and working-class Americans lost a powerful, vigorous champion on pocketbook issues" (143). The labor movement has served as a key force in

American politics, helping elect candidates and lobby on behalf of policies to assist working Americans, while simultaneously mobilizing and engaging a broad swath of voters. But labor's important role in American politics is under threat by declining union density. Public sector unions are the last bulwark of union power, one of the final counterweights to redress rising economic inequality and insecurity in the United States. Why, given that organized labor is the best-positioned group to lobby on behalf of working Americans, particularly to reduce rising income inequality, are unions in decline, their political and economic power waning?

Understanding why public sector unions are vulnerable to retrenchment of their collective bargaining rights and, more broadly, why the labor movement is comparatively weak is of crucial importance. For this reason, this book is focused on studying private *and* public sector unions over the last century—we cannot understand organized labor today without tracing both sectors' historical development. The most recent attacks on public sector unions, the organizational divides between public and private sector unions, and the changing composition of union membership all have their roots in policy decisions made over eighty years ago.

Overview of the Book

The rest of the book follows chronologically the path of public and private sector union development, illustrating how a seemingly minor exclusion in the Wagner Act has set public and private sector unions on separate development paths that continue to resonate today. In doing so, the links between past decisions and today's labor movement as well as the powerful role of federalism in shaping organized labor will become clear. Chapter 2 details the exclusion of public sector employees from the 1935 Wagner Act, setting up the critical moment that is the turning point for public and private sector unions. Chapter 3 discusses the peak of private sector union membership, the 1940s and 1950s, and how public sector unions missed this key moment. This chapter demonstrates how public sector unionism was artificially repressed and reflects on what the labor movement could have achieved with a vibrant public sector union movement growing in tandem with the private sector. Chapter 4 describes events in 1961 that were a watershed moment for the emergence of public sector collective bargaining laws in the 1960s. The chapter further discusses the unique form of these laws—piecemeal and set at the state level—and the consequences of this federal arrangement.

Chapter 5 explores the beginning of organized labor's decline in the 1970s and how the separate development paths of public and private sector unions led to conflict rather than cooperation in facing these challenges. Specifically, public sector unions came under attack during the fiscal crises and tax revolts of this period. Rather than support them, private sector union members were sometimes part of the backlash against government unions. Chapter 6 provides an overview of organized labor from the 1980s onward as a movement on the defensive, one that was just beginning to unify public and private sector unions with mixed results because they had missed the optimal time period for cooperation and success—the mid-twentieth century. Chapter 7 examines the wave of legislation that attacked public sector collective bargaining rights across the country in 2011 and situates the book's broader argument within the events that occurred in Wisconsin in 2011, illustrating how the course of labor's development has led to today's weak labor movement and rendered public sector unions vulnerable and under attack. Chapter 8 brings together the historical story of earlier chapters to assess the consequences of labor's dual trajectories, linking the historical overview to larger conclusions about federalism and labor's current political weakness. The chapter concludes by offering an outlook for the future of organized labor, the dangers of a weak labor movement, and specific policy suggestions, namely a unified, national labor law.

Chapter 2

The Wagner Act: A Critical Exclusion

To understand labor's comparative weakness and the distinct paths of public and private sector unions in the United States, we must begin with the 1935 National Labor Relations Act (NLRA). Also known as the Wagner Act, the NLRA was a cornerstone of New Deal legislation and the foundation for modern-day private sector labor law. The Wagner Act provided federal protections to private sector workers' efforts to unionize, outlined anti-union practices employers could no longer utilize, and put in place the National Labor Relations Board (NLRB) to oversee union representation elections, adjudicate complaints, and interpret the Act in subsequent cases.

The NLRA is known as the Wagner Act because of the pivotal role Senator Robert F. Wagner played in the Act's drafting and passage. It was Wagner's singular persistence that enabled the labor disputes bill to overcome employer opposition and White House indifference to become law (Morris 2005, 64). Senator Wagner was inspired to draft the Act because of his time serving as head of the National Labor Board (NLB) from 1933 to 1934 where he experienced mounting frustration as existing statutes lacked the specificity and enforcement tools to protect the right to unionize in the face of employer resistance. During his tenure on the NLB, Senator Wagner instructed his legislative aide, Leon Keyserling, and his staff to draft a new law that would specifically outline illegal employer practices and enable American workers to bargain collectively. The resulting Wagner Act is notable for its bold commitment to employee rights, particularly the opening proclamation that "employees shall have the right to self-organization, to form, join, or assist labor organizations, to bargain collectively through representatives of their own choosing, and to engage in other concerted activities for the purpose of collective bargaining or other mutual aid or protection" (NLRA 1935, Sec. 7). By establishing employees' right to self-organize and collectively bargain, the Act affirms employees' right to join unions, placing the federal government firmly in the middle of industrial relations (Gross 2003, 1).

The bold and unswerving commitment to workers' rights did not apply equally to all workers, however. In an acknowledgment of the tenuousness of the New Deal coalition, particularly the southern Democratic wing, the definition of "employees" in the Act excluded agricultural laborers and domestic servants (Bernstein 1950, 91; Labor Department 1934). In addition, employers in the Act were defined as "any person acting as an agent of an employer, directly or indirectly, but shall not include the United States or any wholly owned Government corporation, or any Federal Reserve Bank, or any State or political subdivision thereof," thereby excluding public sector workers (NLRA 1935, Sec. 2). The exclusion of agricultural and domestic workers was a de facto barring of many African Americans, women, and southern laborers from the Act's protections, which generated some controversy during the Act's passage.[1] In contrast, there was virtually no discussion of the exclusion of public sector workers from the Act.

Our knowledge of the drafting of the Wagner Act is limited by the documents that have survived—a variety of personal and public papers on the drafting, debate, and passage of the Act[2]—which do not clarify explicitly why Keyserling, Wagner, and the other drafters chose to exclude public sector employees. In early drafts of the bill, public sector employees were not specifically mentioned. Their exclusion did not come until Keyserling's fifth draft, sometime between January and June 1934 (Keyserling 1934; Casebeer 1989). Keyserling's drafts include many notes and asides, but unfortunately the exclusion of public sector employees is typed with no notes on the topic to elucidate his intentions. Keyserling's first four drafts of the Act did not contain the exclusion, and the issue of public sector unionism did not animate debate over the bill. Thus, the exclusion was placed in the Act, but it appears this was done without full recognition of the significance of this omission. A little-discussed or -debated decision at the time has had far-reaching consequences for public sector unions and labor as a whole.

Keyserling likely felt little need to discuss or explain the exclusion of public sector workers because those most affected, public sector employees, were not organized around the idea of inclusion. For established government unions, their focus was pulled in two directions because the public sector already had a central body of laws governing employment, the civil service.

Thus, a great deal of government union activity was devoted to civil service reforms, which included much of the demand-making that would normally take place under a collective bargaining framework.[3] As will be discussed in the next chapter, however, most public sector unions recognized the negative consequences of exclusion from the Wagner Act in the decade after the bill was enacted.

For emerging government unions, many were not in a position to lobby on behalf of their own inclusion. In many of the leading public sector union publications, the Wagner Act was not mentioned before or after passage, and the *American Federationist*, the official magazine of the American Federation of Labor (AFL), includes much discussion on the Wagner Act but never addresses the exclusion.[4] Even more intriguingly, within the papers of the Wisconsin State Employees Association (WSEA), the founding local of the American Federation of State, County and Municipal Employees (AFSCME), the discussion of the Wagner Act is limited to wholehearted support. Arnold S. Zander, the secretary of the WSEA and later the first president of AFSCME, wrote letters to Wisconsin's two senators as well as the representative for Dane County (which encompasses Madison, Wisconsin), urging them to vote in favor of the Wagner Act without any mention of the exclusion of public employees (Zander 1934a, 1934b, 1934c).

The silence of an up-and-coming government union on the exclusion of public sector workers may seem surprising but, for the WSEA, pursuing collective bargaining rights would have been ambitious given the challenges facing public sector unions at the time.[5] During this period, many policymakers, thinking of the inherent differences between the private and public sector, as well as influenced by negative memories of earlier public sector strikes, viewed public sector unionism as a threat to democratic sovereignty.

The greatest impediment to public sector inclusion in the Wagner Act was the pervasive fear of government unions, provoked by memories of the 1919 Boston police officers strike. During the 1800s, police and firefighters associations formed to provide pensions and insurance programs for their members, but they quickly expanded to more closely resemble unions (Kearney and Maraschal 2014, 14). In 1918–1919, there was a particularly high number of strikes by police and firefighters as part of the broader 1919 postwar strike wave. In September 1919, the majority of Boston's police force went on strike for several days. Caught up in the postwar red scare, critics saw the strike as a Bolshevik takeover (Slater 2004). The police commissioner, in concert with Massachusetts governor Calvin Coolidge, refused the police officers' demands and did not recognize them as a union, and the strikers were ultimately replaced. After a plea for leniency from AFL president Samuel Gompers, asking for the strikers to be allowed to return to their jobs, Coolidge responded in uncompromising terms: "There is no right to strike against the public safety by anybody, anywhere, any time" (Sobel 1998, 144). During the strike, there were several nights of mild lawlessness in the city that were heavily reported on by the media. Critics of the strike came to see it as an embodiment of what public sector unionism would become: unbridled chaos and a Bolshevist threat to America.

The 1919 Boston police strike illustrated the severity of hostility toward striking civil servants. Joseph Slater argues that this hostility extended to public sector unionism more broadly. He asserts that "memories of the Boston strike inhibited the growth of public sector unions for decades" (2004, 36) and, looking particularly at judicial decisions, contends that one of the central themes of these decisions was "hostility toward unions" (72). The antagonism toward government unionism that manifested in Boston was fed by the view that several features of public sector unionism were inherently different and dangerous. First, the public sector is primarily involved in service provision of non-tradable goods rather than industrial production. Thus, when public sector unions strike, rather than halting the production of tradable goods, they instead can halt vitally important services like police and fire protection, public education, and mass transit. Second, public sector employers, unlike their private sector counterparts, are often elected officials. Thus government unions can influence their employers through collective bargaining *and* political action.[6] Finally, the nature of public sector labor relations is different in a multitude of ways including that profit and marketplace demands do not solely govern labor relations and the employer and employee are not the only actors in the bargaining relationship; voters and interest groups are just two of the additional players (Kearney and Mareschal 2014, 89–90). As a result of these differences, some fear that the balance between union and employer may be disrupted with public sector unions exerting undue influence, thereby subverting the democratic process.

For judges and legislators during the 1930s and 1940s, public sector workers were seen as wholly separate from private sector workers because their employer was the state, local, or federal government. In an open letter to the president of the National Federation of Federal Employees and the president of the CIO, President Roosevelt outlined the dominant position of the time: "All government employees should realize that the process of collective bargaining, as usually understood, cannot be transplanted into the public service.... The very nature and purposes of government make it impossible for administrative officials to represent fully or to bind the employer in mutual discussions with government employee organizations" (Federal Union Policy Told 1937). By the "very nature and purposes of government," President Roosevelt likely meant the differences listed above, which led him and other policymakers to conclude that public sector unionism was fundamentally different from private sector unionism and threatened the democratic, accountable relationship between an elected official and the voting public. An article in the *Wall Street Journal* succinctly stated the dominant fear of the time in the article's title: "Governed by Our Servants" (1928). Judges and policymakers worried that government unions would tie the hands of policymakers and wrest power from elected officials to an outside group threatening state sovereignty (Slater 2000a, 996). The courts and policymakers coupled their fear of devolving democratic power to a private entity with concerns that public sector unions would be identical to their private sector counterparts, which would mean that they could engage in militant strike activity.

Given the widespread fear of government unionism at the time, public sector unions were likely hesitant to expect something as generous as inclusion in the Wagner Act. For instance, in a 1934 letter to the secretary of the Minnesota State Employees Association, Zander explained that "it is our hope that we will get some measure of recognition, at least from the next legislature ... I doubt that we will make a direct request for recognition, but will present several bills, the passage of which would get our name in the statutes and give us some measure of recognition, although it might be indirect" (Zander 1934d). Zander's wish that the Wisconsin legislature would offer an indirect acknowledgment of the name and existence of the WSEA is a vivid illustration of the difficulties public employee unions faced for even basic recognition, much less full inclusion in the Wagner Act, in the 1930s.

Public sector unions were silent on their exclusion and for the most part others were as well. The omission of government employees was only mentioned twice in the available documents. First, on June 5, 1934, the ACLU wrote a letter to Senator Wagner, which outlined their opposition to the Act because, tellingly, they recognized many of the shortcomings of the bill and feared it "will inevitably serve as a weapon in the hands of employers to crush organized labor" (ACLU 1934, 1). Among the ACLU's fifteen pages of disagreements with the bill, they briefly noted that "we see no reason why the

United States should be exempted from the employers governed by the Act and, therefore, urge the amendment of section 3 (2) by deleting the United States from the exemption" (11). The letter has handwritten asides by Leon Keyserling that include his reactions and check marks next to proposed amendments; other portions of the letter are crossed out. Next to the ACLU's suggestion on public sector employees, Keyserling put two lines through the section and an "x" next to it. We cannot know Keyserling's thinking on the matter, but his notations suggest he either did not agree with the ACLU's suggestion or felt it could not or should not be included in the Wagner bill.

Public sector employees were mentioned a second time during the House Committee on Labor debate of the bill on March 19, 1935. Francis Biddle, chairman of the interim labor board, testified on behalf of the bill. Representative Robert Ramspeck (D-GA) framed a theoretical question for Biddle in reference to mail carriers. Representative Aubert Dunn (D-MS) asked for clarification on whether mail carriers would be covered under the bill. This exchange followed:

> *Mr. BIDDLE.* That is true; I was taking it as a theoretical question. They [mail carriers] would of course have no relief here. I suppose Mr. Connery [chairman] in drawing the bill thought it wise to exclude Government employees as that is suggesting a debatable question and he did not want to overload the bill.
> *The CHAIRMAN.* We thought that Mr. Ramspect's [sic] committee will have to take care of that eventually.
> *Mr. RAMSPECK.* I was not objecting to that feature of the bill. I think the States and Government should be excluded.
> *The CHAIRMAN.* And I felt it would be a very good example to the Government and very unselfish. (NLRB 1949, 2653)

Biddle suggests that public sector employees were excluded from the Wagner Act because there was a lack of consensus over their standing and including them in the bill would have overloaded the bill, likely meaning that public sector inclusion may have created undue controversy that could have prevented passage through Congress. The chairman, Representative William Connery (D-MA), who was the House sponsor of the bill, responds by pointing out that he expects public sector employee collective bargaining to be handled by Ramspeck's committee, which was the House Civil Service Committee. Ramspeck went on to say that he agreed with the exclusion of public sector employees to the Wagner Act, and the chairman added that he thought the Wagner Act would be a nice example for public sector workers to follow.

This brief aside in a legislative history over three thousand pages long cannot tell us conclusively why public sector employees were explicitly denied protection by the Wagner Act. However, the scant documentary evidence suggests three implications. First, Senator Wagner, Leon Keyserling, and other drafters of the bill were at the very least aware and consciously choosing to exclude public sector employees. Second, this exclusion was not discussed extensively and received little attention from those following the bill, particularly in comparison to other key exclusions like agricultural workers. Finally, government employees were likely excluded from the Wagner Act because there was no consensus on their inclusion: it likely would have generated controversy, perhaps even legal challenges to the law, and public sector labor law was seen as perhaps belonging in a separate discussion on civil service because the nature of public sector employment did not entitle public sector workers to the same rights as their private sector counterparts.[7] During the Wagner Act's drafting and passage, its supporters could not be sure whether the Supreme Court would even uphold the law. The Court's "switch in time that saved nine" would lead it to ultimately affirm the constitutionality of the Wagner Act, but this was not a foregone conclusion in 1935. This uncertainty may have contributed to the decision to exclude public sector workers rather than increase the risk that the Supreme Court might overturn the law.

Although the possibility of public sector employees being deliberately included in the Act would have been difficult given the uncertainty and fear of public sector unionism at the time, six factors suggest that opposition to public sector collective bargaining rights in the 1930s was not as dominant, uniform, or far-reaching as Slater and others contend and that inclusion was a possibility. First, public sector unions were not a new idea in the 1930s. Indeed, there was a rich variety of government unions at the time, many dating back to the nineteenth century. The first public sector employee actions can be traced back as early as the 1830s when workers in federal shipyards fought for a ten-hour workday (Kearney and Mareschal 2014, 14).[8] There were several strikes by Government Printing Office employees in the 1860s as part of the broader movement for the eight-hour workday (U.S. Civil Service Commission 1944). The 1862 strike by printing office employees lasted seven weeks and resulted in wage increases but no reduction in hours. Postal workers formed organizations beginning in the 1860s and the first teachers, firefighters, and police organizations emerged in the late 1800s as well (Kearney and Mareschal 2014). Teachers and firefighters locals started affiliating with the AFL in 1902 (AFSCME 1976). At the national level, the post office clerks affiliated with the AFL in 1906, the National Federation of Federal Employees and the American Federation of Teachers both followed suit in 1916, and the International Association of Fire Fighters followed shortly thereafter in 1919 (U.S. Civil Service Commission 1944; AFSCME 1976). These organizations were active employee associations but also bona fide unions. In 1940, David Ziskind sought to document the number of strikes by public sector employees to date. He counted 1,116 strikes beginning in 1835 and believed many more had occurred that he was unable to document (Ziskind 1940, 187). Although still small, government unions were a growing portion of the labor movement.

Second, inclusion was possible because the broader labor movement supported public sector unionism. As early as 1919, the AFL included public sector employees' collective bargaining rights as one of its key principles (American Federationist 1919, 132). Likewise, during the infamous Boston police strike, public sentiment was firmly against the striking policemen, but the AFL and its president, Samuel Gompers, continued to advocate for and support the fired Boston policemen (Gompers 1920). From its inception, the CIO also backed government unions. When they broke from the AFL in 1935, the CIO almost immediately launched plans to organize and advocate for public sector employees.[9] Had the CIO emerged earlier, they could have potentially lobbied on behalf of public employees' inclusion in the Wagner Act.

The third reason inclusion was possible was because these early government labor organizations encountered hostility but also made important breakthroughs. Most famously, at the federal level, President Theodore Roosevelt in 1902 responded to postal worker political activism by issuing a gag rule forbidding federal employees from lobbying for legislation on their behalf (Kearney and Mareschal 2014, 134). Although Roosevelt's gag rule is remembered as emblematic of hostility toward public sector unionism, the federal government was not uniformly hostile to government unions; just ten years later, the Lloyd-LaFollette Act overturned Roosevelt's gag rule and created employment protections for federal workers. Likewise, the 1924 Kiess Act established collective bargaining for printers in the Government Printing Office (U.S. Civil Service Commission 1944).

Fourth, the 1930s was a period of greater acceptance of organized labor, and this included government unionism. Many elected officials acknowledged their employees' unions, worked in concert with these government unions, and spoke at their meetings and conferences. The National Federation of Postal Clerks noted the change in attitude at their annual convention in 1935. Speakers asserted that the Postal Clerks were having the most "cordial relations" with the Postal Service ever and declared that "this administration of the Postal Service believes in collective bargaining. This administration of the Government believes collective bargaining is necessary" (Union Postal Clerk 1935). Representative Robert Ramspeck of Georgia, chairman of the House Civil Service Committee, spoke on several occasions at meetings of the National Federation of Federal Employees. At these meetings, Ramspeck was openly supportive of federal employee union organizing.[10] Likewise, the Tennessee Valley Authority (TVA) established collective bargaining with its employees already affiliated with trade unions from 1935 to 1937. Collective bargaining was extended to TVA white-collar workers by 1940 (AFSCME 1976).

Fifth, the NLB, formed under the 1933 National Industrial Recovery Act (NIRA), also signaled government acceptance of, or at the very least uncertainty over, public sector unionism when it adjudicated a case involving a government employee. The ultimate ruling in this case could have served as a precedent for including public sector workers in the Wagner Act. The National Recovery Administration (NRA), formed under the NIRA, was charged with helping industries develop codes to govern such things as fair competition, workplace standards, and union rights. NIRA was a precursor to the Wagner Act because it included an earlier version of Section 7(a), the portion of the Wagner Act guaranteeing employees collective bargaining rights. The NLB considered the implications of NIRA's 7(a) for government employees when John L. Donovan, president of a union local representing NRA employees within the American Federation of Government Employees (AFGE), was fired by General Hugh S. Johnson, head of the NRA. Donovan "aroused General Johnson's wrath by his conduct while heading a grievance committee of thirteen to present employee demands," including demanding an immediate meeting with Johnson to present the grievances (Spero 1948, 192). Donovan and his union claimed that he was fired for his union activities and appealed the decision to the NLB. General Johnson agreed to allow the board to rule on the case (Chicago Daily Tribune 1934).

The case garnered public attention because of the irony that the agency tasked with administering 7(a) was accused of violating that section. As the *Chicago Daily Tribune* noted, "Here was the labor relations board, constituted by the President and by congress to arbitrate industrial labor disputes, seeking to find the facts regarding the treatment of labor in the National Recovery Administration, constituted by the President and by congress to write a new chapter of harmony in industrial relations. Here also . . . was the champion of unionism [Hugh S. Johnson] on trial for anti-unionism" (Chicago Daily Tribune 1934). Members of federal unions fed this narrative, picketing NRA headquarters "carrying placards taunting Johnson with violating the spirit of the act he was supposed to administer" (Spero 1948, 192). Picket signs read "Johnson betrays labor" and "What about 7a, general?" (New York Times 1934a). The ACLU appealed directly to President Roosevelt. In a letter calling on FDR to repudiate Johnson, the ACLU wrote, "If the National Recovery Administration cannot set its own house in order and deal fairly with its own employes [sic] . . . it is folly to expect employers throughout the country to pay serious attention to Section 7A" (New York Times 1934b). The case generated national news coverage also thanks in part to Donovan's vociferous outcries in the press (Union Postal Clerk 1934b) and to senators who were already critical of General Johnson and condemned the firing (Washington Post 1934a). The event and public attention were "exceedingly embarrassing" to the NRA (Spero 1948, 192).

The attacks on General Johnson were perhaps unduly harsh. By many accounts, including the NLB's ruling, Donovan's conduct "had been far from polite," but without proper grievance procedures, "conduct more temperate" could not be expected (New York Times 1934c). While the board criticized General Johnson for Donovan's termination, they did note in the ruling that Johnson "seemed not to have been opposed to the existence of the union" and had even conferred with the union previously over the issue of overtime (National Labor Relations Board 1935, 27). This is in line with other accounts of government officials' and agencies' greater openness to public sector unionism in the 1930s.

Although the NLB noted General Johnson's pro-union stance, they took issue with his firing of Donovan. The board referred to Section 7(a) of the NIRA in making their decision, stating that "in deciding this case, we can adopt no other standard than that of Section 7 (a) of the Recovery Act, and must consider the case as though we were dealing with an employer to whom Section 7 (a) applied" (National Labor Relations Board 1935, 27–28). They went on to rule in favor of Donovan's reinstatement, arguing that "when the NRA is engaged in compelling employers to observe strictly the provisions of Section 7 (a), it should, in dealing with its own employes [sic] carry out the purposes of that section with even more scrupulous care than might be expected of ordinary employers" (28). In other words, if it is illegal for private sector employers to fire union leaders seeking to bargain collectively with them, then the federal government should hold itself to the same standard and respect their employees' collective bargaining rights.

The Donovan case thus vividly illustrates an alternative course to excluding government workers from the Wagner Act: a year before the Wagner Act became law, the NLB, chaired by none other than Senator Robert F. Wagner, had ruled in favor of using Section 7(a) to protect a government employee. Thus, under the law, labor board, and Section 7(a), which were the precursors to the Wagner Act, public sector employees were deemed to have the right to join a union and collectively bargain with their employer. Labor leaders interpreted this decision as lending "impetus to the movement to unionize all Government employes [sic]" and affirming government employee collective bargaining rights (Union Postal Clerk 1934c). L. Harold Sothorn, general counsel for AFGE, declared that the decision "makes more secure the right of Government employes [sic] to organize for the betterment of working conditions" and that the board "shows a clear conception of the fundamental rights of the employer and the employe [sic], the application of which will inevitably better the Government service" (Union Postal Clerk 1934b). The president of AFGE, E. Claude Babcock, declared that the decision "definitely recognizes the right of Government employes [sic] to unionize and present grievances to superior officers without penalty" (Washington Post 1934b). In the Donovan decision, the NLB signaled to public sector unions that Section 7(a) applied to them as well. This suggests that public sector employees' explicit exclusion from the updated Section 7(a) in the Wagner Act just a year later was not inevitable but, in light of the momentum of the Donovan decision, somewhat surprising.[11]

The sixth and final reason the inclusion of government employees in the Wagner Act could have been possible is that although there was not a concerted movement among government unions for inclusion, there was discussion and acknowledgment that public sector employees should have collective bargaining rights in the 1930s. Support for government employees' rights was most vocal when discussing NIRA and its industry codes. Government unions expressed both confusion over whether NIRA's Section 7(a) (stating the right of employees to form unions and collectively bargain) applied to them and dismay that they were not included. The *International Fire Fighter*, the monthly newsletter of the IAFF, assumed firefighters were protected under the Wagner Act (IAFF 1933a). A July 1933 political cartoon declared that the firefighters "Will have our code for your O.K., shortly!" implying that firefighters would be helping create industry codes under the framework of NIRA (IAFF 1933b). When the union realized later in 1933 that they and other municipal employees were not included in the Act, they passed a resolution at the national AFL convention calling for their inclusion (IAFF 1933c) and brought the matter up with administrators charged with implementing the Act. NIRA administrators were not opposed to including firefighters in the future and indeed predicted that later codes would include municipal employees once key industry codes had been established (IAFF 1933d). Hence, for the IAFF, their collective bargaining rights seemed guaranteed.

The National Federation of Postal Clerks was likewise upset by their exclusion from the protections in NIRA. They called the line NRA administrators were drawing between public and private sector industries an "artificial distinction" (Union Postal Clerk 1934a). The distinction seemed especially artificial when compared to what was occurring in Great Britain, where the government was successfully implementing industry codes and collective bargaining with their public employees (Union Postal Clerk 1934a). In Great Britain, the Whitley Committee was formed during World War I to study how to improve relations between employers and workers and issued a recommendation for national joint councils across industries. The recommendation was taken up most strongly in the public sector where "'Whitley councils' were established in 1919–20 for civil servants and gradually extended to other public services" (Farnham, Hondeghem, and Horton 2005, 118). The goal of the civil service council, as laid out in its constitution, was to "secure the greatest measure of co-operation between the State in its capacity as employer and the general body of civil servants" (Gladden 1967, 130). It was through the Whitley Councils beginning in the 1920s and 1930s that "full recognition was achieved and collective bargaining machinery was established" for civil service trade unions in Great Britain (Farnham, Hondeghem, and Horton 2005, 118). For government unions in the United States, the Whitley Councils offered a model for the type of business-labor cooperation and creation of industry codes that were described under NIRA. The postal clerks, like the firefighters, did not assume they were excluded from the law but instead were looking across the water for models of how they might fit under NIRA. Both unions were surprised and upset when they realized they were not included. This suggests that the federal climate for public sector employees being included in the Wagner Act was not so clear-cut. Had hostility to public sector unionism been absolute, the postal clerks and IAFF would not have been surprised by their exclusion from NIRA and later the Wagner Act. Instead, their shock indicates that there had been a real possibility for inclusion.

The existence and activity of public sector unions, the confusion and ambiguity around the place of government unions within larger labor laws, the Donovan decision, and the calls for inclusion all suggest that the exclusion of government employees from the Wagner Act was not a foregone conclusion. Legislators needed only to look to the British as an example of a country that already provided collective bargaining rights to public sector employees, albeit with important distinctions from private sector employees' rights (Sires 1953). There was also the possibility that public sector workers would have inadvertently been included.

Despite these possibilities, the exclusion of government employees was incorporated into the Wagner Act and signed into law. The Act became law during a brief moment when the New Deal coalition signaled their willingness to support labor legislation. The coalition, particularly the southern wing, became increasingly hesitant to advance labor rights after passage of the Wagner Act. Eric Schickler and Devin Caughey explain that "labor unions and their liberal allies were engaged in a race against time, seeking to construct a durable political-economic place for organized labor before their opponents could capitalize on growing anti-labor sentiment of the mass public" (2011, 164). Private sector unions succeeded in capitalizing on this moment through passage of the Wagner Act, but government unions lacked the size and power on their own to push for such a law. An "Officer's Report" from the State, County, and Municipal Workers of America (SCMWA) written just four years after passage of the Wagner Act already recognized this crucial missed opportunity. The report notes that when the Wagner Act, "labor's bill of rights," was passed, "the government employee was not sufficiently well organized and did not have a sufficiently powerful voice to demand those rights and prerogatives won by the rest of labor" (SCMWA 1939, 32). By 1939, government unions had grown and were recognizing the need for such protections, but "it was felt however necessary the claims of the government employees, the moment for realizing these claims was not a favorable one" (32). With the New Deal coalition's support for labor wavering, the labor movement feared that beginning the process of amending the Wagner Act "would also lay it bare to enemy destructive forces" by opening it up to harmful amendments in Congress (32). Thus, missing their chance with the Wagner Act, the moment for public sector employees to gain collective bargaining rights in the 1930s had passed. It would not be until the 1970s that government unions would have enough momentum on their own to pursue a national-level law—after the window of opportunity to pass such legislation had closed again—and well after the private sector labor movement had already peaked in size and strength.

The passage of the Wagner Act in 1935 marks a critical juncture for the split between public and private sector labor law for two reasons. As Paul Pierson (2000) notes, timing and sequencing matter, and when key moments pass certain opportunities also can be lost, constraining future possibilities. For instance, Jacob Hacker (1998) shows how the United States' passage of national health coverage for the poor and elderly, rather than the majority of working Americans, just as health-care costs were beginning to skyrocket led to a series of developments that made the possibility of universal health care in the United States increasingly remote. The Wagner Act was equally pivotal: the legal exclusion of government employees constrained public sector union growth at the very same time private sector union membership skyrocketed, and it forced public sector unions to focus their demand-making for legal recognition at the state and local levels, setting public and private sector unions on separate developmental trajectories with striking consequences for the size, strength, and effectiveness of organized labor in American politics. It is this legal exclusion, rather than economic or cultural developments, that set the U.S. labor movement apart from those of other nations and further set the public and private sector labor movements apart, both legally and developmentally. Thus, understanding labor today must start with 1935 and the exclusion of public sector employees. The remainder of this book will move chronologically, exploring in greater detail the decades following passage of the Wagner Act to illustrate how this seemingly minor exclusion has had lasting consequences for organized labor. Let us now turn to the two distinct paths public and private sector unions have followed since passage of the Wagner Act.

Chapter 3

After Wagner (1936–1960): Life Without Collective Bargaining Rights

The years immediately after passage of the Wagner Act vividly illustrate how the law served as a crucial turning point for organized labor. For private sector unions, the late 1930s and 1940s were a period of tremendous growth and development facilitated by the Act. As one union leader explained at the time, the law was "a terrific spur to the workers" because "to the vigor of the organizing drive, to the encouragement of victories, of strides taken, to the prestige of the C.I.O., is now added the sanction of law, the often effective support of the Labor Relations Board, the authority of the Federal Government" (AFT 1937). The pro-union legal and institutional environment created by the Wagner Act put an end to active state repression of labor. Combined with massive war mobilization during World War II, the Wagner Act was a "terrific spur" for organized labor, which led to skyrocketing private sector union membership, reaching levels previously unheard of in American history. Private sector union membership grew from just under 7 percent of the American workforce in 1935 to 14 percent by 1939, a doubling of union density in just four years. Union density reached 23 percent by the early 1940s (Bernstein 1954, 304).[1] The promises laid out in the Wagner Act were coming to fruition as labor became a powerful force in both size and political impact through its alignment with the Democratic Party and the New Deal coalition (Farhang and Katznelson 2005, 3).

For the public sector, however, the period after the Wagner Act was notably different. Instead of exponential growth and increasing political legitimacy and clout, government employees and unions remained disjointed and unsure of their legal footing or next steps. Public sector unions first experienced confusion and frustration that the Wagner Act did not apply to them. As denial moved into acceptance, the public sector labor movement grappled with what to do next. Public sector unions explored myriad ways to gain collective bargaining rights. Ultimately, they settled on trying to achieve institutional recognition at lower levels of government, with important consequences for the growth of public sector unions and the strength of the labor movement as a whole.

The defining feature of government unions in this period was the drawn-out struggle for institutional recognition. The period of the late 1930s and 1940s is a powerful illustration of federalism at work as government unions, shut out at the national level, turned to the states and localities for legal protections. In detailing the experiences of private and public sector unions in the decades immediately after passage of the Wagner Act, this chapter illustrates the double-edged sword of federalism for the labor movement. Federalism enabled public sector unions to employ innovative strategies and venue shop for more sympathetic levels of government after the window of opportunity at the national level closed; however, this innovation was not without consequences: state-level innovation came only as a result of decades effort, expended resources, countless failures, fragmented organizing, and limited results—all while the private sector labor movement had already reached its peak of power and influence.

Reassessing Venue Shopping

Scholars often describe the multilayered governments of federalism as a vast array of opportunities where political actors can, when they encounter resistance, seek out more sympathetic venues across levels of government. For instance, David Brian Robertson argues that lawmakers employ "federalism as a political weapon," using it as "an advantageous political institution that helps them win political battles or to defeat opponents" (2013, 20). Federalism is a tool in political actors' arsenal to employ to achieve their goals. As Robertson explains, "Federalism is an attractive weapon in politics because when important choices are left to the states, the states produce results different from the national government's" (24). Thus actors may look to the states when they are seeking different outcomes from those they might obtain at the national level. Frank R. Baumgartner and Brian D. Jones likewise see federalism as producing strategic choices. They argue that "federalism in America creates a great number of distinct and partially autonomous venues for policy action," enabling variation and more sites to enact new policies across these subjurisdictions (2009, 216). They describe the multitude of jurisdictions as a "system of policy venues" that creates opportunities for policy advocates who can venue shop, steering policies from a less promising venue to one that offers more advantageous prospects for success (216). Both Robertson and Baumgartner and Jones characterize federalism as producing strategic opportunities to pursue goals in multiple venues to increase the chance of success.

These scholars are correct that savvy political actors can strategically harness federalism to achieve their goals. However, this characterization of federalism rests on the assumption of politically sophisticated actors who see federalism as a strategic opportunity. Public sector unions in the 1930s and 1940s do not fit this mold easily. It would be better to view government unions during this time period as struggling to understand where they fit in the legal regime; trying to define their goals in the face of the uncertainty of their legal status; and, hampered by their inexperience, beginning this new endeavor lacking a clear road map for how to proceed. Further, by depicting federalism as an opportunity, Robertson and Baumgartner and Jones perhaps inadvertently make this process of venue shopping seem full of potential for political actors. However, as this chapter will illustrate, it is not always obvious to political actors that venue shopping is a possibility; it took public sector unions time to identify this as an explicit strategy and use it to their advantage. Moreover, the process of venue shopping and strategically using federalism as a political weapon can also be time-consuming, debilitating, and fraught with missteps and failure. Government unions ultimately were able to take advantage of some opportunities, but there were major costs associated with venue shopping as well.

Government Unions Face Uncertainty over Their Exclusion and Next Steps

When President Roosevelt signed the Wagner Act into law on July 5, 1935, government employees were unsure how the law related to them. The exclusion of public sector employees from the Act was little discussed or debated, so many workers and unions likely were not aware of the exclusion, leaving them to wonder if perhaps the law protected their collective bargaining rights as well. Fred Baer, the editor of the *International Fire Fighter*, the publication of the International Association of Fire Fighters, did not read the law as a decisive exclusion. He argued that statements made by FDR and his cabinet "declared that Federal employes [sic] have a perfect right to belong to labor unions and to be represented by such unions," and municipal employees might "indirectly or by implication" fall under both the Wagner Act and the statements made by the president and his cabinet (Baer 1937, 1). This suggests that Baer did not see the Wagner Act as explicitly excluding government employees.

The secretary-treasurer of the American Federation of Teachers (AFT) was so unsure about the law's effect on public sector workers that he asked the National Labor Relations Board (NLRB) to clear up the matter. The NLRB responded to the request with this statement: "The only opinion which the Board can issue must be reached after a full hearing of the evidence in a case. This is true not only of the merits of a case involving an alleged violation of the Act, but also is true of any decision the Board may make to take jurisdiction under the National Labor Relations Act" (AFT 1937). Rather than clearing up the confusion, the board's statement suggested that the matter of whether the Wagner Act protected government workers was not straightforward and only rulings by the NLRB on actual cases would determine the matter. The Wagner Act defined employers as not including "the United States or any wholly owned Government corporation, or any Federal Reserve Bank, or any State or political subdivision thereof" (NLRA 1935, Sec. 2). While this language may seem clear-cut, the NLRB response suggests that there was uncertainty over who would fall under the "public sector" and that this would need to be decided on a case-by-case basis. The AFT saw the NLRB's response as very promising and directed their locals "to a study of the possibility of securing protection under this act" because a favorable ruling would establish protections "on a national scale" and "teachers should have the same rights of citizenship as all other Americans" (AFT 1937). Uncertainty over whether they were protected or not left government unions unsure about their legal footing and whether what they were doing—forming unions and seeking to collectively bargain—was legal.

Subsequent rulings by the NLRB over the next decade did affirm the exclusion of public sector employees in specific instances but with notable exceptions. The first case to uphold the government employee exclusion was brought by the International Longshoremen and Warehousemen's Union, which was seeking to organize a variety of workers at the port in Mobile, Alabama (Mobile Steamship Association 1938). The NLRB granted the longshoremen's union representation of workers at the port from banana handlers to cargo handlers but ruled that warehousemen employed by the State Docks Commission, an agency created by the State of Alabama, were excluded because they were employed by a political subdivision of the state. Not all NLRB rulings were as clear on the exclusion, however. For instance, a year earlier, the NLRB had ruled that striking engineers onboard vessels owned by the U.S. government but contracted out to a private company were not excluded and possessed protection under the Wagner Act (Cosmopolitan Shipping Company 1937). Likewise, a hospital in the District of Columbia argued that its employees were exempt from the Wagner Act because it was "semipublic" due to the fact that it received appropriations from Congress and entered into contracts with the D.C. Department of Public Health (Central Dispensary and Emergency Hospital 1942). The NLRB was unconvinced and allowed hospital workers to organize under the Act. Thus, while the NLRB did affirm the public sector exclusion on a case-by-case basis, they also illustrated that this provision was not a hard-and-fast rule.

As public sector unions came to understand that they were not covered under the Wagner Act, they almost immediately began calling for collective bargaining rights, although they differed in terms of which level of government and through which venue they thought these rights would come. Looking just at the two main unions of state, county, and municipal workers, both unions suggested and at times supported a variety of ways to gain collective bargaining rights. In 1938, the AFL-affiliated American Federation of State, County and Municipal Employees (AFSCME) adopted a motion at their convention to try to "amend the Wisconsin Labor Relations Act to bring public employees under the act" (AFSCME 1938, 46). By 1940, however, AFSCME had passed a resolution urging its locals and the AFL to push for public sector employees' inclusion in the Wagner Act at the national level (AFSCME 1940, 129). That same year, AFSCME president Arnold Zander wrote that, "for the most part, our local unions find promotion and adoption of civil service legislation and ordinances the most effective way to approach this problem in the public service" (quoted in Spero 1948, 217).

The CIO's AFSCME counterpart, the State, County and Municipal Workers of America (SCMWA), also defined and redefined their goals in this period. In 1938, SCMWA praised a New York City agency that incorporated collective bargaining rights into the civil service. At the same time, the union went on to argue that "there can be no full democracy unless there is real democracy in the administration of government personnel. Real democracy today means nothing less than the passage of S.C.M.W. of A. legislation conferring upon government employees the inalienable right to organize, to petition for redress of grievances and to a fair hearing" (SCMWA 1938a). This legislation essentially called for a public employee Wagner Act for New York City (SCMWA 1938b).

At the CIO convention later that year, the union introduced and the convention adopted a resolution calling on state and local governments to "pass appropriate legislation or issue appropriate executive orders" guaranteeing collective bargaining rights (SCMWA 1938c). The union also met with the governor of New York and requested he issue an executive order affirming collective bargaining rights for state employees. In their meeting with the governor, SCMWA leaders "pointed out that the absence of a uniform policy at present served to leave the way open for administrative acts of anti-union discrimination, deliberate mishandling of employee ratings, and the institution of anti-labor practices such as existed in one state hospital whereby new employees were asked to sign undated statements of resignation" (SCMWA 1938d). By their 1941 convention, the SCMWA had set their sights higher than the city or state; they identified inclusion in the Wagner Act as their single, central legislative task. However, still keeping the door open for alternative routes, in the same sentence they also call for inclusion "in state and local acts of a similar character" (SCMWA 1941, 4).

Among other public sector unions, the way to gain collective bargaining rights was equally unclear. In 1944, the United Federal Workers of America (UFWA) called for the right to request union recognition elections from the NLRB directly (UFWA 1944). One CIO pamphlet from 1955 called for collective bargaining rights extended through civil service law (CIO 1955). The United Public Workers of America (UPWA) formed when the UFWA and SCMWA merged in 1946. At their 1946 convention, the newly formed UPWA passed a resolution that accurately sums up the strategy of public sector unions in this period: "THEREFORE BE IT RESOLVED, that the UPWA . . . urges the various government bodies to establish a 'Wagner Labor Relations Act' policy for their own employees" (UPWA 1946a, 20). Government unions were clear as to the goal—collective bargaining rights—but the UPWA's vague term "various government bodies" is emblematic of their uncertainty over the means of achieving their goal. In the decades after the passage of the Wagner Act, public sector unions remained unclear and in disagreement over who—a boss, the city council, a state legislature, the governor, an executive agency head, Congress, or the president—might make this goal happen and how—informal agreement, local ordinance, executive order, civil service reform, or legislation—this goal might be achieved.

Hostile Organizing Environment

The confusion over where to target activity and what methods to use to achieve collective bargaining rights was compounded by the hostile organizing environment. The SCMWA described their treatment in 1943 as that of "second-class citizens" facing discrimination that "more than anything else gives the government employee a feeling of not belonging, a feeling of being excluded, and a feeling of not counting" (SCMWA 1943a, 29, 16). The union put it even more strongly in a 1946 political cartoon, depicting this legal second-class citizenship as a literal stone wall standing between them and economic and political security (SCMWA 1946). The exclusion of public sector employees from the Wagner Act meant that it remained unclear whether the public sector had collective bargaining rights. In this void, long-standing anxieties about and opposition to public sector unionism flourished without the competing narrative of legally legitimate public sector unionism to dampen these fears.

Judges in particular reinforced in their rulings the perspective that government unionism was dangerous; for example, they continued to refer to the Boston strike well into the 1930s and 1940s. Private sector union strike activity was growing, and judges were fearful of enabling militant strikes among public sector workers by granting them collective bargaining rights. They rejected the possibility that government unions could be defined on different terms than their private sector counterparts (Slater 2004, 82–88). The near universal dominance of this shared understanding of public sector unionism among judges and policymakers meant municipal agreements between unions and elected officials were a rarity as courts and legislatures sided unanimously against public sector unions. In 1941 and 1946, the National Institute of Municipal Law Officers (NIMLO), a group that sought to promote cooperation among municipalities on legal matters, surveyed state attorneys general, available court decisions, and 365 city attorneys. Citing the threat to state sovereignty, they found unanimity that collective bargaining agreements between public employees and municipalities were illegal (NIMLO 1946).

The findings of NIMLO are not surprising; through the 1950s, the courts, state legislatures, and municipalities largely decided against public sector unionization. Government workers could be fired without legal recourse for joining a union. Yellow-dog contracts—whereby a worker agreed not to join a union as a condition of employment—were outlawed for private sector unions in 1932, but they were still permissible in the public sector well into the 1960s (Slater 2000b, 500). Laws recognizing unions as the collective bargaining unit of public employees would not be passed until the 1960s. Public sector unions were not strong enough on their own to push for such legislation, particularly given the public's and policymakers' fears of government unionism. Because the national and state legislatures refused to recognize public sector unions and the courts routinely sided against them, government unions only made headway by (a) organizing public sector workers without the guarantee of legal protections or collective bargaining, and (b) finding individual towns, departments, or officials who were willing to acknowledge the union in negotiations.

While the organizing environment was overwhelmingly hostile to public sector collective bargaining rights, in the 1940s and 1950s cracks began to appear in this unified legal thinking. The success and growing legitimacy of private sector unionization, the dimming fears of government takeover by labor, the fading memory of the Boston police strike, and pressure mounted by public sector unions helped challenge the dominant thinking on government unionism (Slater 2004, 156). However, the cracks that began to form provided small, limited opportunities rather than transformative change.

Struggling for Institutional Recognition and Legitimacy in a Hostile Environment

Faced with a hostile organizing environment, public sector unions struggled to gain institutional recognition and legitimacy. Without legal recognition, government unions possessed limited bargaining tools. They experimented with a variety of tactics and sites of demand-making to alter the legal environment, with varying levels of success.

Ten years after the Wagner Act was signed into law, there was little change in the legal environment for government workers. Favorable rulings, like applying Section 7(a) to the National Recovery Administration and reinstating John L. Donovan, did not create national public sector collective bargaining rights, but, taken together, these decisions served as "a moral rather than a legal rule" (Ziskind 1940, 243). AFSCME president Arnold Zander, speaking at the union's biennial conference in 1946, could just as easily have been describing government employees' experiences in any of the preceding decades: "In public service we know the burning shame of yellow dog contracts, the sting of the black list and the bite of anti-union favoritism and discrimination" (quoted in Stern 1946, 1). The struggle for institutional recognition was often met with resistance. New Deal liberalism at the national level did not likewise transform state governments. Instead, as Margaret Weir has argued, the New Deal "reform impulse . . . had no enduring counterpart in the states," and in some ways states became less receptive to reform during this period (2005, 158). Thus government employees who turned to the states and localities did not experience the same reception private sector workers did during the FDR administration.

After passage of the Wagner Act, states and municipalities across the country continued to pass ordinances banning strikes, requiring employees to sign yellow-dog contracts, and, at times, outright banning government workers from forming or joining unions. Joseph Slater chronicles numerous instances of teachers being forced to sign yellow-dog contracts or fired for union activity, as well as other examples of "discrimination against unionized teachers" (2004, 68–69). For instance, the city of Dallas, Texas, instituted an ordinance in 1942 forbidding city employees from organizing or becoming a member of a labor union. This ban was upheld by a district court and an appeals court in Texas under the justification that city employees "had no constitutional rights to remain municipal employees" (Spero 1948, 30–31).[2] The Supreme Court waded into the issue in 1946 when it refused to take up a case from the State of Mississippi where the State Supreme Court had upheld the firing of policemen in Jackson for joining a union. As Spero notes, "The highest court in the land thus, by implication, endorsed the doctrine that, as long as there is no legislation prohibiting employing authorities from limiting or preventing the organization of their employees" such actions are "a proper exercise of administrative discretion" (1948, 37). In 1947, reacting against the massive postwar strike wave that swept the country, New York State passed the Condon-Wadlin Act, which banned strikes "by all employees of the state and its subdivisions" (Spero 1948, 34). The Act had an expansive definition of a strike and called for the automatic firing of employees found in violation of the Act (34). Ohio, Michigan, and Texas passed similar anti-strike legislation that same year (Eaton 1975, 149). Virginia (in 1946) and Texas (in 1947) prohibited collective bargaining in the public sector, and Maryland (in 1945) and Florida courts (in 1945) refused to extend collective bargaining rights to public employees (Spero 1948, 344–345).

The legal environment thus continued to deliver setbacks to the public sector labor movement.

Government unions did have some victories, but they were of a limited and vulnerable kind. One way government employees had success in obtaining collective bargaining rights was when they had previously been private sector workers. For instance, Ohio passed a law in 1945 allowing publicly owned utilities under contract with private operations that had existing union contracts to continue using those contracts. This enabled the Transit Board in the city of Cleveland to enter into a contract with their employees who had been acquired from a private transit firm (Spero 1948, 344). Government employees also had some success gaining union recognition and bargaining in the area of public utilities. For instance, the Tennessee Valley Authority, the Bonneville Power Administration, the Alaska Railway, and the Inland Waterways Corporation all entered into agreements with unions representing their workers (346). Government unions may have had more success in these instances because they were venturing into new areas of government activity, taking over what had previously been private sector work, and the government entities continued to be organized and operated like private corporations. Perhaps these overlaps with the private sector enabled attitudes about private sector labor relations to seep into the public sector in these instances.

The NLRB and, during World War II, the War Labor Board also entered into formal agreements with organizations representing their employees. Both boards insisted that these employee organizations not be affiliated with the AFL or CIO, owing to the types of cases they would be ruling on (Spero 1938, 363–366). Given the central role these two boards played in upholding the collective bargaining rights of private sector workers, it is not surprising that they would seek to model the employer-employee relationship they were tasked with regulating.

The firefighters in Washington, D.C., also found themselves in a unique situation to pursue change because their collective bargaining rights were set by legislation unlike that which applied to other federal, state, or local employees. After the 1919 Boston police strike, Congress passed a law banning D.C. firefighters from forming or joining a union with any affiliate organization that used strikes as a bargaining tactic, effectively preventing firefighters from affiliating with any national union (IAFF 1939, 3). In 1938, District of Columbia firefighters contacted the International Association of Firefighters (IAFF) for advice and assistance on getting the law changed.

The union and D.C. firefighters lobbied members of the House Committee on the District of Columbia, successfully getting legislation introduced to amend the law. In the 1939 session, the bill unanimously passed both House and Senate committees and floors (IAFF 1939, 13). While a clear victory for the D.C. firefighters, the ultimate law was limited in scope. Nicknamed the "Affiliation Bill," the law simply allowed the association of D.C. firefighters to affiliate with the IAFF. The law created new language prohibiting strikes and provided no means for the union local to serve as the sole representative of the firefighters or to collectively bargain with the organization over wages and working conditions.

Unions in the more "traditional" public sector, lacking unique public/private arrangements or special subcommittees to target their lobbying, were forced to use creative methods to pursue their goals. Joseph Slater chronicles how the Building Service Employees International Union (BSEIU) turned to political tactics including "conventional means such as campaigning for sympathetic politicians and lobbying for new or improved laws" (2004, 105). At the same time, lacking legal protections, "at least as frequently . . . locals used informal channels and political connections: cajoling friendly government officials, soliciting public support, and meeting with administrators to work out unwritten, unofficial 'agreements'" (105). Such informal agreements were the bedrock of many of the advances made by public sector unions in the 1930s and 1940s. For instance, by 1943, the SCMWA reported 38 collective bargaining agreements, mostly with municipalities, covering over 5,000 employees. This meant that 17 percent of the union's locals and 15 percent of the union's membership had some sort of agreement with their employer; however, only 20 of these 38 agreements allowed collective bargaining (SCMWA 1943a, 4).

Police unions also relied on informal agreements and recognition with limited success. In 1944, the International Association of Chiefs of Police (IACP 1944, 3) circulated a questionnaire to all 198 cities with populations of 50,000 or more. Of the 168 cities that responded, only 15 reported having police unions.[3] Of those 15, only two—Flint, Michigan and Augusta, Georgia—reported having received official recognition. Police in 38 other cities had tried to unionize, but "in each instance a ruling by the city council or commission, the city attorney, or head of the police department . . . prohibited the department members from affiliating with the proposed union" (4). For instance, in Jackson, Mississippi, 36 officers were fired when they refused to obey an order from the mayor to disband their union (4). As this report illustrates, police unions were scattered and limited in their success in the 1940s.

The case of municipal sanitation workers in Newark exemplifies the uncertainty government employees faced without settled national-level protections. In October 1942, approximately 400 Newark Department of Public Works employees from Local 277 of the SCMWA voted to go on strike over wages (New York Times 1942a). The workers had been agitating for over a year for recognition of their union and improvements in wages and working conditions. The Newark director of Public Works, Joseph M. Byrd, had refused to recognize or negotiate with the union and proceeded to fire sixty-five of the strikers. The mayor of Newark suggested mediation but Byrd refused; garbage was not collected for seven days before Governor Charles Edison asked the War Labor Board (WLB) to intervene (New York Times 1942b; SCMWA 1943b). This was the first time that the WLB got involved in a strike against the government. If public sector employees could gain recognition and perhaps redress from the WLB, this could set a precedent for government employees' collective bargaining rights, providing justification for them to take future grievances after the war to the NLRB. However, Newark contested the jurisdiction of the WLB to intervene in the dispute precisely because it involved a city and its employees (New York Times 1942d).

A WLB mediation panel ruled in November that the board did have jurisdiction, noting that "it is unthinkable that the National War Labor Board would endanger the war effort by failing to concern itself with the problems of municipal employes [sic] to the same extent that it concerns itself with the problems of those employed by private individuals or corporations" (New York Times 1942c). In addition, the board recommended that the fired workers should be reinstated, and Newark should recognize Local 277 and develop procedures for negotiation and settling grievances (New York Times 1942c). Byrd appealed the panel's ruling.

The United States Conference of Mayors, the New Jersey Civil Service Commission, and New York City mayor Fiorello La Guardia—himself facing a similar WLB case with his city transit workers—all condemned the strike and the WLB's claim to jurisdiction (New York Times 1942e, 1942g, 1942h). The Conference of Mayors disagreed with the WLB's jurisdiction on principle but also argued that "any alleged dispute with city employes [sic]" is "fully covered and provided for in the State laws, city charters and ordinances of our respective States and cities" (New York Times 1942h). This claim vastly overstated the legal clarity over public sector employees across the country during this time and also with regard to the case at hand; Governor Edison asked the WLB to intervene because—likely referring to the recalcitrant Byrd—city officials refused mediation and the State Civil Service Commission was "not adequately set up by law to intervene" (New York Times 1942f). Governor Edison's actions suggest that he was open to government unionism or at the very least recognized that the state lacked the tools to address government unionism and, thus, the federal model and federal authority were needed to step in during the wartime emergency. Strikes are often the most polarizing activity unions engage in, generating powerful opposition, particularly during wartime when strikes are often portrayed as unpatriotic. However, even in this charged climate and after the Wagner Act exclusion, Governor Edison and the WLB panel supported federal jurisdiction in dealing with a public sector union, and the WLB panel further advocated for the collective bargaining rights of municipal employees with federal oversight.

At the hearing of the full WLB, those arguing that the WLB did not have jurisdiction pointed to the Wagner Act as evidence that municipal employees were exempted from federal labor law, while those advocating for the Newark sanitation workers called local government "the last stronghold of anti-unionism" (New York Times 1942i). The board issued a unanimous ruling on December 15, 1942, overturning the initial WLB panel decision. The board ruled that it did not have jurisdiction in the case because it would constitute "a clear invasion of the sovereign rights of the political subdivisions of local State government" (New York Times 1942j).[4] Although the ruling seemed to repudiate municipal employees' ability to have federal collective bargaining rights, in actuality it was not so clear-cut. The board also stated that while government employees possessed no right to strike, they did have the right "to organize and participate in a limited form of collective bargaining with government." The board also said that "in the interest of a more successful prosecution of the war, it is to be hoped that mutual cooperation and a reciprocal use of State and Federal labor relations machinery will characterize . . . the relationships between the Federal and local governments in labor matters, including disputes with government employees" (New York Times 1942j). Although the board supported public sector collective bargaining rights, they ruled in favor of federalism and limited federal interference in municipal labor matters. For the sanitation workers of Local 277, the hope that they might have found in the November decision was dashed by the full board's ruling in December. The language in the ruling affirming collective bargaining rights for public sector workers did not actually grant them those rights; it merely demonstrated the board's support. Moreover, the ruling did not lay out specifically how they might obtain collective bargaining rights given the board's lack of jurisdiction.

The WLB ruling was just one chapter in long-standing efforts to gain collective bargaining rights for sanitation workers. Just two months after the WLB ruling, the *New York Times* included a short update on Local 277. The article noted that Public Works Director Byrd, who "long had resisted efforts of the C.I.O. local to gain recognition," no longer "had jurisdiction" over the sanitation workers (New York Times 1943). Instead, Parks and Public Property Director Ralph A. Villani was in charge and announced that he would recognize and negotiate with the union. The story behind this story is unclear. Perhaps Byrd had been an outlier within the Newark bureaucracy and some agreed with the WLB's affirmation of collective bargaining rights and sought to achieve the outcome the original WLB panel had suggested. Perhaps Byrd was removed for other reasons unrelated to Local 277. The outcome for the union was the very thing they had struck for in October 1942. The president of Local 277 praised Villani for "his enlightened approach to the problem" (New York Times 1943). However, the gains made by Local 277 are notable as much for what they did not achieve as for what they did. Local 277 gained recognition, but it was not through national federal protection of collective bargaining rights or even state-level rights but rather through the good graces of an "enlightened" boss. Local 277 is emblematic of the chaotic, uncertain efforts to gain collective bargaining rights in this period and the limited gains government unions were able to obtain. The limits of Local 277's gains are obvious when we ask a simple question: What if Director Villani moved on and a new boss took over?

Informal agreements, like the one between Local 277 and Villani, were one of the major victories for government unions in this time period but lacked the institutional guarantees of legislation. As just mentioned, one danger of such agreements was that the "enlightened" boss would move on and the agreement would dissolve with their departure. Another danger of these informal agreements was that others would not respect them. For example, the UFWA requested that Fourth Assistant Postmaster General Smith W. Purdum put into writing his oral assurances that it was the policy of the Post Office to "deal with and recognize union activities among its employes [sic]" (UFWA 1939). Without Purdum's guarantee in writing, the UPWA complained that other Post Office officials were not adhering to the verbal promise, including not allowing union representatives to be part of negotiations. Without written, institutionalized guarantees, the union had no recourse when they were denied access.

One of the central weaknesses of these informal agreements is that they were haphazard and piecemeal. Unions had to lobby each individual school board, city council, agency head, police chief, and so forth. When they succeeded in receiving an informal agreement, the content of this agreement varied tremendously and usually was a far cry from full collective bargaining rights, as was the experience of the SCMWA. In 1938, the SCMWA gave an overview of the successes their union had gained to date. The union praised agreements made with the New York City Department of Welfare and Pennsylvania's highway and liquor control boards (SCMWA 1938e, 6). However, these agreements had just two central components: recognition of the union and the formation of a grievance committee. In other words, these departments agreed to acknowledge the union exists and hear complaints. Not present in the agreement were protections for employees joining this union, a procedure for formally electing which union will represent workers, or an obligation for the department to collectively bargain with the union. Other victories included agreements to recognize the union and form a grievance committee in Washington State's Department of Social Security in Seattle and with employees of the Maybury Sanatorium in Northville, Michigan (6).

Although the SCMWA frames these examples as victories, as government unions sought recognition and collective bargaining rights wherever they could find them, their gains were small and haphazard compared to national, institutionalized collective bargaining rights. The Seattle Department of Social Security may have recognized the union, but what about the rest of the department, or the many other state departments, not to mention the Washington municipal employees, other states' employees, and federal employees? The Maybury Sanatorium may have achieved union recognition, but what about the countless other employees in public health-care facilities in Michigan and across the country?

Government unions took their victories where they could find them, but the costs are clear. Excluded from national-level protections, public sector unions expended precious resources to achieve limited victories. When thinking about federalism, some might argue that the various lower levels of government provided opportunities for government unions, enabling them to make some advances when they were shut out at the national level. The victories made by Tennessee Valley Authority workers, Newark garbage collectors, and New York City Department of Welfare employees, among others, certainly support this perspective. But the opportunities of federalism are not without costs. Each of these localized victories represented a significant expenditure of the union's time, effort, and resources on a single campaign rather than national-level change. For instance, the UPWA reported at their 1948 convention on the various avenues they had to pursue to try to gain wage increases for their members, including "negotiation with administrative officials," "the passage of local ordinances," "oral arrangements either with the mayor or the city manager," "the promulgation of new civil service rules by the civil service commissions," and "public education and publicity campaigns" to put pressure on elected officials (UPWA 1948, 55). Without a national law fostering routinized collective bargaining in the public sector, unions like the UPWA were forced to wage battle across multiple levels of government, only winning marginal victories for small pockets of workers.

This history of government unions after passage of the Wagner Act challenges the characterization of venue shopping as strategic. Public sector employees were essentially kicked out of one venue and left scrambling to regroup. Rather than public sector employees strategically shopping for the best venue to gain collective bargaining rights, the exclusion of government employees from the Wagner Act punted the question of public sector unionism to other levels of government. During the 1940s and 1950s, a variety of lower levels of government struggled to establish clear policy in the face of federal inaction on the matter. For government unions, significant time and resources were spent understanding that they did not have national-level protections and then trying to figure out how they might achieve collective bargaining rights. This history suggests that in policy areas that are in their infancy, political actors may be characterized less by strategic choices than by confusion, missteps, and instability.

Furthermore, turning to the states and localities for rights was costly for the public sector labor movement. In general, informal agreements were achieved through each local union working directly with their boss. As a result, the public sector union movement was highly fragmented. Rather than coordinated efforts by government unions to achieve either state-level or national-level collective bargaining rights, unions focused much of their energy venue shopping for their own opportunity to advance their members' rights. Eleven years after passage of the Wagner Act, the SCMWA and the UFWA recognized the price that they had paid with this strategy and decided to merge into the UPWA: it had become clear to the two unions that "what

UFWA has been fighting for" for navy yard workers is "almost entirely what" SCMWA and the City of Detroit agreed to for railway maintenance workers (UPWA 1946b). Fragmented venue shopping meant fewer unions reaped the benefits of the hard work; the victory one SCMWA union achieved would have been even greater if it had applied to other unions and workplaces as well. On the merger, the two unions noted that "in dealing with many city governments SCMWA-CIO has . . . made substantial progress toward establishing full union rights for municipal employees in many cities. But its campaigns must, of necessity, be localized." The merged unions would be better able "to set a national pattern for union rights of government workers" (UPWA 1946b). After more than a decade of struggle, SCMWA and UFWA had come to realize the failure of their localized campaigns and set their sights on achieving national-level collective bargaining rights.

SCMWA and the UFWA's decision in 1946 to merge coincided with an overall realignment within the public sector labor movement as they finally came to realize that national-level rights would provide a measure of protection and the ability to expand that more localized efforts could never match. It was only in the 1960s that government unions really came to understand the limits of venue shopping and invest heavily in trying to achieve national collective bargaining rights. Part of the reason for this slow recognition was that government unions were focused on their successes: across the country, locals were achieving handshake agreements, union recognition, and workplace representation through grievance committees and appeals boards. But the period after the Wagner Act is also notable for the continued resilience of anti-union actions against public sector employees: firings, yellow-dog contracts, refusal to recognize unions, and adverse court rulings were commonplace. Over time, labor increasingly came to recognize the need for national and/or state legislatures to change the law and finally institutionalize public sector collective bargaining rights, but this recognition and the coordinated effort of unions to achieve this goal took decades to develop with costly results.

The Closed National Window of Opportunity

Public sector unions' slow recognition that national-level collective bargaining rights were needed was costly because the window of opportunity for such rights to pass through Congress was already closing. In 1939, the SCMWA "Officer's Report" delivered at their national convention focused on the need for government employees to be included in the law. The officers reported having met with the CIO general counsel to draft an amendment to the Wagner Act that would eliminate the public sector exclusion. However, just four years after passage of the Wagner Act, the CIO and SCMWA already were recognizing that "the moment for realizing these claims was not a favorable one" (SCMWA 1939, 32). The greatest fear that these labor leaders had was that introducing an amendment to the Wagner Act in Congress would open the Act up to other amendments for the "enemies of labor," ultimately laying it "bare to enemy destructive forces" (32). In fact, the next time the Wagner Act was altered by Congress it was at the hands of the "enemies of labor" with the passage of the Taft-Hartley Act in 1947, which largely closed the window of opportunity at the national level.

During World War II and the years that followed, in the face of private sector labor's tremendous gains, anti-union forces did not fade away. Instead, employers increasingly believed that the Wagner Act put unions not on equal footing with management but rather on higher ground (Lichtenstein 2002, 105). Anti-union efforts were assisted by southern Democrats who had formed a critical part of the New Deal coalition but increasingly turned away from the New Dealers in the face of threats to sustaining the racialized labor system in the South (Farhang and Katznelson 2005). Management resistance and southern Democratic defection created an opening for legislation that would scale back the positive rights commitment to unionize and collectively bargain enshrined in the Wagner Act. The Taft-Hartley Act passed in 1947, over President Truman's veto, and weakened private sector unionism in America by strengthening the power of management.

Taft-Hartley drove some of the most active, radical labor leaders from the movement by requiring members to sign legal affidavits asserting they were not Communists. It further outlawed many of labor's most potent tools including wildcat and solidarity strikes. Moreover, it eliminated foremen and supervisors from labor-law coverage, a crucial exclusion in the years to come as such positions expanded within the labor market. The Act further limited unions by enshrining employer free speech rights, which were later interpreted as protecting employer anti-union free speech during organizing campaigns, enabling more virulent anti-union efforts by employers hindering union organizing. Lastly, states that were hostile to unions gained a new tool with Section 14(b), which banned the closed shop and allowed states to enact "right-to-work" laws whereby employees in unionized workplaces are not compelled to join the union, enabling them to free ride on the efforts of unions.

The Act also took aim at federal public sector unions. The law prohibited federal employees from participating in strikes and stated that "any individual who strikes shall be discharged immediately from his employment, and shall forfeit his civil service status, if any, and shall not be eligible for reemployment for three years" (Korns 1957). An AFSCME history of public sector unionism noted the cruel irony of the strike prohibition in the Act: "Taft-Hartley . . . becomes the first U.S. general labor law to cover employees of the federal government with a provision forbidding them to strike and establishing specific penalties for those who do" (AFSCME 1976). Thus, the first recognition public sector employees received in a national labor relations law is in the very law that organized labor continues to see as a major step backward for the movement.

The Taft-Hartley Act signaled the resurgence of anti-union forces in Congress and the closing of a window of opportunity for progressive labor legislation, including public sector collective bargaining rights. The provisions in Taft-Hartley changed the course of private sector industrial relations in the United States. Whereas the Wagner Act affirmed the right of employees to unionize, Taft-Hartley strengthened the power of employers and states to oppose unionization efforts. Momentum has largely been on the side of Taft-Hartley supporters ever since. Most notably, there have been no revisions to private sector labor law on the scale of the Wagner and Taft-Hartley acts since 1947, and the smaller revisions that have occurred have continued Taft-Hartley's anti-union approach. For instance, the Labor Management Reporting and Disclosure Act of 1959, also known as the Landrum-Griffin Act, regulated unions' internal affairs, allowing greater federal oversight of labor unions' financials, internal elections, and membership. The Act signaled that Taft-Hartley was not a one-off event but instead an enduring turn away from the original intent of the Wagner Act in private sector labor law.

Serious attempts at labor law reform to try to revive the original intent of the Wagner Act during the Johnson, Carter, Clinton, and Obama presidencies all met with failure. Circumstances unique to each reform effort certainly contributed to their failure, but one central feature of American politics has proven a consistent barrier: the institutional features of the U.S. Senate. The Senate is marked by (a) malapportionment whereby states with high population density and rural, low population states receive equal representation, and (b) supermajoritarianism whereby, barring the 60 votes to reach cloture (from 1917 until 1975, 67 votes were required for cloture), individual senators have the ability to stall and/or block legislation. These institutional features are detrimental to organized labor because union strength is geographically concentrated, making a pro-union supermajority unlikely and instead granting the anti-union coalition the power to obstruct labor law reform (Dark 1999; Warren 2011).

The obstructionist powers in the Senate have been used to great effect since Taft-Hartley to stymie reform. A telling example is the 1965 attempt by labor, Democrats, and President Johnson to overturn Section 14(b) of the Act. Placing labor reform near the end of the legislative session's agenda certainly played a role in the failure of the reform effort,[5] but the crushing blow was obstructionist senators' use of the filibuster. As the legislative session drew to a close, labor supporters were unable to muster the votes to invoke cloture and end the filibuster. Given the Democratic supermajority in the Senate, it was twenty-one Democratic senators who proved the decisive votes by joining with twenty-six Republicans to vote against cloture on October 11, 1965 (Foley 1965). These Democrats were a unique subsection of the Senate: of the twenty-one, seventeen were from states that already had right-to-work laws on the books. This is striking because only seventeen states had right-to-work laws at the time (NRTLDF 2012). Only four Democrats from right-to-work states *voted for* cloture. Thus, of the twenty-two Democratic senators from right-to-work states in 1965, seventeen of them voted against cloture, ensuring that repeal of Section 14(b) would not pass.[6]

It is not surprising that Democrats from right-to-work states would oppose the repeal of the law that allowed their states to pass such provisions. However, what this example illustrates is how, once the existing legal framework of Taft-Hartley was put into place, labor opponents utilized obstructionism to great effect in the Senate to maintain the status quo. Anti-union Senate Democrats could be effective in opposing unions simply by blocking future reforms. Obstructing labor reform efforts has been effective because it has prevented the existing legal and institutional framework of labor law from adapting to modern-day labor relations, resulting in policy drift in the area of labor law (Hacker and Pierson 2010). As Streeck and Thelen note, "Institutions do not survive by standing still" but rather "require active maintenance; to remain what they are they need to be reset and refocused . . . in response to changes in the political and economic environment in which they are embedded" (2005, 24). By failing to update private sector labor law, the current institutional framework atrophied and now lacks the capacity to properly coordinate and regulate modern-day labor relations. The erosion of national private sector labor law is not simply the result of the passage of time but rather the product of deliberate "nondecisions" and obstructionism by federal policymakers (Streeck and Thelen, 2005, 25; Hacker and Pierson 2010).

The consequence of this purposeful obstruction is what Cynthia L. Estlund describes as the "ossification of American labor law," by which she means that "the core of American labor law has been essentially sealed off—to a remarkably complete extent and for a remarkably long time—both from democratic revision and renewal and from local experimentation and innovation" (2002, 1530). The term "ossification" is apt because it implies that labor law is becoming increasingly rigid and out of date. The congressional impasse is "the linchpin of the process of ossification," which has prevented the repeal of Taft-Hartley and created an out-of-date legal framework for dealing with labor relations that has hampered labor's organizing efforts (1527). By orchestrating policy drift in this area, obstructionists have helped create an antiquated labor law that is just as harmful to labor's efforts to maintain membership levels as the Taft-Hartley Act's original provisions.

The legislative impasse over private sector labor law was accompanied by significant development of private sector labor law in the judicial branch. As Karl E. Klare (1978) has demonstrated, the judicial branch, rather than a means for labor to bypass legislative gridlock, has "deradicalized" the Wagner Act with court decisions upholding aspects of the Act in line with liberal capitalism and denying more revolutionary interpretations. For instance, subsequent interpretations of the strike provisions within the Wagner Act resulted in the strike being "rendered negotiable, predictable, less effective, and less likely" (McCammon 1990, 224). Further, the evolving NLRA legal doctrine set forth by the courts and the NLRB has "deferred to employer property rights rather than employee self-organization rights or union interests" at the expense of union organizing (Block, Wolkinson, and Kuhn 1989, 238). These "deradicalizing" private sector labor judicial developments have made the importance of new legal doctrines, generated in Congress, all the more pressing but no more likely to pass.

Thus the only area where we have seen movement on private sector labor law—passage of right-to-work provisions and judicial decisions—has diminished the federal commitment outlined in the Wagner Act to promote the right to collectively bargain in the private sector. Having the locus of decision making at the national level meant private sector unions nationwide benefited from pro-labor policymaking during the New Deal, but it has also meant that private sector unions are beholden to the multiple veto points at the national level and limited in their alternative strategies if the federal government does not reform existing labor law.

For the public sector, Taft-Hartley was not much of a step backward in the sense that there were no national collective bargaining rights to ossify. However, passage of Taft-Hartley does represent a turning point at the national level in attitudes toward organized labor and the possibility for any kind of labor law reform, including public sector collective bargaining rights. Government unions, excluded from the protections of the Wagner Act, did not experience the massive organizational gains that the private sector experienced in the 1930s and 1940s. Instead, government unions struggled to find their footing, seeking out a variety of venues, experimenting with different methods, and ultimately achieving limited, fragile forms of success. These achievements represented decades of effort, countless hours of work, and significant resources that were devoted to selective, often highly localized victories while, at the same time, the private sector labor movement achieved the height of its power and influence. It was this process of exhausting work, and recognizing the limited gains, that ultimately led government unions to coalesce around the strategy of state- and national-level legislation to obtain collective bargaining rights, but this strategy came late, missing the private sector labor movement's peak and the window of opportunity in Congress before anti-union opponents coalesced around Taft-Hartley. Many public sector unions were focusing their efforts in workplaces, municipalities, and states, trying to gain handshake agreements at the very time private sector unions were battling Taft-Hartley.

Federalism and venue shopping separated the labor movement during this crucial period. Government unions' efforts at the state and local levels eventually paid off, but there would never come another opportunity like the Wagner Act or the 1940s when labor was on the rise. The next chapter details the breakthrough moment when many public sector unions succeeded in securing collective bargaining rights in the 1960s. However, this moment of optimism and potential for the public sector labor movement can be fully understood only in light of the events of the 1930s–1950s, when the private sector movement had already peaked and received the devastating blow of Taft-Hartley. The successes detailed in the next chapter are notable for both tremendous innovation and incredible limitations as the timing of government unions' appeals and federalism limited what was possible for the public sector labor movement.

Chapter 4

1961: The Public Sector's Watershed Moment

While private sector labor law reached an impasse following Taft-Hartley, after decades of effort, major changes were creating a window of opportunity for public sector laws to pass at the state and local levels (Kingdon 1984). Public sector employees drove the change by pressing for recognition of their grievances and defiantly organizing and joining unions regardless of legal provisions, forcing policymakers to take notice. During and after World War II, public sector employment increased as the New Deal expanded the size and scope of local, state, and federal government. The number of state employees rose from 804,000 in 1946 to 1,592,000 in 1960. Likewise, the number of local government employees increased from 2.8 million in 1946 to 4.8 million by 1960 (Bernstein 1991, 208). Government employment rose from just under 11 percent of the total workforce in 1930 to well over 15 percent by 1960 (U.S. Census Bureau 2003). Wages and salaries in these expanding fields still lagged behind those in the private sector, creating tensions among the growing public sector workforce and feeding a demand among federal, state, and local workers for representation (Bernstein 1991, 208).

As a result, public employees were increasingly forming and joining unions in spite of the lack of legal recognition and protection. As Irving Bernstein notes, exclusion from the Wagner Act "did not forbid public workers to engage in collective bargaining, but prevented them from doing so within the carefully crafted NLRB system" (1991, 205). Public employees seeking to redress grievances formed employee organizations, but these unions lacked many of the key hallmarks of private sector unions including employment protection, NLRB certification elections, arbitration processes, and the guarantee of employer recognition. These organizing efforts were more successful at the municipal level. For example, under Mayors Joseph F. Clark Jr. and Richardson Dilworth, Philadelphia developed collective bargaining procedures and negotiated agreements for police officers, firemen, and city employees during the latter half of the 1950s (Bernstein 1991, 209). This was done despite the lack of state law empowering Philadelphia's mayors to take such steps. Founded in 1932, the American Federation of State, County and Municipal Employees (AFSCME) was at the forefront of driving such change. AFSCME grew from 9,737 members in 1936 to 286,283 members by 1966 (Donoian 1967). AFSCME and other public sector unions like the American Federation of Government Employees, which represented federal workers, as well as teachers, firefighters, and police unions, actively sought to change the legal climate for public sector bargaining through political activity. They represented an increasingly organized workforce with unaddressed grievances and no legal framework to cope with their demands.

Public sector unions were also emboldened by the civil rights movement. African Americans often found greater success and acceptance in government employment, and they gained recognition and leadership positions within public sector unions and helped push for union progressivism on civil rights and heightened politicization overall (Moody 1988, 182). AFSCME consistently was on the progressive wing of the labor movement and was particularly active in the civil rights movement, but the American Federation of Teachers' and other public sector unions' activities overlapped with the movement as well (Levy 1990; McCartin 2006; Moody 1988). The social foment of the time over civil rights occurred in tandem with and helped fuel public sector unions' efforts to gain legal recognition.[1]

In an era of growing social unrest, government unions began to obtain both formal and informal recognition. They engaged in heightened levels of demand-making including strikes, despite the legal prohibitions against them; public employees' growing militancy forced the issue of government unionism onto the legislative agenda. Public sector union leaders and members faced jail time and financial punishments for striking but, in some instances, succeeded in gaining union recognition and getting their demands met. It is difficult to measure the climate of public opinion at the time, but newspaper coverage, academic discourse, and legal opinion from the period suggest a growing acceptance that government workers had the same need for representation as private sector workers. Rising tolerance was undoubtedly helped by the fact that private sector union density reached its peak in

1953 with over a third of the workforce unionized, making labor unions an accepted part of American life.

Robust private sector unionism served as a powerful example for public sector employees to emulate, and the labor movement also offered support to the emerging public sector unions. Since the 1940s the CIO had been a vocal proponent of pro–public sector labor laws, and after the merger with the AFL in 1955, the AFL-CIO increasingly moved from a vocal supporter to an involved ally in the effort to get new legislation passed (Slater 2004, 131, 162). However, it would be misleading to attribute public sector success to the AFL-CIO. The AFL-CIO did not form a public sector unit until the 1970s and disbanded it a decade later. Moreover, relations between the more progressive (and rapidly growing) AFSCME and the AFL-CIO were strained at times—after all, government union power would require the current AFL-CIO leadership to relinquish some of their influence within the movement. In the end, powerful and active public sector unions and employees demanded acknowledgment from their employers and the labor movement. It was their activism that drove the change in laws and within organized labor.

Government unions' demands were ultimately translated into law by the election of Democratic mayors, legislatures, and chief executives. Democratic politicians owed much of their success to the politically mobilized and active private and public sector unions (Greenstone 1969). In New York City, Mayor Wagner promoted public sector unionism because it provided him with loyal supporters independent of the city's political machine (Shefter 1992, 73–75). In Wisconsin, Governor Gaylord Nelson had served as a field representative for the municipal employees union and remained friends with the union's leaders prior to signing the state's public sector collective bargaining law as governor (Slater 2004, 180). In the decade leading up to passage of the law, Democrats received 20–30 percent of their political funds from unions (180). For Democrats and public sector unions, "each side in that relationship knew well how much it needed the other" (McCartin 2006, 79). Public sector labor laws served as the fruits of the marriage between labor and the Democratic Party (79). Newly elected Democrats attributed their success to labor's political prowess, and Democrats were self-interested in promoting increased government unionization.

Public sector unions' efforts and the assistance of Democratic politicians created a window of opportunity to pass state laws acknowledging the legal standing of government unions. As Slater notes, "The legal regime had become brittle, as popular opinion and actual practices increasingly tolerated unions of government workers" (2004, 158). Several key factors made some states more likely than others to pass pro–public sector labor legislation. Berkeley Miller and William Canak found that "the presence of strong statewide labor movements and earlier private sector union successes, the long-term incumbency of especially northern Democrats, and high levels of interparty competition" all were correlated with state laws favorable to public sector collective bargaining (1988, 181). Interparty competition, Democratic Party electoral success, and an already strong and established labor movement were evident in events that marked the turning point for public sector labor law.

Three events were particularly important during this period; they helped break open the "brittle" legal regime for government unions. First, in December 1961, in a highly publicized episode, the United Federation of Teachers (UFT) went on strike in New York City. Through negotiations, the UFT was recognized by the city as the collective bargaining representative of all city teachers. New York City municipal workers had agitated for decades to little avail until Robert F. Wagner Jr. was elected mayor in 1953. Wagner's support for labor could be traced back to his father, the architect of the Wagner Act. Upon entering office, Mayor Wagner created a department of labor and tasked it with creating a labor policy for city employees.

Wagner issued Executive Order 49 in 1958, in essence creating "a little Wagner Act for the city" that, through expansions over the next decade, would come to cover all of the city's employees (Bernstein 1991, 210–211). While the 1958 order was a milestone, the Act initially did not cover many of the city's workers, including teachers. The UFT formed in 1960 to address teacher grievances in a more confrontational fashion than had previous New York City teacher professional associations. On November 7, 1960, the UFT organized a strike involving over one-fifth of the city's teachers. The strike only lasted a day, but afterward the school board was amenable to holding a vote among the city's teachers to choose which union would represent the teachers in future negotiations (Buder 1962). On December 16, 1961, the UFT won the right to represent the city's 43,000 teachers (Katz 1961). Teachers, school boards, and unions across the country closely followed the events. The *Los Angeles Times* called it "one of the most significant events in the teaching profession," and a *New York Times* editorial declared that the success of the UFT in New York City had "a significance that extends far beyond New York. It will set patterns for school systems everywhere and for the still ill defined systems of collective bargaining in government" (Turpin 1962;

"A Union for Teachers" 1961).² The developments in New York City inspired increased teacher activism and organizing to demand similar treatment in cities across the country.

The second key event was President Kennedy's signing on January 17, 1962, of Executive Order 10988, which recognized and protected the right of federal employees to join unions. The election of Kennedy, a Democrat from a northern, union-friendly state, created an opportune time for the passage of new policies dealing with federal workers. In addition, federal employees were already organizing. By 1961, fully one-third of federal employees, 762,000 workers, were members of employee organizations, but the executive branch had no definitive policy for addressing these groups' demands (Bernstein 1991, 206). Recognizing the need to deal with federal employee organizations, Congress introduced nineteen different federal employee collective bargaining bills in early 1961. One of these nineteen bills was likely to pass but whether the form of the legislation was to the executive branch's liking was unclear.

If President Kennedy hoped to influence the outcome, he could not wait for Congress to act. Instead, the president created an informal study group to explore the issue and, after they recommended an executive order to sidestep the chaos of nineteen different pieces of legislation, formed a task force to draft the order (Bernstein 1991, 212–213). The task force's recommendation of a comprehensive policy permitting many of the rights outlined in the Wagner Act but with key limitations, including barring the right to strike and upholding the primacy of civil service laws, was incorporated into Executive Order 10988 (214). While it limited the rights granted to federal employees, the order was a milestone for public sector unionization and led to a rise in union organizing; over a million federal employees belonged to a union only five years later (216). For the public sector labor movement more broadly, Kennedy's recognition of federal workers' right to unionize finally displaced the fear of government unionism and legitimized public sector workers' demands for legal recognition. However, the majority of public sector employees worked (and still do) for the state and local rather than the federal government, making Kennedy's executive order largely symbolic: absent a national law, collective bargaining rights would still have to be won in each state or locality for the majority of government workers.

Finally, on January 31, 1962, this newfound legitimacy was realized when Wisconsin became the first state to pass a comprehensive collective bargaining law for municipal public sector workers.³ The law was the culmination of a decade of work by the founding AFSCME local, the Wisconsin State

Employees Association (WSEA). WSEA had been politically active on behalf of its members since its founding in 1932. AFSCME's continuing demand for legal recognition in Wisconsin finally gained sway in the 1950s as a result of evolving public support for government employee unionization. Moreover, in the 1950s there was intense party competition in Wisconsin between Democrats and Republicans, with labor forming the core support for Democratic politicians (Slater 2004, 168). Democrats were keenly aware of the role labor had played in their success, and this spurred their support of labor law reform. The legislature nearly passed labor laws several times in the 1950s. The ultimate breakthrough came from the continued efforts of AFSCME and the election of the first Democratic governor in decades, Gaylord Nelson, and a Democratic state assembly (179). Over the next several decades, other states followed Wisconsin's example in passing public sector labor legislation.[4]

The recognition of the UFT in New York City, Kennedy's issuing of Executive Order 10988, and the passage of a collective bargaining law in Wisconsin all occurred within the span of two months. They highlighted the fact that existing labor law—or the lack thereof—was out of step with the nation's new understanding of public sector unionism. The change in attitude was reflected by the activities of the National Institute of Municipal Law Officers (NIMLO). In the 1940s, NIMLO surveyed its members and found overwhelming opposition to granting collective bargaining rights to public sector unions (NIMLO 1946). Now, in 1968, NIMLO held a labor relations seminar devoted to the subject of public employment unionism. Instead of summarizing the wealth of legal and public opinion opposed to public sector unionism as they had in the 1940s, NIMLO in 1968 displayed a dramatic turnaround by discussing public sector collective bargaining rights as a foregone conclusion for municipalities. The seminar was held just days after Martin Luther King Jr. was assassinated while assisting striking public sanitation workers in Memphis. In the shadow of this violent act and the subsequent rioting, participants believed "a revolutionary change in the employee relations picture of cities" had occurred (25). As a result, municipalities must accept this "new endeavor" and plan, prepare, and adapt to this changed environment by passing new labor legislation (27). The participants in the NIMLO seminar were not exaggerating; the 1960s was a period of dramatic change in both public sector union density and legislation.

The pressure for change in public sector collective bargaining rights had reached a boiling point and manifested itself in specific ways: the majority of activity took place at the state and local levels and involved disparate union locals in separate movements for union recognition. The exception, of course, was federal employees, who simultaneously lobbied at the federal level for changes to the civil service laws. Public sector unions lacked the size and influence to pursue legislation at the national level and, because the Wagner Act left public sector unionism an open question, the states and localities became the locus to address government employee collective bargaining. The dispersed movements for public sector legislation reflected the federalized nature of American labor law. Excluded from the Wagner Act, and lacking their own national-level law, public sector unions had to fight the battle in every state and locality.

Over the next two decades, dozens of states followed Wisconsin's example by extending collective bargaining rights to public sector workers. Quantifying just how much legislative change occurred during this period is difficult because laws varied both in the degree to which they were universal or targeted specific workers, like teachers, and in the generosity of their collective bargaining rights. In an attempt to capture the magnitude of legislative change, Richard B. Freeman and Robert G. Valletta compiled a data set to measure the degree of pro-bargaining or anti-bargaining laws for public sector workers in the United States. Using their most stringent measure of pro-bargaining, only five states qualified as pro-bargaining in 1969. By 1984, twenty-one states qualified as pro-bargaining (1988, 406). Looking at change over time, forty of the fifty states moved in a pro-bargaining direction from 1969 to 1984 (416). Henry S. Farber used the same data set to assess the development of laws allowing collective bargaining for public sector workers in four categories of workers. Overall, "the total increased from one state in 1955 to over 40 states for firefighters and teachers and to over 30 states for police and state workers by 1979" (2005, 15–16).

Figure 2 illustrates the magnitude of change in state employee labor law from 1955 to 1980. In 1955, every state either prohibited or had no statute allowing state employee collective bargaining, save Illinois.[5] By 1980, only nine states still had no provision regarding state employee collective bargaining. Thirty-four states now granted state employees some degree of collective bargaining rights: six authorized but did not require the employer to bargain collectively with employees, one allowed employees the right to present proposals, four gave employees the right to meet and confer with their employers, eighteen had laws with an implied duty of employers to collective bargaining, and, most generously, five states explicitly required employers to

1955 State Employee Collective Bargaining Laws

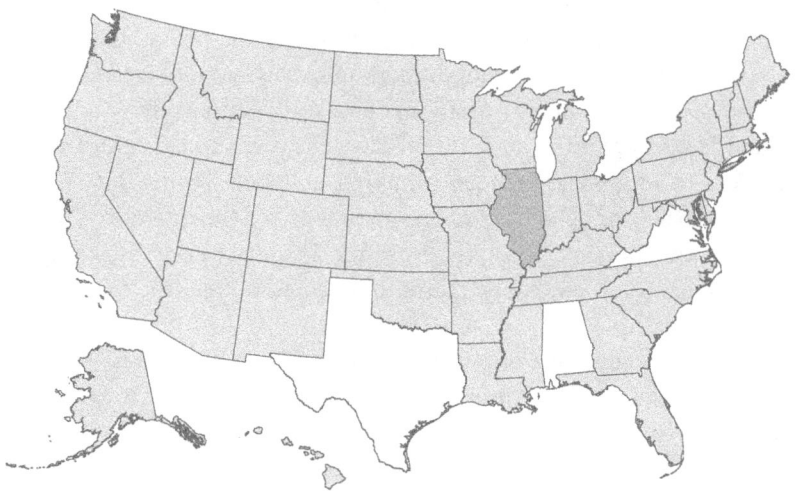

1980 State Employee Collective Bargaining Laws

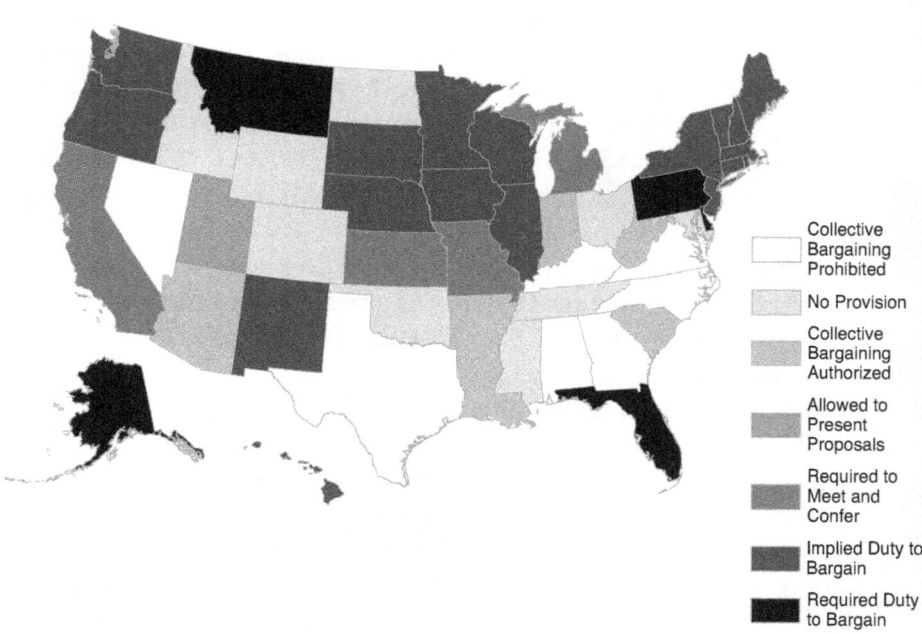

Figure 2. The proliferation of public sector collective bargaining laws. Valletta and Freeman 2012 (see Valletta and Freeman 1988 for data set documentation).

collectively bargain with employees (Valletta and Freeman 2012). No longer was an entrenched opposition to public sector collective bargaining dominating the legal landscape.

Pro-bargaining public sector legislation has been associated with rising union membership (Freeman and Ichniowski 1988), and this was certainly the case during this time period. Public sector union density rose from 10.8 percent in 1960 to over 35 percent in the 1980s (Jamieson 2013). However, pro-bargaining public sector legislation is not enough to explain the rise of public sector unionization. With the Wagner Act, the private sector was granted a foundation for robust organizing, but, as discussed in the last chapter, the Taft-Hartley Act and labor law ossification led to rising employer resistance that has hindered private sector organizing. Public sector union density has grown not only because of new legislation but also because employer resistance is much less prevalent. Without employer hostility, and with new legal protections, government unions have had greater success in organizing new workers.

Two major factors led public sector employers to be less likely than private sector employers to resist unionization and engage in unfair labor practices. First, public sector employers receive less pressure to resist and more pressure to behave civilly during organizing campaigns. Government employers are not beholden to shareholders' financial performance expectations and largely lack a profit motive that might encourage them to oppose unionization. Instead, they face pressures from their constituents to behave civilly and not break labor laws during union representation campaigns. As Kate Bronfenbrenner and Tom Juravitch note, "Many public officials are elected and regardless of their individual attitudes are constrained from engaging in activities that the public might perceive negatively" (1994, 21). Moreover, public officials likely face greater punishments for breaking labor laws (like removal from office) compared to the limited punishments at the NLRB's disposal: "put crudely, management opposition to unions can gain profits in the private sector; in the public sector, it can cost votes" (Freeman 1988, 85). In general, employers in the public sector have more to lose by opposing unionization.

Second, public sector employers lack the tools of union resistance deployed by private sector employers. In the private sector, employers can threaten to move operations to other states and/or overseas to avoid unionization, and often they follow through on these threats (Cowie 2001). Most public services cannot be moved in the same way. Private sector workers seeking to unionize who are fired by their employer for their efforts can appeal to the NLRB, but remedies often come too little and too late. Government workers do not operate under employment-at-will rules that allow discharges for any reason. Instead, most public sector workers are protected under civil service laws and can only be fired with "just cause" and enjoy due process rights if they are fired. Thus, "if a union organizer is fired in the midst of a campaign, the burden is on the employer to establish that this was not a retaliatory dismissal and that there was a *good* reason (not just any reason) apart from the organizing campaign to fire the employee" (Fischl 2011, 49). Unlike private sector employers, public sector employers must justify firing an employee who is seeking to organize, and due process rights prevent immediate firings without review. Thus, one of the most potent tools for private sector employers seeking to hamper unionization efforts is largely unavailable to public sector organizing campaigns. Bronfenbrenner and Juravich found that "workers in the private sector were almost six times more likely to be fired and not reinstated before a union election than they were in the public sector" (1994, 18).

These factors combine to discourage hostile employer opposition in the public sector. Without the virulent opposition private sector workers face, government workers have found greater success in union representation elections. Looking at all certification elections from 1991 to 1992, Bronfenbrenner and Juravitch found that unions win 85 percent of certification elections in the public sector versus just 48 percent in the private sector. Remarkably, "in almost one quarter of all campaigns in the public sector, the employer did not campaign at all against the union" (1994, 1). Employer resistance is not unheard of in the government sector, but it does not dominate the landscape. Instead, "private sector employers are six times more likely to commit unfair labor practices such as discharges for union activity, and more than twice as likely to use other tactics such as captive-audience meetings, employer leaflets and mailings, supervisor one-on-ones, and illegal wage increases" (1). In the 1960s, the passage of pro-bargaining legislation in many states combined with more amicable labor relations in the public sector to promote union organizing efforts (Farber 2005; Freeman and Ichniowski 1988). Once the political and legal barriers to public sector unionization were overcome, the more cooperative employer relations in the public sector enabled government union density to expand.

The public sector union militarism of the late 1960s and 1970s is a vivid illustration of what a growing government union movement buoyed by new

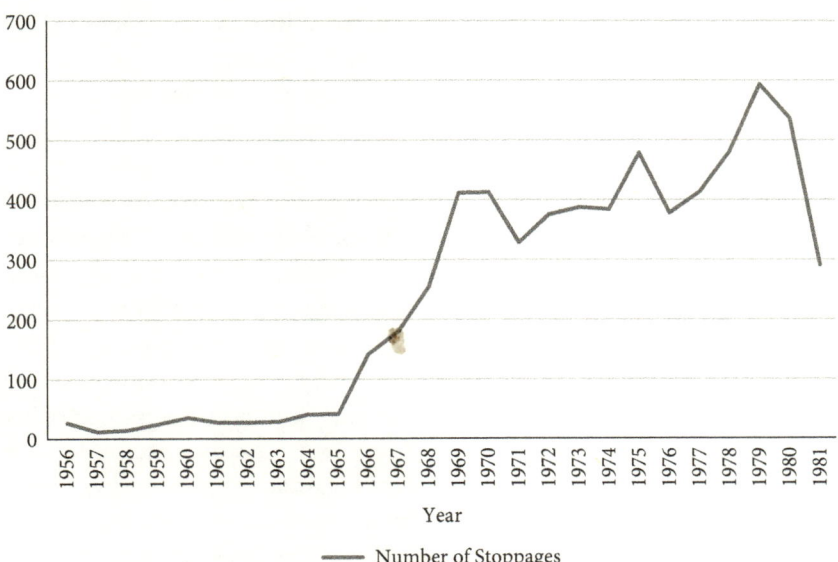

Figure 3. Work stoppages in the government industry, 1956–1981. Bureau of Labor Statistics 1968, 1977, 1980, 1983.

state, local, and federal laws had become. For instance, Martin Luther King Jr. was in Memphis on that fateful day in 1968 not to support a civil rights demonstration but rather to show solidarity with striking AFSCME municipal sanitation workers. While strikes were (and remain) technically illegal for the vast majority of public sector workers, this did not stop teachers, policemen, firefighters, and other public workers from taking such action in increasing numbers.[6] In 1958, there were 15 public sector strikes involving 1,730 workers. In 1980, there were 536 strikes involving 223,600 workers (PSRC 1982). Figure 3 illustrates the dramatic rise in work stoppages[7] by government workers as measured by the Department of Labor. Prior to 1965, there were less than 50 such stoppages each year. After 1965, work stoppages rose into the triple digits, peaking at 593 stoppages involving over 254,100 public sector employees in 1979. This number is remarkable considering the fact that many of these stoppages were illegal owing to a lack of collective bargaining rights or legislation that granted limited rights that did not include striking. Such activity is indicative of the rising prominence of organized public sector workers and their implementation of disruptive techniques to accomplish their goals. At the time, thanks to the watershed moment in government collective bargaining laws, public sector unions appeared to be a permanent fixture with growing influence in local, state, and federal politics.

However, this moment of tremendous success for government unions was fragile. Even in 1966 after the public sector movement had experienced their watershed moment, underlying problems were evident. As the general counsel to the AFT, John Ligtenberg, noted at the time, "Much of the chaos that existed in labor relations before 1935 when the National Labor Relations Act became law, still survives in the field of public employment" (Ligtenberg 1966). In other words, there still was no uniform, solid legal foundation for public sector employees across the country. Indeed, state laws governing public sector labor relations varied in virtually every respect including whether they granted collective bargaining rights; which workers were granted rights (e.g., state or municipal employees, workers in certain occupations but not others); what issues unions were allowed to bargain about; and whether strikes were permitted or other means of resolving disputes were mandated.

Correspondence between George W. Tayler and David L. Cole, who were serving on the New York governor's Public Employee Relations Committee, which would help draft the legislation to legalize collective bargaining for New York state employees, perfectly captures the troublesome underside of the government union success in the 1960s. Tayler, writing in 1966 to Cole, opens his letter by noting the remarkable degree of variation in state collective bargaining laws and laments that he "wish we knew _why_" the states were so different. He closes the paragraph by remarking that "the varying results should not be surprising, I suppose, under our federal-state system of government" (Tayler 1966). Tayler's suspicions in 1966 were prescient. Excluded from the Wagner Act and operating in a federated system, public sector unions were able to gain collective bargaining rights at the state and local levels. But even as the government workforce expanded and there was growing public acceptance of government unionism, the gains made during this time were limited. As the following chapters will demonstrate, the unique form of these laws—piecemeal and set at the state level—restricted the success of government unionism, which has had lasting consequences for organized labor in the United States.

Chapter 5

The 1970s: Labor Out of Alignment

When Scott Walker introduced his "budget repair bill" in 2011 to strip many public sector workers in Wisconsin of their collective bargaining rights, he privately alluded at the time that he was specifically targeting government employees rather than all union members as part of a "divide and conquer" strategy (Stein and Marley 2013, 47). Walker was so confident in his strategy and the lack of genuine solidarity within the labor movement that he did not expect that private sector unions would mobilize on behalf of their public sector brethren to challenge the bill (51). Although Walker's intuition about private sector unions in Wisconsin was ultimately proven wrong, looking back we see countless instances where labor solidarity was not the norm. In the 1970s, Walker's "divide and conquer" strategy—driving a wedge between the public and private sector labor movement—was successful. Whereas solidarity is the clarion call of the union movement, it is not always practiced in reality; the divisions within organized labor have deep, long-standing roots.

The most salient divisions at the turn of the twentieth century in the American labor movement were numerous and often debilitating. Racial, ethnic, and gendered divisions of labor led many unions to organize around exclusionary principles. When John L. Lewis left the AFL and formed the CIO in 1935, it was the culmination of decades of disagreement within the labor movement over whether to organize, as the AFL had up until that point, by craft, targeting the most highly skilled workers, or by industry as Lewis suggested, welcoming everyone from the least skilled to the most skilled in an industry into one big, inclusive union. Looking back, David M. Kennedy's observation is apt that "the house of labor was deeply divided" (1999, 298). While the merger between the AFL and CIO in 1955 signified that the conflict between craft and industrial unionism had largely been resolved, divisions within the house of labor remained.

A major remaining division is between public and private sector unions. There are major differences between public and private sector unions: (a) public sector union members, on average, tend to earn higher incomes and be more highly educated; (b) public sector unions have a higher percentage of women and minorities; (c) the public sector deals in non-tradable goods, and thus public sector unions' work actions often threaten vital services rather than halt production; and (d) a public sector union's employer is the local, state, or federal government, and thus public sector unions can and do exert pressure through political activity. Although there likely would have been friction between these unions as a result of their differences, public and private sector unions are not inevitably in conflict; organized labor is inherently diverse along a variety of characteristics and these divisions are not necessarily debilitating.

Yet when government unions finally gained organizing might in the 1970s, the relationship between public and private sector unions was, at its best, disconnected organizationally, and, at its worst, in direct conflict. This raises the question: Why do some divisions and not others become salient within an organization at certain moments in time? In particular, why were public and private sector unions so organizationally divided in the 1970s? It is easy to attribute organizational conflict to a failure of leadership, but such divisions can have deeper, long-standing origins. This chapter explores the division between public and private sector unions in the 1970s to illustrate how institutional forces outside the labor movement—in this case the incongruent timing and sequencing of union development created by divided labor law—can create salient divisions within an organization.

Labor's Incongruent Development

Earlier chapters introduced us to the significance of divided labor law for organized labor's development: the exclusion of public sector employees from the foundation of national-level private sector labor law (the 1935 Wagner Act) meant that public sector employees were forced to target their demand-making at the state and local levels rather than the national level, which resulted in inherently more vulnerable and unequal collective bargaining rights. Previous chapters stressed the importance of *where* collective bargaining rights originated. This chapter focuses on the significance of *when* collective bargaining rights were obtained. As one academic put it in 1967, "In American labor history, the 30s were the decade of the industrial worker. The 60s are proving to be the decade of the public employee" (Hamilton 1967). When we look at Figure 1, it is clear that public sector union development and private sector union development are not aligned. Thus divided labor law not only shaped labor's development by situating private and public sector unions at different levels of government (federal and state, respectively), it further affected when public and private sector unions obtained collective bargaining rights and consequently when each sector's union movement was established.

The causal importance of timing and sequencing is central to understanding the organizational relationship between public and private sector unions (Pierson 2004, 54). As detailed in Chapter 3, the exclusion of government employees from the Wagner Act and the absence of public sector collective bargaining law(s) delayed public sector union growth at the very time that private sector union density skyrocketed in the 1930s and 1940s. In other words, "the law artificially repressed the size of these unions," putting public and private sector union development out of sync (Slater 2004, 199). It wasn't until the 1960s that public sector employees were able to generate the needed pressure to get pro–public sector collective bargaining laws passed, resulting in a period of explosive public sector union growth in the 1960s and 1970s. Public sector union density more than tripled over the span of these twenty years. In contrast, private sector union density declined by more than a third over this same period (Visser 2012).

In the 1970s, public and private sector unions found themselves in conflict with each other, further highlighting their differences. This was not simply the result of the nature of the two types of unions but more the result of the divided labor law in the United States and what Joseph Slater has termed labor's "unsynchronized development" (2004, 202). With divided labor law "artificially repressing" public sector unionism for decades, government unions grew and gained power not in tandem with private sector unions after the Wagner Act but instead in the 1960s and 1970s when private sector unions had already reached their height of power. This sowed discord within the movement. Even more troubling for labor solidarity, the decade of the 1970s was a period of cultural, economic, and political crisis, which amplified conflict between these two domains.

The Importance of Timing and Sequencing

Labor's unsynchronized development is a vivid illustration of the consequential role of timing and sequencing. The analysis in this chapter echoes Jacob Hacker's study of health insurance in Britain, Canada, and the United States. He finds that "the timing and sequence of policy developments shaped what was possible" (1998, 96). In Hacker's case, critical timing elements, like whether national health insurance is enacted before large portions of the population have private health insurance and whether national health insurance comes before or after the dramatic rise in health-care costs, shaped whether these countries successfully adopted national health care. Hacker is concerned with how the sequence of developments makes the possibility of a specific policy, national health care, more or less feasible, but the logic can apply more broadly to organizational development. In particular, Hacker identifies how the ordering of events can make certain paths more or less likely; this can be applied to analyzing the likelihood of organized labor working more or less cooperatively.

Cohesion within the labor movement was shaped by when public and private sector unions developed (at separate times or in tandem) and by the external conditions during this development: economic growth/contraction and political support/backlash. Inter-union cooperation is promoted when sectors develop in tandem, fostering organizational identities and connections as they grow together. Conflict is created when one sector develops late and has to fight its way into an entrenched movement. Further, cooperation is promoted when the external environment creates a sense of abundant resources and optimism, whereas economic contraction or political backlash can amplify conflict by pitting unions against each other. Thus when the timing and sequencing align public and private sector unions, a more unified labor movement is likely: both sectors gain their collective bargaining rights together and grow in tandem during a period of economic growth and political support. When these variables do not align, conflict within the labor movement is much more likely. Moreover, when these variables are out of alignment, the potential for a strong, unified labor movement in which both sectors peak in power and influence together is also lost. Labor's weakness today should thus be understood in historical context: labor missed the crucial moment when the movement would have been the strongest possible.

Broadly, this chapter illustrates how incongruent development paths can create salient divisions within an organization. Timing (public sector union growth occurring late and during a period of cultural, economic, and political crises) and sequencing (public sector growth occurring well after private sector union growth) amplified the public/private conflict within the labor movement. For organized labor, the salience of the public/private division became an internal weakness that diminished labor's political effectiveness. This chapter also sheds light on some of labor's "failures" over the last several decades, including why the 1970s marked the end of the New Deal agenda; the failure of labor law reform in the late 1970s; and why private sector unions did not embrace the dynamic, growing, explicitly political, and social movement oriented–public sector union movement in the 1970s. Recognizing the important ways divided labor law has patterned the behavior and development of public and private sector unions vividly illustrates why the 1970s was a missed opportunity for the emergence of a revitalized, more equal, diverse labor movement working in concert with an array of social movements to further the cause of working Americans.

Looking Beyond Blaming Labor's Leadership

There is strong pressure within the labor movement to maintain solidarity because this is the source of much of labor's economic and political power. Individuals organize when they share a collective interest that they cannot adequately advance on their own (Olson 1968). A similar logic can apply to organizing across unions: we should see cooperation when labor unions share a collective interest that cannot be advanced independently. Indeed, we see organized labor cooperate when individual unions are organizationally intertwined, they share goals and tactics, and incentives exist—like the potential for a legislative or strike victory—to encourage them to work together. Many factors can intervene, however, to make unions' collective interests less prominent and their differences more visible, making it harder for individual unions to recognize and pursue inter-union cohesion.

A central assumption in this chapter and project more broadly is that a unified, organizationally cohesive labor movement is crucial to the labor movement's political effectiveness. Practically, this translates into a unified AFL-CIO because it is the best-positioned organization today to represent the entire labor movement. Efforts to create alternative labor federations, most recently the Change to Win federation formed in 2005, have been at best marginally successful. Today, Change to Win is a separate federation mostly in name only as both labor federations have recognized the need to work together if they hope to be politically effective. For all its faults, the AFL-CIO is the central organization of the labor movement with an organizational structure spanning the country, a diverse membership of unions, and the history and name recognition to lead the labor movement. Despite these resources, however, the AFL-CIO has not been as politically influential as we might expect—the union defections to Change to Win were the result of legitimate frustration with the AFL-CIO. Thus, given that practically speaking the AFL-CIO is the most promising organization for the union movement, why has it faltered in its efforts to unify and lead the labor movement? Part of the answer can be found in the different development trajectories of public and private sector unions.

This chapter draws on interviews with labor leaders,[1] historical documents, and secondary source accounts to explore the relationship between public and private sector unions in the 1970s. There is a tendency among labor historians to see the public and private sector union movements as wholly separate entities in the 1970s and to describe the government unions as "exceptions" without asking why the two sectors were so different and distinct in the first place (Lichtenstein 2002, 181). In Chapter 3 we learned that the AFL and CIO supported early public sector organizing efforts in the 1930s and 1940s. When the two federations merged in 1955, government employee collective bargaining rights were regularly part of the AFL-CIO's platform. Why did this change just two decades later? This chapter begins with the premise that a labor movement divided by sector is neither natural nor inevitable and instead seeks to understand why the public and private sector union movements were such distinct entities in the 1970s.

Labor historians also tend to blame the intractable leadership of the AFL-CIO for failing to support and join the New Left social movements in the 1960s and 1970s—perhaps labor's last, best chance to stave off their plummeting membership losses and power. A typical account, in asking why labor "missed the boat" of the civil rights, student, feminist, environmental, gay, and other social movements, explains that "to a large extent, it was the conservatism bred by business unionism in which many labor leaders presided over increasingly narrow member-oriented organizations that had lost a broader vision and passion for social justice. This combined with ideologically intense cold war anticommunism made many labor leaders (led by George Meany and the AFL-CIO) suspicious and at times quite hostile to new political stirrings on the left, whether it was civil rights, antiwar protests, or the women's movement.... Most labor leaders ... gave their primary loyalty to the status quo" (Turner and Hurd 2001, 14–15). Thus revitalization was "blocked by defensive, threatened leaders" who were able to "cordon off their organization from the radical currents of change" (17). While labor leaders certainly made poor decisions in this period by eschewing these other movements, it is important to recognize that labor leaders and their decisions occur within a much broader context. Institutions and outside political forces can make certain decisions and behaviors, such as whether to align with or turn away from potential allies, more or less likely.

Timing and sequencing affected many of the factors that shaped union leaders' decisions about the New Left movements. Private sector and public sector unions' distinct organizational identities were in part products of when they each developed: private sector unions gained clout when the Cold War mind-set was dominant, whereas public sector unions rose to power and adopted the tactics of their contemporaries including those of the civil rights movement. Further, the labor movements' decision about how to treat the up-and-coming public sector unions was shaped by the era: rather than the prosperous 1950s when the debate was over how to share the wealth, the 1970s were marked by economic crises and discussion of tightened budgets and austerity measures. Thus divided labor law and the delayed development of organized labor helped foster a context that discouraged cooperation between public and private sector unions.

As a result, when trying to understand the failure of organized labor to join forces with the New Left social movements, we cannot simply look to the decisions of the leaders of the AFL-CIO and its affiliate unions. Lowell Turner and Richard W. Hurd note that at the very time that organized labor was eschewing the new social movements, "the main exception to the predominant pattern of the 1960s and 1970s lay in the public sector" (2001, 17). Many public sector unions were part and parcel of the New Left social movements and, rather than seeing public sector unions as the main exception, this chapter instead asks why they were not the vanguard of change for the labor movement, ushering organized labor into New Left politics. The answer lies not simply in the decisions of a few leaders but rather in the delayed growth of public sector unions, which amplified the conflicts between public and private sector unions, ultimately making private sector unions less likely to embrace their public sector brethren and the New Left social movements.

Comparing public and private sector union development temporally emphasizes that we need to understand labor leaders' behavior in context and vividly illustrates how the fortunes of labor's two sectors were out of alignment—growth and decline happened simultaneously. Moreover, this growth and decline occurred under the specter of cultural, economic, and political upheaval. The incongruent development of public and private sector unions in the face of a decade of turmoil heightened the public/private conflict in the 1970s and weakened organized labor's effectiveness in American politics.

Incongruent Timing and the Cultural, Economic, and Political Cleavages of the 1970s

For organized labor, the years 1970 and 1971 were an auspicious start to the decade. These years were described by the media as plagued by strikes and confrontation (Labor: The Year of Confrontation 1970; Labor: A Plague of Strikes 1971). Longshoremen, teamsters, mine workers, autoworkers, teachers, postal workers, and countless others participated in a massive strike wave at the outset of the decade: "In 1970 alone there were over 2.4 million workers engaged in large-scale work stoppages, thirty-four massive stoppages of ten thousand workers or more, and a raft of wildcats, slowdowns, and aggressive stands in contract negotiations" (Cowie 2010, 2). A variety of factors led to the strike wave including: the happenstance of numerous contracts expiring in a short period of time, the spirit of protest carried over from the civil rights and New Left movements, a young and energized union membership frustrated with the less confrontational approach of union leaders, and invigorated public sector employees just beginning to see dividends from their struggles for recognition. It was a heady time for organized labor as private sector unions wielded significant power and influence (not yet able to see that economic conditions generating their strike activity would only worsen, crippling union bargaining power), and public sector unions were experiencing tremendous organizing and legislative success.

Rather than presaging a decade of coordinated public and private sector union militancy, 1970 and 1971 can be seen as a brief moment when public sector labor's ascendance overlapped with a still relevant and powerful private sector labor movement. Through the rest of the decade, the fortunes of the public and private sector unions would not overlap in the same way again. By the middle of the decade, the change was stark; as one article noted at the time, "The twin symbols of organized labor" were "the unemployed Detroit autoworker and the striking San Francisco cop. Joblessness in the private sector and militance in the public employee sector have dominated the labor news for the past 12 months" (Broder 1975b). And by the second half of the decade, conditions led reporters to declare that "solidarity, a once sacrosanct word," was, for labor leaders, "difficult to use any more" (Pryor and Steiger 1977). Thus the "year of the strike" was just that, one year, rather than the beginning of a sustained, vibrant, and growing private *and* public sector labor movement. After this brief moment of overlap in 1970 and 1971, public and private sector union development became increasingly incongruent. The timing and sequencing of public and private sector union growth increased the saliency of their differences because public sector unions were outsiders to an already established labor movement trying to force their way into an entrenched, complacent leadership when cultural, economic, and political crises pitted public sector and private sector union members against each other.

Distinct Identities amid Cultural Upheaval

Private and public sector unions developed different organizational identities that often contributed to a lack of understanding and empathy between them. Private sector craft and industrial unions matured during the 1930s–1950s when there was one dominant union model: the private sector. These unions came of age during the post–World War II labor/business compromise that, while still marked by strikes, included a greater acceptance of private sector union members' collective bargaining rights on behalf of business. In contrast, public sector unions matured in the 1960s and 1970s when the dominant union model—the private sector—was well established but could not apply to them because they still had to obtain their fundamental right to collectively bargain. Further, they came of age during a period of new political tactics embodied by the nonviolent protests, sit-ins, and other actions of the civil rights movement.

Private sector unions understandably viewed labor conflict through the lens of the private sector model that had been dominant for several decades. But this dominant model was ill-suited for public sector labor relations. Thus, while private sector unions generally supported pro–public sector collective bargaining laws, in practice they often resisted sharing power and failed to sympathize with government union issues. In interviews labor leaders often mentioned hostility among private sector unions toward their public sector brethren. Jerry Wurf noted in 1981 that "one thing that has always irritated me is that large pieces of the private sector, not just conservative folks in the building trades, would not accept the fact that public workers should have the rights of trade unions" (quoted in Serrin 1981). Many government unionists worked in white-collar jobs, were more highly educated, and earned higher incomes. One former state AFL-CIO president explained that "many leaders thought public employees were not real union members because they were not blue collar" (Interview #20). In addition, in interviews, some leaders mentioned that private sector union members did not understand the different environment of public sector collective bargaining.

Because of the limitations on their collective bargaining rights, such as strike bans, public sector unions would often turn to other unions for help when they had problems with an employer. As one former American Federation of Teachers (AFT) leader explained, "The public sector would bring collective bargaining issues to the [state AFL-CIO] convention and the private sector would wonder, why are you bringing it to us, take it to the shop floor. Well, the public sector doesn't have a shop floor. There was frustration getting the private sector to understand that the public sector is working in a different environment. They didn't want to be bothered with public sector pension issues. The private sector doesn't understand why the public sector can't just hand out flyers and agitate at work" (Interview #23).

Given the economic crises private sector unions began encountering in the 1970s, public sector pension issues could seem rather trivial at times to private sector union members. As one AFT union leader recalled, "There was some feeling that public employees had it awfully easy because they had no plant closings, layoffs, etc. Thus, we often had less sympathy in a labor dispute from the private sector unions" (Interview #23). An AFSCME leader further remarked in our interview, "I used to think it was a very lonely fight when we called to raise taxes" (Interview #38). The private sector union model of blue-collar workers exercising their collective bargaining rights to negotiate with their employers did not fit with the often white-collar public sector employees who were still fighting for collective bargaining rights. Public and private sector unions' different organizational challenges—one to gain any legal recognition, the other to negotiate, at times quite forcefully, for the best contract within an established system—promoted a lack of cohesion. Because they operated in different legal environments, one expanding collective bargaining rights and one ossifying, the private sector unions at times failed to understand the needs of the public sector unions joining their movement.

Government unions displayed their own lack of empathy and understanding toward private sector unions because of their distinct organizational identities. In many interviews, leaders recalled public sector workers' snobbish attitude toward blue-collar union members, preferring to think of themselves as professional associations rather than unions. The private sector union members may have incorrectly seen the public sector jobs as cushy. In one respect, however, their perceptions were accurate because government workplaces in general were relatively milder union organizing and bargaining environments with less hostile employer resistance. One labor leader emphasized that government employees—who were fortunate enough to have gained collective bargaining rights—sometimes forgot "what the private sector was going through" because, when contract negotiations broke down, "public employees could just go to arbitration whereas private sector employers would just bypass the union" (Interview #23).[2] In addition, many states and localities continued to outlaw strikes for government employees but developed other mechanisms for those times when negotiations broke down, including mediation, whereby a third party helps negotiate and suggests resolutions to disputes; interest arbitration, whereby a third party considers all evidence, testimony, and positions of both sides and usually makes a binding decision; and fact-finding, whereby a third party investigates the dispute and usually makes a non-binding recommendation. All three of these alternatives to the strike offered public sector workers ways of managing conflict with their employers at the very time that the private sector was struggling to cooperate with their employers. Increasingly, hostile employer resistance was largely a private sector phenomenon, and this fact was not fully appreciated within the public sector.

The lack of empathy was enhanced by the fact that, in many cases, public sector unions were literally outsiders in the labor movement because they were not affiliated with the AFL-CIO. Due in large part to the fact that yellow-dog contracts barred many government employees from forming unions and their employee associations from affiliating with labor unions, many public sector workers were forced to form associations unaffiliated with the AFL-CIO (Slater 2004, 69). Absent a national collective bargaining law, states and localities continued to employ yellow-dog contracts well into the 1960s (70). As a consequence, some of the largest public sector unions, including the National Education Association (NEA), the National Federation of

Federal Employees, and the Fraternal Order of Police, were not affiliated with the AFL-CIO. Thus, divided labor law created an organizational barrier between the public and private sector labor movements.

The clashes of organizational identity between the public and private sector were amplified in the 1970s by the cultural upheaval of the decade. The 1970s witnessed a clash of cultures as mainstream Americans' older, more established values conflicted with the radical and diverse viewpoints of African Americans, intellectuals, gays and lesbians, feminists, and others involved in the New Left social movements, as well as their calls for recognition. Public and private sector unions' organizational identities tracked onto opposing sides of the cultural clashes: private sector union identity was firmly entrenched in the Cold War liberal consensus of the 1950s, whereas public sector unions largely arrived on the scene in the 1960s when connections with the civil rights movement and later the antiwar movement helped forge a very different identity.

Organized labor was staunchly entrenched in the old mind-set, which was vividly depicted by the Hard Hat Riot in New York City on May 8, 1970. Several hundred antiwar protestors had gathered on Wall Street protesting the Kent State shooting. Two hundred Building and Construction Trades Council members soon arrived to oppose the protestors. The confrontation quickly turned violent as the construction workers "proceeded to storm the steps of City Hall, chasing student protestors through the streets of the financial district, and bloodying around seventy people in the process" (Cowie 2010, 135). Demonstrations continued throughout the month of May, culminating in a rally of one hundred thousand in support of the war sponsored by the Building and Construction Trades Council of Greater New York (135). The conflict was portrayed in the media as a clash of cultures as the hard hats worn by the construction workers in the riot became "a powerful metaphor for the deepening conflicts that had developed during the 1960s over politics, gender roles, and cultural values" (Freeman 1993, 736). The "hard hats"—staunch Cold Warriors in favor of the war in Vietnam and the cultural status quo that ensured their unions and union jobs were not integrated—were a strong presence in the leadership and rank and file of much of organized labor in the 1970s, except the public sector.

Indeed, the sharp cultural divide between the New York construction workers and antiwar protesters encapsulates much of the difference in organizational identity between public and private sector unions at the time. On one side, "most labor leaders . . . stood in an increasingly stolid, unresponsive center, not on the dynamic frontier where they had once defined, and stretched, the limits of conventional politics" (Lichtenstein 2002, 187). These leaders were the same people who "had battled the Communists in the 1940s and accommodated themselves to the constraints of the Cold War and the narrow compass of the Taft-Hartley labor relations regime" and thus they "remained entirely out of tune with the multiple insurgencies that began to animate left-liberal politics in the 1960s" (187). On the other side, public sector unions and their leaders, particularly teachers and government employees, were an integral part of the New Left, demanding equal rights, respect, and compensation on par with white, male, private sector employees who had seen such dramatic improvements in their working conditions and compensation in the postwar era.[3] To be sure, this distinction masks important variation within the private and public sector unions at the time—police unions in particular were and remain a much more conservative group—but it is no coincidence that the antiwar vanguard in the labor movement found strong support among the unions of teachers and government employees.

Whereas the private sector was an entrenched part of the political order, favoring backroom lobbying, public sector unions were taking to the streets to gain legal recognition. Government unions utilized tactics drawn from the civil rights movement including protests, marches, and defiance of laws including strike bans. Moreover, because public sector unions represented a diverse membership that included many women and minorities, they frequently collaborated on social justice issues that the other social movements of the time were championing (Zieger and Gall 2002, 210). Thus, at the very time the public sector was fighting to gain entry into the leadership circles of organized labor, their differences from the private sector in terms of organizational identity were amplified by the larger national conflicts over politics and values brought about by the New Left, making cooperation that much more difficult.

How cultural upheaval amplified public/private sector conflict is embodied in the power struggles between the existing leaders of the union movement and the up-and-coming public sector unions in the 1970s. While the AFL and CIO initially offered support to government union efforts in the 1930s and 1940s, the relationship became strained as public sector unions expanded, becoming some of the most liberal and militant union voices, and demanding recognition and influence within the labor movement. Labor leadership in the 1970s was largely a stalwart group of aging, industrial unionists led by George Meany. Meany became president of the AFL in 1952 and then oversaw the merger of the AFL and CIO in 1955; he was president of the AFL-CIO until 1979, when he was eighty-five.

George Meany did not fit the model of the politically disruptive, radical unionist. Instead, he led the AFL-CIO in a more conservative, business-oriented direction focused on backroom lobbying in Congress and tough contract negotiations. Meany's leadership reflected the times: after World War II, organized labor gained a more prominent and accepted position among political elites, but labor's newfound status was premised on their acceptance of the liberal consensus, ridding unions of many of the most radical leaders (especially the Communists), and full-fledged support of the United States in the Cold War. Meany, a former plumber, embodied midcentury organized labor's focus on the skilled trades, maintaining the gains that had been made and negotiating for increasingly better contracts for existing union members. Because labor's organizational identity had been forged in the postwar years, Meany did not endorse the March on Washington and had a strong Cold War mind-set, vehemently supporting the war in Vietnam and refusing to endorse Democratic candidate George McGovern in the 1972 presidential race.

Meany's refusal to endorse McGovern is particularly striking because McGovern had had a strong pro-labor record throughout his career, and labor had endorsed the Democratic presidential candidate for the previous twenty years (Zieger and Gall 2002, 219).[4] One of Meany's political advisors anonymously analyzed the AFL-CIO's decision to remain neutral in cultural terms saying that "this is our showdown with the new politics" and "at some point the movement within the Democratic Party had to be stemmed, and this is it" (quoted in Shabecoff 1972). This echoes the analysis of Nixon campaign leader Clark MacGregor that the AFL-CIO saw the Democratic ticket as "a new McGovern élite accepting within its ranks radical professors, student agitators, professional welfarists, extremists of virtually every sort, an élite which makes the ordinary working man feel unwelcome and unwanted" (quoted in Shabecoff 1972). Such descriptions cast the Democratic Party as two opposing sides: the old-line New Deal liberals and the up-and-coming New Left movements. The labor movement mirrored this opposition: George Meany and the AFL-CIO Executive Council on one side and the public sector unions largely on the other.

In sharp contrast to Meany's intractable leadership, Walter Reuther, president of the United Automobile Workers (UAW) and former president of the more activist CIO (then vice president of the merged AFL-CIO), was the champion of the more liberal wing of labor. It was Reuther who helped stage the March on Washington, stood beside Martin Luther King as he delivered his "I Have a Dream" speech, advocated more radical policies like profit-sharing plans, and eventually pulled the UAW out of the AFL-CIO in opposition to the Vietnam War. Reuther accused the AFL-CIO of becoming "historically obsolete" and criticized the Executive Council for being "increasingly comfortable custodians of the status quo" who displayed "complacency," "indifference," and a "lack of social vision" (quoted in Cowie 2010, 43). Reuther died in a plane crash in 1970, leaving the more radical elements of the labor movement without a spokesperson.

One of the best candidates to take up Reuther's more radical mantle was Jerry Wurf, the president of the quickly expanding American Federation of State, County and Municipal Employees (AFSCME). Wurf was a civil rights veteran unwilling to toe the line of AFL-CIO positions and, as the head of an expanding union, gained a seat on the AFL-CIO Executive Council. Despite his seat at the table, existing union leaders bristled at Wurf's quick rise and more radical politics. As Jefferson R. Cowie explained, "AFSCME and Jerry Wurf were regarded as barely tolerated mavericks and outsiders in mainstream labor circles" (2010, 62). A profile of Wurf in 1976 captured the divide between Wurf and the AFL-CIO leadership: "At A.F.L.C.I.O. headquarters in Washington, old line union leaders—in particular, George Meany—don't seem to know what to make of an international union president whose alliances extend outside the labor federation and whose militancy is sometimes turned against it" (Shapiro 1976). Jerry Wurf himself told a reporter at the time that "people resent us" and that "our role in the AFL-CIO was that of being the oddballs, the peculiar ones" (Pryor and Steiger 1977; Goulden 1982, 184). Resentment stemmed from AFSCME's rapid growth and activist membership at a time when the industrial unions were struggling to maintain their membership levels. Other unions shared Wurf and AFSCME's sentiment. Though not affiliated with the AFL-CIO, National Education Association executive secretary Terry Herndon remarked publicly in 1975 that public employee groups had been "struggling valiantly, with at best tolerant silence from the AFL-CIO" (Broder 1975a). Whereas the private sector unions were already powerful entities, with long-standing contracts protecting their members, government unions—embodying the radical, social movement tradition of the period—continued to battle for legal recognition and acceptance within the union movement.

The timing of public sector union growth did not align with that of the private sector, heightening their differences. Private sector unions and the AFL-CIO leadership were largely content with the gains they had made, convinced that the bureaucratized labor relations crafted in the postwar era that had brought them to power would remain intact. George Meany perfectly encapsulated this mentality when, in the face of declining membership in the 1970s, he told reporters, "Why should we worry about organizing groups of people who do not want to be organized? . . . Frankly, I used to worry about the membership, about the size of the membership. But quite a few years ago, I just stopped worrying about it" (quoted in Lichtenstein 2002, 247). Private sector unions' satisfaction with the status quo and public sector union growth and militancy at times led to an organizational divide between AFSCME and the AFL-CIO. As one AFSCME leader remembers:

> As we grew, we sought to increase our presence and influence inside the house of labor, the AFL-CIO. That involved the playing out of a strategic argument between us and George Meany and the mainstream of the house of labor. We didn't go along with the support of the AFL-CIO for the Vietnam War. When the AFL-CIO was neutral between Nixon and McGovern, we were for McGovern. Federal employees that were kicked out of another union because they were antiwar found their way into our union. In 1972, we operated a political action coalition for the presidency that functioned independently from the AFL-CIO. We continued growing and adopting our own strategy and stance in regard to national politics. That sometimes resulted in votes on the [AFL-CIO] Executive Council of 32–1 against whatever we were putting forward. (Interview #40)

In the face of an existing AFL-CIO leadership that was out of step with the New Left movement and more radical politics of the 1960s and 1970s, AFSCME and Jerry Wurf were often forced to act alone (Cowie 2010, 72).

AFSCME's outsider status was shared by other public sector unions. The United Federal Workers of America (UFWA), a CIO union, recognized and advocated for its diverse workforce from its inception. The union established anti-discrimination and interracial unity committees in the 1940s and later, in response to Truman's anti-discrimination executive order, created agency fair employment committees that used the order to advocate against specific instances of workplace discrimination (UFWA 1948). They emphasized to their members that "we must . . . not permit ourselves to be trapped into approaching the questions of jobs for Negroes as a fight for position between

Negro and white workers" and argued that maintaining the gains made by African Americans during World War II is "the issue which affects every American worker, whether white or Negro" (UFWA 1944, 13). Likewise, the union advocated for paid sick leave and maternity leave, the expansion and support of part-time work, and the expansion of adequate childcare facilities to support working mothers. One of the union's goals was to "keep our mothers on the job"; the challenges working women faced in the workplace were "the problems of the community" and not the sole responsibility of working mothers (14).

The UFWA was one of the more radical unions, but its progressivism was not unique among government unions. The American Federation of Teachers (AFT) was an early supporter of the civil rights movement. Their future president, Albert Shanker, when he was president of the New York City teachers in the United Federation of Teachers, marched with Dr. King from Selma to Montgomery and helped fund the A. Philip Randolph Institute to promote relations between the labor and civil rights movements (Kahlenberg 2007, 61, 63). While Shanker himself was a vocal proponent of the Vietnam War, as early as 1967 the membership of the AFT adopted an anti-Vietnam resolution at their annual convention (147). Aside from his ideological reasons for supporting the war, Shanker also recognized what Jerry Wurf experienced firsthand: "George Meany used Vietnam as a litmus test among labor-union leaders. The AFT would not be taken seriously within the labor movement so long as it took a position on Vietnam far outside of labor's mainstream" (148). The AFT membership also, despite Shanker's misgivings, overwhelmingly voted, like AFSCME, to endorse McGovern (157).

The AFL-CIO responded to this by elevating Shanker to the AFL-CIO Executive Council in 1973, bypassing the current AFT president. At the time, Shanker was president of a union local and one of twenty AFT vice presidents. The Executive Council was traditionally filled with presidents of the national unions, so Shanker's election was an unprecedented move by the AFL-CIO. The message was clear, as one union leader put it at the time: Shanker's position on Vietnam was more in line with that of the AFL-CIO leadership than with the rest of the AFT, and as a result, "George loved Al" (quoted in Kahlenberg 2007, 159). Shanker was rewarded for his Vietnam stance, while the AFT's and AFSCME's outspoken positions on the war and McGovern were met with hostility by Meany and the entrenched leadership of the AFL-CIO.

The AFL-CIO's cold response to the public sector unions was reflected in a variety of ways. It was slow to create a public sector department within the federation and to add Wurf to the Executive Council, despite the fact that it was one of the fastest-growing and most dynamic unions within the movement (Goulden 1982, 207–208). The AFL-CIO was also slow at times to vocally back or provide lobbying support for important public sector issues. For instance, the AFL-CIO pulled its support in 1972 from the State and Local Fiscal Assistance Act, a key policy priority for AFSCME that would support precarious local government finances and protect AFSCME union jobs. The AFL-CIO's refusal to support the measure was seen by AFSCME as a "striking betrayal, and for Wurf, it only seemed further evidence that critical public sector issues were at best secondary concerns for the Federation's lobbyists" (Hower 2013, 282–283). AFSCME leadership lamented having to act alone and in effect watch their backs for fear that the AFL-CIO would betray them for another union's interests (282).

AFSCME joined with several other public sector unions in 1971 to form the Coalition of American Public Employees (CAPE) to lobby for a national-level collective bargaining law (CAPE 1975). The group acted independently of the AFL-CIO because the federation had yet to form a public employee department; once formed, CAPE "drew little support from the rest of the AFL-CIO" (Hower 2013, 300). CAPE is just one illustration of how public sector unions had to look outside of the AFL-CIO for organizational support. Likewise, in 1975 AFSCME and the NEA joined with several liberal private sector unions to form the Labor Coalition Clearinghouse to organize electoral efforts after the AFL-CIO refused to take an active role in the Democratic Party nomination process (360). These organizational divides were emblematic of the splits within organized labor.

Jerry Wurf's antiwar stance was certainly part of the rift as Meany's Cold War mind-set maintained the AFL-CIO's pro-war stance, but Wurf's isolation was also emblematic of his outsider status: he represented an up-and-coming group, embodied a new radical cultural and political movement, and tried to force recognition from a stalwart, established leadership. Cowie notes that this conflict was distinct from previous divisions within the labor movement because one side had already won: "the labor question already had its solution" with private sector labor relations conforming to the dominant business unionism model and "a host of institutional interests invested in maintaining those solutions exactly how they already existed" (2010, 72). Public sector unions, lacking the legal standing and size to be included in the answer to the labor question established in the 1940s and 1950s, were relegated, with a host of other insurgents, to outsider status. As a result, they were unable to transform the course of the labor movement in the 1970s.

Economic Crises and the End of the Postwar Boom

Leadership clashes between public and private sector unions, regardless of the time period, were inevitable, but organized labor's leaders were encouraged to dig in their heels when public sector unions came knocking in the 1970s because this was not a period of plenty; a series of economic crises threatened all of the advancements labor had gained in the postwar years. For the private sector, the postwar boom and the ascendance of organized labor, which had led to a remarkable thirty-year period of economic and social empowerment for the working class, was coming to a close by the 1970s. As Cowie notes, "By mid-decade the record-breaking strikes, rank-and-file movements, and vibrant organizing drives . . . were reduced to a trickle in the new economic climate" and "were then replaced by layoffs, plant closures, and union decertification drives" (2010, 12). While union contracts insulated private sector unions for a while from the economic downturn, over time they too were affected by decreased manufacturing productivity and stagnant wages.

The end of the postwar industrial boom, the oil shocks, deindustrialization, and other forms of economic restructuring hit the private sector hard, gradually pressuring unions to make concessions in the face of declining company profits and manufacturing unemployment (Pizzolato 2009, 234). Just six years after the "year of the strike," things had changed dramatically with "labor's tired leaders" facing a union movement "in a quiet state of crisis" (Kotz 1977). The difficult economic climate was worsened by increasingly virulent employer resistance to union organizing and contract negotiations, out-of-date labor laws, weakened strike effectiveness, and union leaders who had yet to fully recognize the problem or devise solutions. The result was a private sector union movement on the decline in terms of both density and power and influence.

In contrast, public sector unions in the mid-1970s were thriving and using their energy and aggressive tactics to finally bring their members' pay and benefits on par with those of the private sector. Government unions became increasingly militant, as is evidenced by the increase in strike activity. As Figure 3 demonstrates, by the mid-1970s there were over 350 to a high of nearly 600 work stoppages each year. Public sector unions coupled their strike activity with increased political pressure. As one newspaper article put it at the time, "It used to be said you could tell a civil servant by his white socks, the pencils in his shirt pocket, and the tattered briefcase that smelled of apples and peanut butter. Today, add a union card, a checkbook, and, conceivably, a primer on what makes the political system tick" (Skelton and Endicott 1974). Whereas private sector labor was in crisis, public sector labor was ramping up the political pressure.

In interviews, public sector labor leaders recall the period as one of great potential. As one AFSCME leader explained, "Change trends were gathering momentum and new entrants into the movement had the ability to look to the future. I count myself as one of the people" (Interview #40). A leader within the AFT described the period as "big organizing and mobilizing days. Teachers found a voice through their unions." The bottom line, she explained, was that "we were building a movement" (Interview #34). Caught up in the energy and excitement of the public sector union movement, it is not surprising that the public sector unions were not as acutely aware of or involved in what was going on in the private sector. As a leader within the AFT explained, "We didn't see it [private sector decline] happening. We were not as aware of it because it wasn't impacting us directly. It's human nature, if the public sector felt secure in their own right, [then they were] not worried about the private sector" (Interview #40). Several of the labor leaders I interviewed noted that it wasn't until the mid-1980s that public sector unions truly began to worry about private sector decline. It would be a gross generalization to say that government unions were ignorant of and did not care about the trouble in the private sector. However, the momentum of the public sector union movement masked private sector problems; it is harder to worry about a sinking ship when you are riding in a newly built boat that is just starting to sail at full speed.

The economic crises of the mid- to late 1970s further amplified the divergence between the public and private sector unions. The energy crises, the economic slowdown, and other conditions combined to produce stagflation whereby economic growth slows, unemployment remains high, and inflation rises. Stagflation placed cities and states across the country in the precarious position of having to manage declining tax revenues, ballooning deficits, and rising expenditures.

Government unions had to navigate negotiating with employers in severe financial situations. New York City nearly went bankrupt, and the city's large and influential public employee unions were forced to navigate how they would respond to the city's fiscal crisis without the support of the rest of organized labor. In their response, one AFSCME leader recalls, "[we] had to grapple with that on our own" because "it was our problem to solve" (Interview #40). When Jerry Wurf, recognizing how dire the situation was in New York City, suggested meeting with other public sector unions to devise a strategy, including the building trades union that had raided members, he encountered indifference: "Most of their [building trades union] members worked in the private sector, they could care less about city employees. 'Howie McClellan [building trades union president] sat at the end of the table and smiled at Wurf, as if he was powerless to do anything'" (quoted in Goulden 1982, 223). Ultimately, government unions in New York City, particularly AFSCME's District 37, voluntarily deferred and gave up benefits; they also used pension funds to buy $3.5 billion in Municipal Assistance Corporation bonds to help bail out the city. Despite these life-saving measures for the city, as Wurf noted, they "still ended up the villains" (quoted in Goulden 1982, 240).

The grim economic situation facing cities and states put public and private sector unions in difficult, uncompromising positions, which amplified their differences. The economic crises pit the interests of government union members, whose paychecks relied on shrinking local, state, and federal funds, against those of private sector union members, whose tax burdens remained steady even as the value of their paychecks decreased. Public sector union members felt the economic strain their employers were facing, making it hard for them to acquiesce to benefit cutbacks. In contrast, private sector union members were in difficult financial straits, and a high tax burden during an economic slowdown caused them to see the public sector struggle in a different, negative light.

Private sector union members, facing a tough economic climate, became receptive to growing animosity toward public sector union members. This was partly a natural reaction to public sector union militancy, especially during a period of economic crisis. However, there was also a deliberate, coordinated effort to discredit government unions by conservative think tanks, politicians, and advocacy organizations. For example, the tax revolt in California spearheaded by Howard Jarvis primarily targeted high property taxes, but his criticism of big government included public sector workers. Jarvis argued that California needed tax relief because the ratio of local government employees to residents in the state was, he claimed, 1:15 and these government jobs paid 25 percent more than comparable private sector jobs, which he saw as "a case of the poorer supporting the richer" (Jarvis 1979, 110–111).

At the same time, new organizations formed to study the negative effects of public sector unions, most notably the Public Service Research Foundation (1977), which was founded by members of the National Right to Work Committee. The group produced a newsletter (the *Government Union Critique*) and an academic journal (the *Government Union Review*) and also had its own lobbying organization (Americans Against Union Control of Government) (McCartin 2011a; Hower 2013, 373).[5] In one typical pamphlet, the organization warned that "union officials are seizing power over the country through their rapidly growing control of government officials," even going so far as to describe "union barons" as developing a "Master Plan" to wrest power from "legitimate representatives of the people" (PSRC, n.d.). Conservative academics furthered the anti–public sector union effort with a string of publications emphasizing the fundamental difference between private and public sector labor relations and reviving earlier fears of being "governed by our servants." The most influential analysis on the subject was Harry H. Wellington and Ralph K. Winter's 1971 book, *The Unions and the Cities*, which held that public sector unions possessed tools their private sector counterparts did not that enabled them to exert excessive power over their employer, the government. Other conservative academics buttressed this claim by reviving the history of the 1919 Boston police strike as a "city in terror" (Russell 1975), stressing the threat public sector unions posed to state sovereignty (Petro 1974) and emphasizing the danger of public sector strikes (Toledano 1975).

The press aided this effort to discredit public sector unions, frequently placing the blame for city and state budget woes squarely on public sector workers and unions (e.g., Goulden 1982, 241; Broder 1975a, 1975b). A *New York Times* editorial argued in 1976 that striking Massachusetts state employees, by "defying the state law and a court order to return to work," had "lashed out not against some hard hearted employer but against their hard pressed fellow citizens." Likewise, an article in the *Christian Science Monitor* discussing a strike by firemen in Kansas and Chicago argued that "striking firemen refused to answer alarms and inexperienced outsiders had to be brought in to protect the public, human lives and homes became bargaining chips" (Christian Science Monitor 1980). During a particularly heated strike in Baltimore, Maryland governor Marvin Mandel, after a meeting with Jerry Wurf, alleged that Wurf threatened that "Baltimore city would burn to the ground unless the city gave into the demands [of AFSCME]." While Wurf claimed Governor Mandel's story was an "absolute lie," his alleged threat to "let the city burn" was reprinted in anti–public sector union forums as well as mainstream media for years to come as a symbol of the dangers of public sector unionism (Goulden 1982, 243–244).

The demonization of public sector union members gained traction with the general public for two reasons. First, government unions continued to demand expanded benefits and cost-of-living increases in the face of economic crises and state budget collapses. As McCartin notes, "'Stagflation' had the perverse effect of simultaneously ballooning government deficits" and "goading government workers into increasingly unpopular strikes for wage increases to offset raging inflation" (2009, 749). The vast majority of these strikes were illegal, but that did not dampen public sector militancy. In 1975 and 1978, two years in which economic crises were at a boiling point, public sector strikes rose by 24 and 18 percent, respectively (McCartin 2008a). Returning to Figure 3, public sector work stoppages did not decline in the latter half of the 1970s but instead rose to a high of 593 stoppages in 1979.

Public sector strike activity during the economic crises turned public sentiment "so ferociously against striking civil servants that nongovernment union members won't even support them" (Pryor and Steiger 1977).[6] In 1972, the public was mostly evenly divided on the legality of government employee strikes: 42 percent said the law should be changed to permit strikes, and 47 percent said it should not be changed (Nixon Poll 1972). Just six years later, 59 percent of those surveyed disagreed that public employees should be allowed to strike (Clymer 1978). Only African American survey respondents sided with public employees: 50 percent were in favor of allowing them to strike and 36 percent were against. Thus, the increase in government union strikes and disruption of public services in the midst of a period of economic uncertainty was a difficult pill for the public to swallow. As one former NLRB board member noted at the time, "A strong current of public support is growing for officials who take positions that would once have been considered antiunion. There is a growing reluctance to pay the bills for collective bargaining" (Raskin 1975). One article noted that labor leaders were "frankly astounded by the depth of anti-public-employee sentiment"; AFSCME president Jerry Wurf called it "the season of darkness for our union" and his assistant stated that "we recognize that we're under public attack" (Dembart 1976). It is understandable that government unions would resort to heightened demand-making and strikes in the face of losing their recently gained benefits, but this activity helped fuel a massive backlash against government unionism.

The demonization of public sector unions was also successful because Americans, including private sector union members, came to see government unionization through the lens of their own struggles. Some private sector union members, "increasingly worried about plant closings, facing give-backs at the bargaining table, and inflation in their own tax bills," felt public sector unions were part of the problem (McCartin 2009, 751). As Jefferson Cowie (2013) notes, "When the taxpayers are flush, it's much easier to argue that we deserve a first class public sector." In the latter half of the 1970s, taxpayers felt far from flush. Jerry Wurf admitted in an interview at the time that the growing anti-tax revolt attitude "flows over into our relationship with our colleagues" (Pryor and Steiger 1977). For the most part, labor leaders sought to keep clashes between the two sectors private, but some leaders spoke publicly about the discord between the unions. The president of the UAW, Douglas Fraser, said that "if public employees make demands that 'go way beyond' what the taxpayers themselves have, 'then I think you're going to have this conflict. And I think it's happened'" (quoted in Flint 1978). Likewise, the president of an "old-line craft union" speaking anonymously to a reporter reputedly "questioned whether public employees ought to be organized at all, expressing concern for higher costs and whether the United States could become 'another England'" (Pryor and Steiger 1977). Further, "in California, lobbyists for one of the most progressive industrial unions are privately opposing collective bargaining rights for public employees—on the grounds that its members' taxes will have to pay the higher benefits that collective bargaining will yield for state workers" (Broder 1975b). Rather than banding together in the face of difficulties, public and private sector unions were pushed apart by their separate struggles. As Cowie notes, "From the perspective of their brothers and sisters in private jobs, public sector raises were costing them tax dollars—a problem that would become a crisis with the tax revolts at the end of the decade" (2010, 62). Private sector unions were already in difficult straits when government unions came under duress, making it easier for the criticisms against public sector unions to resonate among private sector union members.

The differences between public and private sector unions were magnified by the deteriorating economic climate, which hit just as public sector unions' militant efforts began to pay off. Public sector unions became "political lightning rods" and "scapegoats" that "serve[d] as a fulcrum for a lurch to the right in political life" (Johnston 1994, 13). Government jobs were portrayed as cushy, with overly generous benefits at the taxpayers' expense. In a 1972 survey, 51 percent of respondents said government employees had average or above-average productivity relative to other workers (Harris Survey 1972). Just five years later, a Gallup Poll asked respondents whether federal employees "work harder or not so hard as they would in non-governmental jobs" (Gallup Organization 1977). Only 9 percent responded that federal employees worked harder, 15 percent thought they worked about the same, and a staggering 67 percent said they worked less hard. The public's deteriorating image of government employees led many public sector unions to begin advertising campaigns to counteract public sentiment. For instance, in New York, "aware of the hostility that's out there" from the public, union leaders began a half-million-dollar advertising campaign with the theme: "Public Employees, where would you be without them?" (Lynn 1979). AFSCME's District 37 in New York had its own ad campaign, which included spending $2,000 a week to run radio spots with city workers that concluded with the line, "These are New Yorkers you can be proud of" (Lynn 1979). Similarly, AFSCME ran ads with such messages as, "After the parades, after the promises, someone has to work to keep our states and cities running" (Flint 1978). These efforts do not appear to have stemmed the tide of growing public frustration over striking government employees.

In Washington State, the growing divide between the perceived entitled, lazy government unions and the struggling, hardworking private sector unions erupted in a very public fashion. When Seattle mayor Wes Uhlman faced a recall election in 1975 spurred by firefighters angry over the mayor's firing of a long-time firefighter, the King County Labor Council remained officially neutral. While the council was strategically hedging their bets in case Uhlman prevailed, it was also noted at the time that "there is little rank-and-file union sympathy for the firefighters, who make $15,000 a year after four years . . . and enjoy greater job security than private sector employees" (Broder 1975a). That very same year, when school levies failed to pass in several communities in Washington, the NEA sought a sales tax increase from the legislature to close the budget shortfall. Joe Davis, president of the Washington State AFL-CIO, refused to endorse the measure, which proved "an unexpected stumbling block" (Broder 1975a). These two public events in Washington illustrate how the economic crises at that time exacerbated the growing schism within the labor movement.

Political Backlash

The economic crises led to direct conflicts between public and private sector unions, which ultimately resulted in much larger political clashes involving the broader public. Nowhere was the divide between public and private sector unions more evident than in the battle over Proposition 13 in California. Across the country, the economic crises fostered a growing resentment against higher taxes and the perception that government unions were to blame. This anger was harnessed in California by Howard Jarvis, who spearheaded the campaign to pass Proposition 13, which would place caps on state property taxes and limit tax increases of any kind by requiring a two-thirds majority in the state legislature. Proposition 13 would severely limit California's ability to raise revenue and thus was a threat to government unions and their members, whose jobs and paychecks were dependent on state and local tax dollars. The "tax revolt" beginning in California and gaining steam elsewhere threatened public sector unions just as the economic downturns and restructuring occurring in the private sector threatened private sector unions. However, during the tax revolt, not all private sector union members were in favor of solidarity because they were also taxpayers and just as susceptible to the anti–public sector union rhetoric.

After Proposition 13 passed, many newspaper articles argued that private sector union members had become "foot soldiers in the so-called tax revolt" and "voted overwhelmingly for Proposition 13, in full knowledge that the 57% cut in property taxes that it called for would wipe out the jobs of many of their brother unionists working in local governments" (Shabecoff 1978; Labor Comes to a Crossroads 1978; Bernstein 1978). A *Los Angeles Times* poll conducted in 1978 just prior to the election suggests that these anecdotes accurately captured a divide between public and private sector union members. Figure 4 displays the percentage of the respondents who viewed Proposition 13 favorably and were leaning toward/intended to vote for the measure. Just 38 percent of public sector union members favored Proposition 13, and 35 percent were considering voting for the proposition. The general public was more favorable, at 49 percent, and 54 percent of the general public planned to vote for the proposition. Private sector union members were the most supportive of Proposition 13 in the poll: nearly 60 percent of private sector union members were in favor of the measure and 63 percent leaned toward voting for it. The poll suggests that private sector union members were receptive to anti-tax rhetoric and measures despite the fact that they would adversely affect their public sector union brothers and sisters.

The tax revolt was a product of the 1970s economic crises, stagflation, and the massive growth of the local, state, and federal government since the New Deal. Public/private sector union differences were amplified because the differences between public and private sector unions aligned with many of the

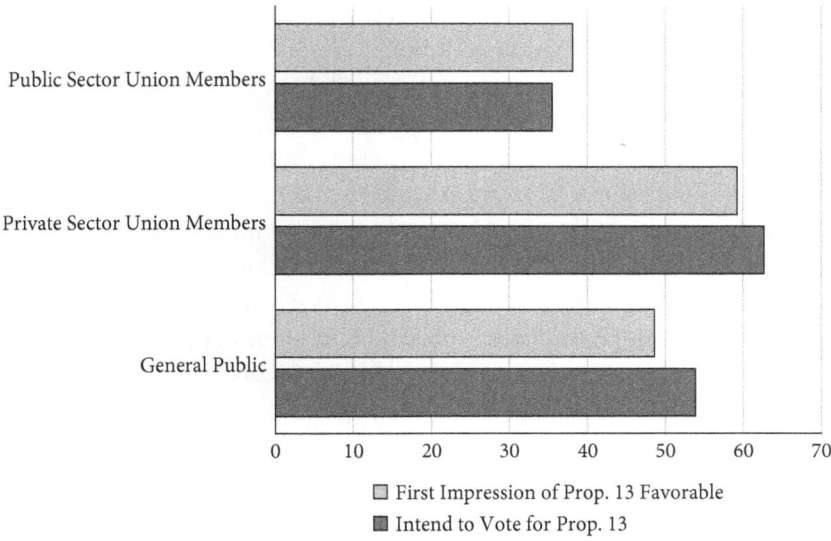

Figure 4. Support for Proposition 13 (percentages). N = 1,003; public sector = 76; private sector = 201. Los Angeles Times 1978.

cultural, economic, and political conflicts animating the decade, and there was little incentive for the two sectors to cooperate. Government unions were still wrapped up in the heady times of astronomical growth, whereas private sector unions were reeling from economic crises and a decade of setbacks following a period when organized labor felt unstoppable. Thus the tax revolt caught organized labor at a time when the public/private divide could easily be amplified and exploited.

Imagining a Different Outcome

The potential for organized labor seemed promising at the outset of the 1970s. Private sector union density was still relatively high and was bolstered by the growing size and political might of the public sector unions. However, instead of forging a cohesive public/private sector movement to tackle the challenges of the decade head-on, organized labor was wracked by schism and discord.

By the end of the 1970s, the United States was unrecognizable in many respects: organized labor's power had waned, the New Deal coalition and liberal consensus were truly dead, a massive transformation of the American economy was underway, and a conservative turn in American politics had begun. On the cusp of this change, President Jimmy Carter and a Democratic legislature entered office, signaling the possibility of the passage of private sector labor law reform in 1978. However, the moment for a public and private sector labor movement to push through labor law reform had already passed. A bill to help make union organizing easier in the private sector died thanks to an unprecedented lobbying campaign by business groups including the Business Roundtable and ultimately by a nineteen-day filibuster by Utah senator Orrin Hatch (Phillips-Fein 2009, 199). The backlash against organized labor more broadly and public sector unions in particular was well underway; even Democrats were hesitant to be associated with the public sector pariahs (McCartin 2009). In general, public support for organized labor had waned. For instance, in 1961 56 percent of those surveyed in a Gallup Poll reported that organized labor had more power than they should really have (Gallup Organization 1961). By 1979, 71 percent of those surveyed reported that organized labor had too much power (Time 1979). The backlash against public sector unions was particularly fierce as evidenced by the very public stand elected officials took against government unions. For example, San Francisco mayor Joseph Alioto, president of the U.S. Conference of Mayors, urged passage of legislation at the conference that would fire any public employee working in broadly defined emergency roles who went on strike (Brown 1975). Likewise, Seattle mayor Wes Uhlman, having survived the recall election brought about by unionized city firefighters, received national attention for his criticisms of municipal unions and call for mayors to stand up to the unions (Negronida 1975). Finally, Atlanta mayor Maynard Jackson, who had long-standing ties to the civil rights movement, fired hundreds of striking black municipal workers, whom he saw as a threat to the city's tenuous municipal finances (Lichtenstein 2002, 232).

As a consequence of this changing sentiment, public sector unions now lacked the power and influence they had held just a few years earlier to pursue labor law reform or a national Wagner Act for public sector workers: "For public sector labor, the decade of the 1970s can be divided neatly in two, with the first half of the decade characterized by aggressive expansion and rising expectations, and the second half by defensiveness and disappointed dreams" (McCartin 2008a, 211). In the early 1970s, they were upstarts fighting their way into the mainstream of American politics and the labor movement. When the opportunity for labor law reform finally presented itself in 1978, it was too late. As will be discussed in the next chapter, the backlash against public sector unions, an increasingly organized and mobilized conservative movement, and *National League of Cities v. Usery* closed the window of opportunity for labor law reform. Ronald Reagan's firing of the striking air traffic controllers in 1981 was a vivid illustration of the dramatic reversal of the public sector unions' fortunes. The timing was never quite right for public and private sector unions to align before the window of opportunity closed at the end of the decade.

When public sector employees gained their collective bargaining rights, both the economic, political, and cultural context and the sequencing of gaining these rights well after the private sector have proven consequential for labor's organizational solidarity; the timing and sequencing of public and private sector union development pushed against a unified union movement. We could imagine a different outcome. If government employees had gained collective bargaining rights in the 1935 Wagner Act or from their own national piece of legislation, their unionization would not have been artificially suppressed in the 1940s and 1950s. Instead, they would have grown and developed at the same time as their private sector counterparts. They would not have had to fight to gain entrance to an already established leadership circle in the 1970s. Likewise, if closer organizational ties and identities had been established earlier, the more diverse membership within the public sector unions and their involvement in the New Left could have emerged from within organized labor rather than public sector unions being associated with the rest of the New Left as outsider insurgents.

Public sector leaders, already integrated into the AFL-CIO, could have led the way in creating a more socially and politically vibrant labor movement. Instead of acting as an outsider and criticizing labor's leadership, Jerry Wurf could have been an insider, promoting the labor movement as "a force that will speak out and influence peace, justice, freedom and equality for all mankind" (quoted in Hower 2013, 295). Thus, private sector unions might have been better equipped to accept and absorb the new social movements, and the divides in organizational identity between public and private sector unions—and the lack of cooperation and understanding they engendered—might not have been so stark in the 1970s. Further, the public sector unions' fight for workplace rights and legal recognition would have taken place during the economic boom of the postwar years rather than in the midst of economic crises that enabled their claims and militant tactics to be easily criticized, alienating private sector union members. Government union demands occurred during a period of scarcity, pitting the public sector's needs for robust local, state, and federal budgets against the private sector's declining incomes. Public sector union growth occurred in a decade complicated by private sector decline, economic downturns, and conservative backlash, fostering moments of conflict and lack of understanding between private and government unions and ultimately limiting the growth of public sector unions and the possibility of a strong, vibrant public/private sector union movement. Thus, the decade of the 1970s is one of missed opportunities, illustrating vividly a union movement with two sectors out of alignment, their differences amplified by cultural, economic, and political crises that pit public and private sector union leaders and members against each other.

Chapter 6

The Late 1970s to the 2010s: Labor on the Decline

By the close of the 1970s and into the early 1980s, the possibility of an expanding, transformative public/private sector labor movement was coming to an end. Just as economic changes like deindustrialization and expanding global markets were putting increased pressure on unionized workplaces, the legal environment was making it difficult for organized labor to adapt to changing circumstances. The next several decades were marked by a labor movement struggling to adapt and survive in the face of mounting difficulties and a constrained legal/institutional regime. The legal framework established in 1935 put in place the foundation for the challenges the labor movement has faced in the last several decades.

The Failure of Labor Law Reform

One of the greatest stumbling blocks for organized labor over the last several decades has been the failure to update the Wagner Act for the modern workplace. Many countries have experienced declines in private sector unionization over the last half century, but the United States stands apart for the steepness of the decline in union density. Economic changes put pressure on private sector unions across the industrialized world, but the existing legal and institutional framework governing private sector labor relations in the United States added stumbling blocks that made it even more difficult for unions to maintain or expand their membership during the past half century. Much research has been done elsewhere on this subject and so will only be briefly touched on here. Two main aspects of the labor policy regime limited labor's ability to maintain union density levels. First, existing private sector labor law hinders labor's ability to organize growing sectors of the workforce because the Wagner and Taft-Hartley acts were designed during a period when the mass-production, industrial workplace dominated American employment. Existing labor law is organized around worksite, preventing organizing across firms and networks that are becoming increasingly integrated. It does not address the growing "contingent workforce," which includes managerial, supervisory, part-time, independent contracting, temporary, and even at-home workers who do not fit the traditional workplace model (Cobble 1994, 286; Carre, duRivage, and Till 1994, 317; Wial 1994, 310).[1] By preventing labor law reform in Congress, obstructionists have ensured that the growing numbers of service, white-collar, and nontraditional workers will remain largely untapped for increasing labor's membership levels.

Second, the current labor policy regime creates incentives for increasingly virulent anti-union efforts by employers. Employer resistance to union organizing has been present throughout American history but has grown in its intensity, organization, and effectiveness since the late 1970s. The NLRB was originally conceived as a non-partisan body, but appointments have become increasingly politicized over time (Flynn 2000; Tope and Jacobs 2009). In the late 1970s and early 1980s, new appointments to the NLRB by Nixon and Reagan and the defeat once again of a labor reform bill in 1978 indicated the growing weakness of unions and "marked the beginning of a far more open resistance to unionization and collective bargaining" (Gross 1994, 51; Hyatt 1977). Employer unfair labor practices that violated existing statutes increased from 9,067 in 1960 to 24,075 in 1990 (CFWMR 1994a). More recently, the number of unfair labor practice charges has ranged from 22,000 to 30,000 over the last decade (NLRB 2012). In addition, Kleiner estimates that the number of illegal firings has risen from one out of every 700 union members in the 1950s to one out of every twenty-five union members in 1995 (2001, 523). Bronfenbrenner, looking at a random sample of union certification elections in the late 1980s, found that more than 75 percent of employers deployed active anti-union tactics (1994, 80). Employer resistance was facilitated by a growing industry of consultants who showed employers how to resist unionization campaigns.

Since the late 1970s, employers have felt increasingly emboldened to resist unionization efforts in part because management consultants encouraged such behavior. These consultants advise employers on how firms can eliminate the demand for unionization and, barring that, prevent and/or defeat union organizing drives (Hyatt 1977; Martin 1979; Lublin 1981).[2] Consulting companies contact employers whose workers have filed a petition to hold a union election, warning them of the dangers of a unionized workplace and offering their services (Phillips-Fein 2009, 206). They hold seminars to train managers and supervisors in how to quash organizing drives (206). Most important, these consultants are experts on labor law and advise employers on the best ways to utilize, manipulate, and even break the law to fight unionization campaigns (206–207). Ultimately, the rise of the union-avoidance industry is notable because it demonstrates the growth of employer resistance during this time period and, most important, how management consultants help employers understand and exploit weaknesses in the labor law to hamper union organizing campaigns.

Three aspects of the ossified labor law have in particular given employers the tools and incentives to challenge union organizing campaigns. First, legal interpretation of existing labor law prioritized the individual right of employer free speech over the collective right of employees and union speech (Klein and Wanger 1985). The law has "failed to back up workers' associational rights" by denying unions access to the workplace in their efforts to unionize (Estlund 2002, 1591). Whereas employers can express their anti-union position by holding captive-audience meetings, distributing leaflets and letters, and meeting individually with employees, unions face significant barriers to contacting employees such as exclusion from the worksite altogether including non-working areas like parking lots and cafeterias (CFWMR 1994b, 23). Employers often capitalized on this monopoly of speech in the worksite by including "distortion, misinformation, threats, and intimidation" (Bronfenbrenner 1994, 82). Such lopsided labor practices are effective because employers face few deterrents to using them.

Second, employers can capitalize on out-of-date labor law by lengthening organizing campaigns and prolonging first contract negotiations. The way in which union organizing elections are mandated by law creates opportunities for delay. Before an NLRB election can be held, the employer and union can raise legal issues, such as the inclusion or exclusion of particular employees within the bargaining unit, which results in an automatic hearing and significant delay, usually up to seven weeks before workers can secure a vote (CFWMR 1994a, 18). Such delays buy time for union resistance and can prolong the process interminably (Hurd and Uehlein 1994, 65). As it stands, even if a majority of employees elect to join a union in the representation election, employers can still prove recalcitrant in first contract negotiations; one-third or more of certified units fail to reach a first contract (CFWMR 1994b, 21). Reforms that would speed up union certification campaigns, such as permitting a majority of employees signing cards to be sufficient for union recognition (known as card check agreements), have failed to pass Congress.

Third, the NLRB's "toothless" tools for constraining employer resistance enable employers to have a union-free workplace; it is more cost-effective for employers to resist unionization and break the law than to meet the demands of union activists (Rogers 1990, 121). A common form of employer resistance is firing union activists because, under an employment-at-will rule, an employer can easily claim that an employee was fired for a reason other than activism (Hurd and Uehlein 1994, 62). The employee is entitled to dispute this claim and, if the NLRB rules in the employee's favor, he or she must be reinstated with back pay, but the process to obtain reinstatement takes an average of two to three years (Kleiner 1994, 139–140; Fischl 2011). At very little cost, employers can thus remove union advocates during the organizing period when their presence is critical. The NLRB currently lacks the power to even issue an injunction to keep the employee working while they investigate. Morris Kleiner compared the average cost of violating six workplace labor policies in the 1980s and found that NLRB punishments were at the low end of the spectrum. On average, Kleiner found that $2,733 plus legal expenses was awarded as back pay when the NLRB ruled that an employee had been fired unfairly (2001, 533). In contrast, punishments for other workplace violations that included punitive damages were significantly larger: the employment-at-will/wrongful discharge statute averaged penalties of $180,000, and the average payment for violations of the EEOC provision of the Civil Rights Act was $8.5 million (532–533). Such disparities illustrate why employers have shown less respect for unfair labor practices regarding union organizing than other workplace protections like civil rights.

The rise of employer resistance to union organizing has hampered labor's ability to maintain or increase union membership and density. Bronfenbrenner examined a random sample of representation elections and found that unfair labor practices had a statistically significant impact on election outcomes and were associated with 10–20 percent lower win rates. Seventy-one percent of employers utilized a management consultant and this was associated with a 10 percent decrease in the union win rate (1994, 80). The negative effect of employer resistance on union organizing has been noted by several scholars, including Clawson and Clawson (1999), Freeman (1988), Friedman et al. (1994), and Kleiner (2001). Others, using a most similar systems comparison between the United States and Canada, have found that robust union density in Canada can be attributed to Canadian labor laws that better regulate and deter employer resistance than do those in the United States.[3]

Failure to update Taft-Hartley hindered labor's ability to adapt to the modern workplace while providing employers with incentives to fight union organizing at every stage. Absent labor law reform, unions have struggled to adapt to the massive transformations in the economy, such as the rise of the service sector, contracting, and part-time employment. All of these changes have meant employment has expanded dramatically in areas where the traditional mode of organizing under the Wagner Act either doesn't apply or is very difficult to accomplish. For instance, how does the traditional model work for organizing caregivers who work in private homes instead of on a shop floor, freelance tech workers who contract with multiple companies, or Amazon warehouse workers who technically work for a subcontractor who runs their single warehouse? Outdated labor law has not adjusted to the modern economy.

The only area of private sector labor law that has evolved over this time is the provision left up to the states: right-to-work statutes banning union shops. States have been given leeway in their anti-union efforts, but they have not been permitted to pass stronger labor protections than the federal framework provides (Freeman 2006). Certainly decisions made by labor leaders and broad economic forces have contributed to declining union density in the private sector over the last half century. Indeed, private sector union decline has been amplified by the population growth in the Sunbelt, a region hostile to union organizing. These population shifts have empowered right-to-work states at the expense of traditional union strongholds like the Northeast. The growth of the service sector, immigration to the Sunbelt, and other broad changes in the economy and society have weakened traditional labor strongholds and caused unions to lose members. However, the institutional framework of U.S. labor law created an environment whereby it is increasingly difficult for private sector union organizers to recoup lost members. On this point, Dorian Warren's assessment is apt: "the fate of the American labor movement is political, not economic, and labor policy is decisive in shaping its trajectory" (2011, 195). Obstructionism ensured that existing labor law has become increasingly out of date, hampering labor's efforts to organize new members and encouraging employers to resist more forcefully, even in the face of a union movement on the ropes.

The public sector union movement has also failed to pass labor law reform. For the public sector, the early 1970s seemed like a time of great potential. Buoyed by rising public sector union density and the explosion of laws recognizing public sector workers' collective bargaining rights, Jerry Wurf, the president of AFSCME, aimed to pass a national Wagner Act for public sector workers (McCartin 2008b, 129). A series of proposals sought to either set up a legal framework akin to the Wagner Act or simply extend the Wagner Act to cover public sector workers (130, 132). McCartin argues that such a proposal might have passed were it not for the summer of 1975. Public sector union militancy was already high when municipal and state fiscal crises rocked the country. States responded to severe budget crises by slashing spending, which hit government employees especially hard. Public employees were loath to accept such measures and strike activity rose 24 percent in 1975 (2008b, 137). Massive strikes in New York, Seattle, and other cities became front-page news, and angry mayors (Republicans *and* Democrats) lashed out at public sector unions, which were seen as frustrating their efforts at fiscal austerity.

The strikes damaged Democratic support for federal public sector labor law, fueled the public's perception that public sector unions had become too powerful, and provided an effective rallying point for the conservative backlash that would follow. During this time, AFSCME hired a marketing firm to help combat the negative image of public sector employees and unions. The marketing firm's recommendations illustrated the changed environment: AFSCME should "moderate its confrontational rhetoric," "curtail its broader political agenda," and "drop its demand for a national collective bargaining law" (Hower 2013, 393). The public sector union movement's faltering image was not simply a product of declining economic conditions and rising strike activity.

In the 1970s, businesses began forming new organizations and mobilizing with greater urgency to push a conservative economic agenda including opposing private and public sector unions (Phillips-Fein 2009, 185–212). Kim Phillips-Fein describes these efforts as the "business activist movement" and details the myriad ways groups like the U.S. Chamber of Commerce, the Business Roundtable, and the National Association of Manufacturers sought to enhance their political clout (2009, 185). With respect to unions, these groups were instrumental in opposing labor law reform with unprecedented lobbying efforts (199, 207) and encouraging their member companies to resist unionization efforts. In addition, they employed substantial resources to shape public perceptions of labor including marketing campaigns with advertisements in magazines; lobbying; the production of think tank research; the formation of corporate PACs and public affairs departments; and public speaking engagements (185–212). This massive public relations campaign sought to paint business and the free market in a positive light and "to make sure that the economic slowdown was blamed primarily on labor unions and excessive government regulation" (189). The efforts of the "business activist movement" helped fuel the backlash against public sector unionism at the very time they were seeking to pass a Wagner Act for government employees.

Union activists' hopes for new public sector legislation were dashed in 1976 when the Supreme Court decided in *National League of Cities v. Usery* that extension of the Fair Labor Standards Act to state and local workers violated states' rights (McCartin 2008b, 146). If the Supreme Court found the more benign extension of minimum wage and overtime laws to state and local employees unconstitutional, then it was assumed that a national public sector labor law would surely be defeated on a legal challenge. The dramatic turnaround of the Supreme Court in the late 1930s to uphold Roosevelt's New Deal legislation is well known. The Wagner Act benefited from the Court's reversal when it upheld the Act in the 1937 decision *National Labor Relations Board v. Jones & Laughlin Steel Corporation*. By 1976, when public sector unions finally had the numbers and organizational capacity to push for a national labor law of their own, the Court's position had changed.

The 1976 decision in *National League of Cities* brought public sector labor's dream of their own Wagner Act to an end, marked policymakers' turn against public sector unions, and forced public sector unions to continue their efforts to obtain collective bargaining rights at the state and local levels. The year 1976 was a moment of possibility when the institutional legacy of the Wagner Act could have been changed in the form of a national-level law governing public sector labor relations. Instead, *National League of Cities* entrenched the existing legal divide: public sector labor law remained situated at the state and local levels. *National Leagues of Cities* was reversed less than ten years later, but the window of opportunity for change had already closed.[4] The brief period of public sector union growth was over, replaced by a movement holding steady but not gaining new members.

How far the tide had turned against organized labor became clear in 1981 when the Professional Air Traffic Controllers Organization (PATCO) went on strike for improved wages, lowered hours, and staffing and equipment improvements to more safely manage the nation's air traffic. The strike of over 12,000 air traffic controllers crippled the nation's air travel.

As federal employees, the controllers were subject to a civil service law that banned strikes by federal employees. Public sector employees had previously disregarded the ban, but President Reagan took a hard line with the strikers. In a nationally televised address, Reagan issued a warning: "I must tell those who failed to report for duty this morning that they are in violation of the law and if they do not report for work within 48 hours they have forfeited their jobs and will be terminated" (quoted in McCartin 2011b, 290). Approximately 1,000 controllers returned to work after Reagan's threat, but the rest, more than two-thirds of the total union and non-union workforce, held the picket line. Two days later, the Federal Aviation Administration issued 11,345 dismissal notices to strikers and used a combination of the remaining controllers and their supervisors, military personnel, and new recruits to keep air traffic moving (301). Public sentiment stood behind the president and turned viciously against the controllers. The *New York Times* (1981) argued that "an illegal strike by key Government workers is simply not tolerable" and noted that the support of organized labor for PATCO "can barely be heard over the public's cheer for the Government." With the nation's airplanes still flying, the president refusing to negotiate, and with few friends willing to stand with PATCO, the strike and the union crumbled.

President Reagan's breaking of the PATCO strike reverberated through the labor movement, signaling a shift to a more hostile government stance toward labor. Although PATCO was a public sector union, Reagan's actions also legitimized the increasingly aggressive employer resistance to unionization in the private sector, especially the use of replacement workers during strikes (McCartin 2011b, 344). The strike became a less viable labor tactic, and major strikes have largely disappeared since PATCO: "the annual number of major work stoppages" never again reached "even one-third of pre-PATCO levels" (351). The breaking of the PATCO strike "acted as a powerful catalyst" for the decline of organized labor (361).

Efforts at Renewal: Too Little, Too Late

The failure to pass labor law reform, declining membership numbers, the breaking of the PATCO strike, and other troubling signs led the labor movement to rethink its tactics and seek out new paths to renewal. When AFL-CIO president George Meany stepped down in 1979, he was replaced by his long-time friend and mentee, Lane Kirkland. Kirkland continued many of Meany's policies (Serrin 1999). Nelson Lichtenstein describes Kirkland as "the near-perfect embodiment of the Cold War labor bureaucracy," as he had little actual union experience, a "visceral hostility" to the New Left, and an affinity for President Reagan's foreign policy (2002, 247–248). Like Meany, he did not emphasize rebuilding the union's ranks through massive organizing drives, which ultimately proved costly (249). Under his sixteen-year leadership, there was a precipitous decline in union membership from 24.1 percent of the workforce unionized in 1979 to 15.5 percent in 1995 (Hirsch and Macpherson 2017).

By the 1990s, some wings of the labor movement viewed declining membership numbers as a growing crisis and felt that organized labor had become complacent and had lost the energy and membership activism that had made labor successful in the mid-twentieth century. Led by Service Employees International Union (SEIU) president John Sweeney, this "insurgent faction" forced Kirkland to resign in 1995, successfully defeated the mainstream candidate, and elected Sweeney as the next president of the AFL-CIO (Lichtenstein 2002, 255). Sweeney came from one of the fastest-growing unions in the movement, the SEIU, whose membership was made up of many of the frontiers of union organizing: public sector employees, service workers like home health aides and janitors, workers from diverse backgrounds, and women and immigrants. The Sweeney insurgency sought to broaden labor's membership and tactics, advocating a "willingness to play a disruptive, insurgent role in society" (256). They called for a renewed focus on organizing (particularly previously ignored workers like women and minorities), greater political activism, and grassroots mobilization of members (Zieger and Gall 2002, 252). Just as important, "the 'Iron Curtain' that once divided official labor and the American left—academic, feminist, cultural and gay—is rusting away" (Lichtenstein 2002, 261–262). The changes ushered in by Sweeney and his supporters were exactly the kind of reforms public sector unions had been attempting since the 1960s and 1970s, but it was only after over a decade of crises, when government unions had become a much larger share of the union movement, that they were able to force the kinds of change needed to revitalize the labor movement.

However, this new effort at renewal and growth has had limited success. Labor law reform failed once again during the Clinton administration owing to the Republican-controlled Congress. President Sweeney argued that "labor must organize without the law . . . so that we can later organize under the law" (quoted in Lichtenstein 2002, 261). This optimism does not capture the fundamental challenges of organizing new workplaces and new workers under the existing legal regime, as illustrated at the start of this chapter. Labor tried again to revise national labor law under President Obama with the Employee Free Choice Act (EFCA), which sought to strengthen the Wagner Act. Among other things, the Act would have given employees the right to unionize through the signatures of a majority of workers rather than the traditional election procedure, which has been marked by hostile employer resistance, and would have required binding arbitration if a collective bargaining agreement had not been met within 120 days of the union being established in order to prevent employers from simply refusing to negotiate with a new union. On at least five occasions, the EFCA failed to pass Congress, despite a Democratic majority and president (Kearney and Mareschal 2014, 343). As had been the case with previous efforts at labor law reform, the major stumbling block for the EFCA was the sixty votes needed in the Senate, which Democrats were never able to obtain. Amending the Wagner Act in the modern era appears to be a nearly impossible task.

Similar Crises, Different Labor Movement

The 2008 financial crisis illustrates how much the labor movement has transformed but how little these changes seemed to matter in the face of a movement in crisis. The Great Recession was an economic crisis on par with those faced in the 1970s, yet there was not the same level of conflict between public and private sector unions as in the past. Certainly there are some episodes that are reminiscent of the amplified public/private divisions of the 1970s. The negative association between public sector unions, big government, and high tax burdens has persisted over time, and private sector union members have remained receptive to this interpretation.

The continued resentment toward government union members demonstrated by private sector unions (including some of the more liberal unions like the UAW and the United Mine Workers of America [UMWA]) may have been exacerbated by the continuing decline of the private sector union movement. A leader in the AFT described private sector union members' "envy and resentment" of the benefits the public sector has managed to hold onto that have been lost in the private sector (Interview #34). Another union leader related a secondhand story in which a former president of a national teachers union went to a school board that included private sector union board members and received no sympathy because "we have become islands of benefits" (Interview #34). Yet another union leader described how, as private sector union density declines, "more and more people view unions as something that exists in the public sector." This "affects people's experience of unions in terms of competition for public resources which has been a lot of the fight the last decade or so around health care and public pensions" as the public sees government unions as having "a set of privileges they don't have access to and they are paying for" (Interview #31). Many leaders referred to this divide as something that "goes back decades" as "good jobs have been shipped overseas, leaving people without a union and wages depressed for the private sector unions that are left," and "the private sector union members see the public sector and hear these messages about how greedy they are" (Interview #19).

Anti-union opponents play up the differences between the public and the private sector unions, trying to generate conflict. When the law distinguishes between unions, this creates an opportunity for union opponents to sow discord. Examples of politicians seeking to divide unions are prevalent today. Then Governor Chris Christie of New Jersey attacked teachers and government unions but also appeared on the cover of *Time* magazine wearing a NJ Building Trades pin (The Boss 2013). Christie's message to private sector workers, union and non-union, is that they are on the losing side of a divide: "At some point . . . there has to be parity between what is happening in the real world and what is happening in the public-sector world" (quoted in McCartin 2011a). Then Governor Tim Pawlenty of Minnesota declared that "it used to be that public employees were underpaid and over-benefited. . . . Now they are over-benefited and overpaid compared to their private-sector counterparts" (quoted in McCartin 2011a). In Wisconsin, Governor Scott Walker's push to eliminate public sector collective bargaining utilized a "divide and conquer" approach that pit the private sector against the public (Martin 2011). However, legal divides can also create openings for dissension among private and public sector unions themselves.

The Wisconsin act to eliminate public sector collective bargaining specifically excluded police and firefighters. One anonymous interviewee revealed that when the legislation was announced on February 11, 2011, the firefighters union actually initially planned to support the bill. It was only after significant lobbying by more progressive wings of the union over the weekend that a majority of members were willing to stand against the bill. It took a concerted effort over that weekend in February for the Wisconsin

IAFF to see beyond the legal division created between public sector unions in the bill.

Despite these examples, however, the union movement has become far more united across sectors today than it was in the 1970s in the face of economic crises. The massive turnout to protest the attack on public sector collective bargaining rights in Wisconsin, which involved numerous private and public sector unions in coordinated response, was emblematic of this cooperation. Why, given that the 2008 financial crisis strained government budgets, once again pitting the interests of public and private sector union members against each other, do we not see the same amplification of differences and lack of cooperation as we did in the 1970s? Over the past thirty years, total union density has steadily declined. Private sector unions have withered under eviscerated labor law that fails to reign in hostile employer resistance, inhibiting their ability to organize new members. The attacks on public sector unions beginning in 2011 served as a wake-up call for many leaders as the last bastion of the labor movement was threatened.

With the hindsight of time, and with some exceptions, the labor movement seems to have finally recognized that their fates are tied together and attacks on either sector threaten the strength of the entire labor movement. The attacks in Wisconsin are not seen as an isolated event but instead part of a larger crisis. As Lee Saunders, president of AFSCME, explained about the events in Wisconsin: "It's about survival.... What's happened didn't just hurt public-sector unions, it hurt the entire labor movement" (quoted in Greenhouse 2014b). For the first time, public and private sector unions are on parallel trajectories—crisis and decline. As one AFL-CIO leader put it, "I guess it takes a crisis. Our fates are tied together" (Interview #35). Today, the timing of public and private sector decline now coincide and the sequencing of the economic crisis in the private sector and the attacks on the public sector are aligned, promoting a sense of shared fate.

As a result of the most recent attacks, there has been a dramatic effort within the labor movement to forge solidarity. Many government union leaders emphasized that "public sector unions are very aware that... we can't be an island of growth in an ocean of decline. Ultimately, our ability to grow and our strength [are] going to depend on a growing labor movement. We desperately need a stronger private sector labor movement. That is clearly understood" (Interview #29). This is a vastly different situation from that in the 1970s, when public sector unions were less aware of and, to some extent, indifferent to the fate of the private sector. One former state-level AFL-CIO president remembers trying to spearhead a union organizing campaign in the 1980s but "the response from locals was lukewarm at best." He saw that failed effort as representative of "a tipping point for labor [toward decline] that wasn't recognized at the time" (Interview #20). Lacking resources and national networks to help, his state-level campaign to organize new workers failed.

Labor leaders have a general sense that the labor movement is different now, ripe for new initiatives, and that major change is needed. Lee Saunders, president of AFSCME, said in 2013 that "everyone has come to the realization that we need more partners, that we got to rebuild the movement, that we have faced all these vicious attacks. . . . Maybe it takes a bat to your head, but people get it now. People are engaged" (quoted in Greenhouse 2013). The bat to the head of labor appears to be the seemingly irreversible declining total union density and coordinated attacks against both public and private sector unions, made worse by decades of only partial cooperation and shared purpose between unions.

Today, the labor movement is emphasizing solidarity like never before, trying to deliberately forge shared organizational identities. This solidarity is taking the form of tangible efforts at cooperation and coordination. Labor unity tables, formed after the devastating defeats of the 2010 midterm elections, were created in states identified as vulnerable in order to prepare an infrastructure to address any potential attacks. In interviews with labor leaders, they mention meetings, phone calls, and strategizing among unions occurring at an unprecedented level. The breaking off of the Change to Win unions from the AFL-CIO in 2005 is increasingly a division in name only. There is a concerted effort to forge ties with like-minded progressive groups, including those advocating for immigrants' rights and environmental and anti-poverty organizations. It remains to be seen whether this period of solidarity will have lasting repercussions, but it does suggest that when labor's development trajectories align, the potential for a coordinated, unified labor movement that truly embodies the idea of solidarity increases. For labor, the drawback is that alignment has come in the form of shared crises rather than parallel growth.

In this moment when labor leaders express shared purpose and tentative optimism, it is important to recognize that the dramatically different response of the labor movement to the economic crises and political attacks today compared to the 1970s is not simply a matter of new leadership. Public sector unions' delayed legal recognition meant that they emerged as a real force in the labor movement not during the prosperous height of American labor in the 1940s and 1950s but instead in the midst of cultural, economic, and political crises in the 1970s. The timing of their growth magnified the differences between public and private sector unions, making the potential for cooperation in the labor movement that much more difficult. Today, the aligning of both the public and private sector union movements in a mode of crisis has fostered shared purpose and understanding, creating the foundation for cooperation and a stronger labor movement. The house of labor may no longer be deeply divided, but this change has perhaps come too late to have a dramatic effect on labor's fortunes; labor may have been too weak for too long to recover what it lost over the course of decades of missed opportunities and conflict.

Lasting Legal Divisions

While organized labor has placed great emphasis on solidarity between public and private sector unions over the last few decades, the legal separation between the two sectors remains and shapes the behavior of the unions within the movement. One of the lasting consequences is the location of labor's political efforts. Politics at the local, state, and federal levels impact both public and private sector labor unions. Teachers unions care about who is elected to the local school board, state spending on education, and national-level policymaking like No Child Left Behind. State government unions are concerned with state-level budgets and policies but are also affected by federal cuts to state block grants and policies that affect their jobs, such as welfare reform. Construction unions are concerned about government support of building projects at all levels of government. Industrial unions like the UAW care about federal trade policy that affects the competitiveness of American manufacturing, but they are also concerned about local policies that encourage American automakers to keep factories located in the United States.[5] Thus we might expect public and private sector unions to divide their energy and resources relatively equally across the various levels of government. However, as Chapter 2 made clear, one key policy area is not divided evenly across the three jurisdictions: labor law.

Private sector labor law is controlled at the federal level whereas public sector labor law is set by states and localities.[6] The federalized nature of American labor law may thus create different incentives for private and public sector labor union political action. Private sector unions have been hampered in their organizing efforts due to the failure of labor law reform at the federal level. Thus the passage of federal labor law reform is one of the top

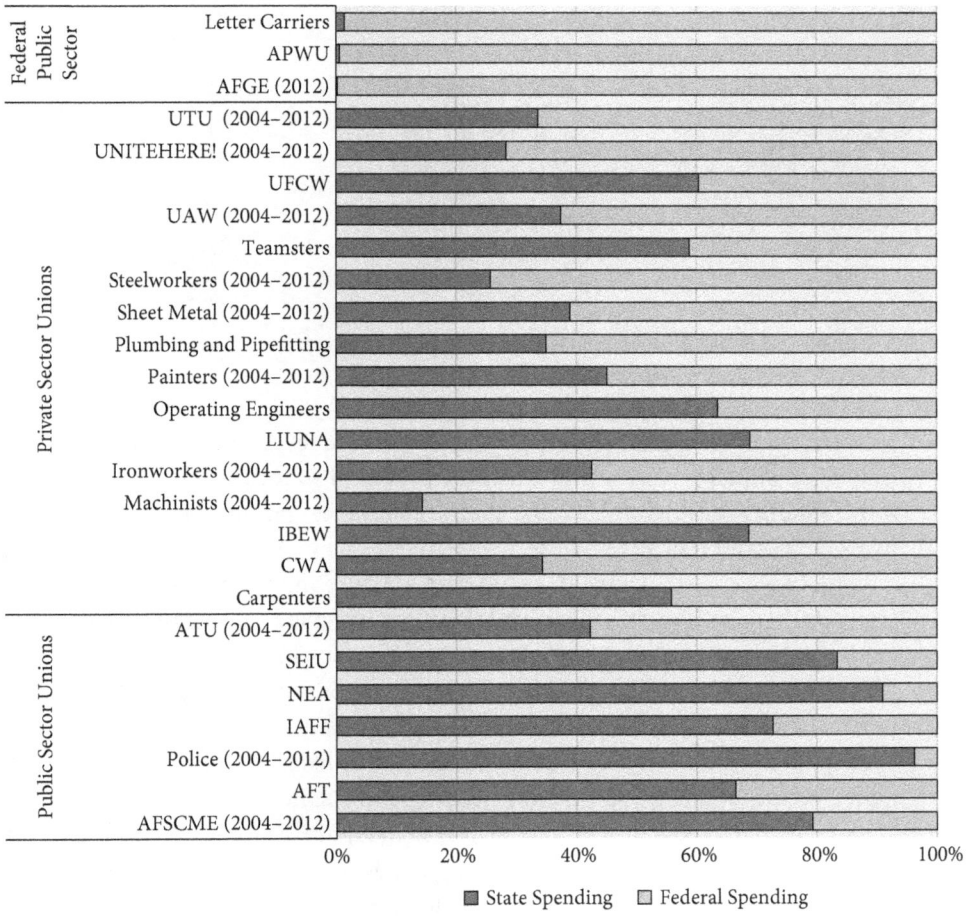

Figure 5. Percentage of total 2000–2012 election spending reported at the state versus federal level by union. NIMPS 2013; CRP 2013.

priorities of private sector unions. In contrast, with the exception of the federal government unions, public sector unions' right to organize and bargain collectively has been more erratic while under the control of states and localities. Thus government unions have a strong incentive to push for state and local labor law protections and maintenance.

Do public and private sector union political activities differ? One way to measure union political activity is through campaign spending. If public sector unions have a greater incentive to influence state-level rather than federal politics, then we should expect to see government unions devote a higher

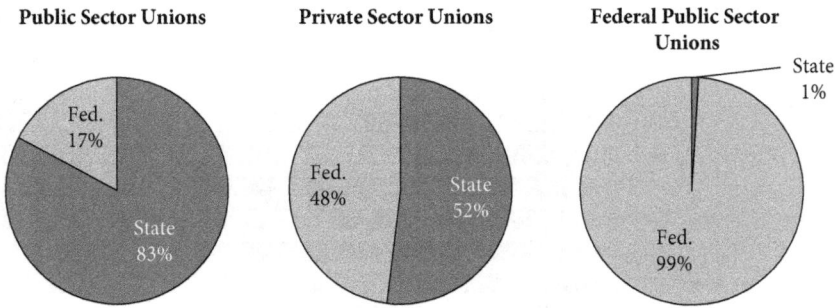

Figure 6. Percentage of total 2000–2012 election spending reported at the state versus federal level by sector. NIMPS 2013; CRP 2013.

proportion of their campaign spending at the state level. The exception is unions of federal workers, who would be predicted to focus on the federal level for policy reasons and because their collective bargaining rights are set by Congress and executive orders.

Figure 5 shows the percentage of twenty-six unions' political spending from 2000 to 2012 on state-level elections versus federal-level candidates, PACs, parties, and outside spending groups. The unions are divided between public sector, private sector, and federal public sector unions. In general, the public sector unions devoted the majority of their spending to the state level, whereas the private sector unions spent more at the federal level. The federal public sector unions spent virtually nothing at the state level. The averages across the three types of unions are displayed in Figure 6. From 2000 to 2012, public sector unions spent 83 percent at the state level, whereas private sector unions spent just over half at the state level. Federal public sector unions allocated less than 1 percent of their total spending at the state level. Figures 5 and 6 demonstrate a clear divide in spending between public and private sector unions. On average, from 2000 to 2012, public sector unions spent $7 at the state level for every $1 spent at the national level. For private sector unions, their money was divided evenly across the two jurisdictions. For federal public sector unions, only one cent was sent to the state level for every $1 spent at the national level.

Not surprisingly, not only do public sector unions devote a higher proportion of their total spending to state elections, but this translates into more total public sector spending than private sector spending at the state level. Figure 7 displays the total spending of private and public sector unions at the state level during the 2000–2012 elections. In every election except the 2001 and

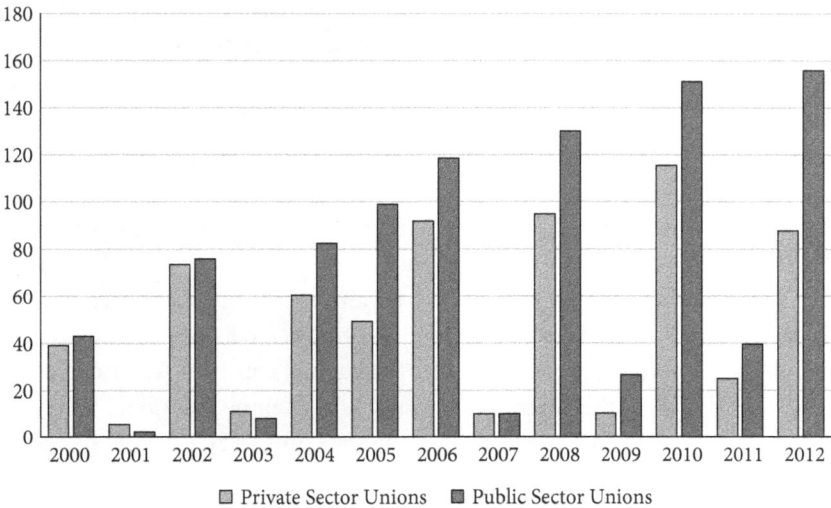

Figure 7. Total state-level spending (in millions of dollars) by public and private sector unions per election. NIMPS 2013.

2003 midterms, public sector unions outspent their private sector counterparts at the state level. In total, government unions spent over $942 million during the twelve-year span compared to just under $674 million spent by private sector unions at the state level. This is a difference in total spending of over $268 million. It is not surprising that public sector unions spend more given that they are the largest unions in the movement. However, this difference is important because the largest unions in the labor movement today have an incentive to spend their proportionally larger share of resources at the state and local levels rather than the national level. As the unions with the most members and money, public sector unions are thus pushing the labor movement to move their time and resources to demand-making at a different level of government. This is an important shift within the labor movement with potentially important ramifications for labor's effectiveness at the national level.

These aggregate measures are suggestive but cannot confirm that the divided legal regime is the cause of the differences in location of election spending. However, for public sector union leaders, focusing electoral spending on the state and local levels is a clear choice given recent events. The most recent attacks on public sector workers in states like Wisconsin and Indiana have certainly made the tenuous nature of public sector labor law abundantly clear to public sector unions, leading them to increase their political efforts. Former AFSCME political director Larry Scanlon, noting the increased political spending, remarked, "It makes sense that our political spending has ramped up over the last year and a half as our members have come under attack like never before." Scanlon estimated that approximately two-thirds of AFSCME's political budget went to the state and local levels (quoted in McGinty and Mullins 2012). For AFSCME, political spending at the state and local levels is a matter of life and death.

Unions have many shared goals and organizational connections, but when it comes to where to devote their political energy and resources, there is a divide that is perhaps promoted by the federalized nature of American labor law. Excluded from the Wagner Act and lacking their own national-level law, public sector unions were relegated to the state and local levels as their sites of demand-making and this appears to still be the case. Government unions devote a higher share of their political spending and a higher level of spending overall to the state level than do private sector unions. As government unions become an increasing portion of the labor movement due to the shifting balance of power, we are likely to see labor's influence at the state and local levels increase. Indeed, in the last few election cycles, AFSCME has led the charge for renewed attention to state- and local-level politics, beginning with the state budget and sequestration battles. In national-level interviews, almost all leaders emphasized a growing emphasis on state- and local-level politics. At their annual winter meeting in 2014, AFL-CIO labor leaders explicitly announced a larger focus on state- and local-level politics. They planned to target four industrial states that have been the site of backlash recently—Michigan, Ohio, Pennsylvania, and Wisconsin—as well as Florida (Greenhouse 2014b).

This growing attention to the state and local levels may help combat the most recent attacks on public sector unions and foster pro-labor policy, but there is a trade-off. Focusing attention and resources at the state and local levels could have negative repercussions for labor's role in national-level politics. Labor may be sacrificing the time, money, resources, and lobbying efforts at the national level for this state-level focus. On important issues like economic inequality, it is unclear who will fill the void at the national level if organized labor pulls back. Labor is a unique voice for working Americans and the focus on the state level, while crucial to the survival of public sector unions and thus labor as a whole, may have unforeseen consequences at the national level.

The past several decades have witnessed a labor movement struggling to survive in the face of a legal environment that makes it difficult for them to organize and encourages the public and private sector wings of the movement to often act separately. The challenges facing the modern labor movement were compounded when many legislatures across the country considered new legislation that challenged public sector collective bargaining rights beginning in 2011. These modern attacks will be discussed in the following chapter.

Chapter 7

The 2010s: The Modern Assault Against Public Sector Unions

The 2011 battle over Act 10 in Wisconsin was the most public struggle over public sector collective bargaining rights in decades, but it was not unique. Act 10 was part of a surge of legislation proposed across the country seeking to scale back government employees' collective bargaining rights in the 2010s. The preceding decades had seen moments of expanded public sector rights—state workers gained collective bargaining rights in Indiana in 1989 and Washington in 2002, for instance—but also retrenchment—New Mexico's Public Employee Labor Relations Act renewal was vetoed by the governor in 1999,[1] and Indiana's state workers' rights were rescinded in 2005, for example (Malin 2012). What led so many states to take up public sector collective bargaining rights at this time?

One of the most important factors was the 2010 midterm elections, which was a Republican wave at the national and state levels. Before the election, Democrats controlled 52 of 88 state legislative chambers. After the election, Republicans controlled 53 of the 88 chambers (Ballotpedia 2010). Republicans won ten new governorships and netted five gubernatorial races overall, including in Ohio, Michigan, Pennsylvania, and Wisconsin. After the election, Republicans controlled both chambers of the legislature and the governorship in twenty states (Ballotpedia 2010). In Wisconsin, the Republican wave was especially strong; the party gained control of both houses and the governorship for the first time since 1938 (Stein and Marley 2013, 3). The Republicans not only took control of both houses but unseated the top lawmakers in each house, the Senate majority leader, and Assembly speaker (3). Just as Democratic control helped the public sector gain collective bargaining rights in many states in the 1960s, the Republican wave helped lay the groundwork for the retrenchment of these rights.

The massive Republican gains in the 2010 midterms laid the foundation, but it was well-organized conservative groups that encouraged Republican lawmakers to focus on the public sector. These organizations have grown in size, strength, and influence relative to other more traditional political organizations, like the Republican Party, in recent decades (Skocpol and Hertel-Fernandez 2016). Through campaign donations, lobbying, funding research, advertising, and other activities, these groups have pushed states to take on public sector collective bargaining rights, even as polling conducted at the time showed that the majority of Americans did not support such attacks (694). In Wisconsin, the major conservative groups that backed Walker's actions included Americans for Prosperity, created and partly financed by the Koch brothers, the Wisconsin-based Bradley Foundation, and the American Legislative Exchange Council (Stein and Marley 2013, 35). These and other conservative organizations across the country provided money, lobbying, public information campaigns, model legislation, and other support to state legislators and governors willing to pursue attacks against public sector unions. Their efforts were so successful in Wisconsin that it has become a model for efforts across the country (Kaufman 2018). More recently, these organizations, in tandem with their legislative efforts, have pursued a coordinated legal strategy to weaken organized labor, including the recent efforts to pass "paycheck protection" legislation (i.e., non-member government employees should not have to pay agency fees to the unions that represent them) (Scheiber and Vogel 2018).

Public sector unions were an obvious target for these conservative groups because, by 2010, public sector union members outnumbered private sector union members for the first time in American history (Greenhouse 2010). It is not surprising that the slew of attacks on public sector collective bargaining in 2011 occurred just one year after public sector union members made up the majority of the labor movement. As one labor leader noted, "I think the Right realizes that the strength of the progressive movement is rooted in the public sector and it is trying to kill, going for the jugular, kill the remaining strength of the progressive movement. The Democratic Party barely exists, the organizational muscle is rooted in unions, and the strength of that is rooted in the public sector ... the Right sees that very clearly" (Interview #29). The organizing and financial might public sector unions can mount for Democratic candidates are not lost on Republicans. After the Republican landslide in the 2010 elections, conservative commentator Dick Morris wrote, "We may, at long last, have a way to liberate our nation from the domination of those who should be our public servants but instead are frequently our union masters" (quoted in McCartin 2011b, 365). It is not a coincidence that states that sought to weaken public sector unions followed up by trying to weaken private sector unions. In Wisconsin, after the crippling blow of Act 10 dramatically decreased public sector union membership, the legislature passed a right-to-work law in 2015, weakening private sector unions. Hurting public sector unions was seen as first step toward weakening the entire labor movement.

Anti-union opponents were also emboldened to act against government unions during this time because economic conditions made the public more receptive to rhetoric against public sector unions. As was discussed in the last chapter, the 2008 Great Recession helped revive many of the same critiques of public sector unions that had gained traction in the 1970s, in particular, blaming government unions for state budget woes and high taxes in the midst of economic turmoil. During the Great Recession, states struggled to uphold their pension commitments to state workers—which were often unfunded promises[2]—just as private sector employees were getting laid off and watching their retirement accounts plummet in value. This messaging gained particular resonance in places with a growing divide between rural and urban areas, such as Wisconsin. In her work on the attitudes of rural residents in Wisconsin, Katherine Cramer-Walsh uncovered a distinct rural consciousness that included resentment of government workers in the city who were seen as lacking a strong work ethic and as a drain on taxpayer money (2012, 524). These rural Wisconsinites were thus predisposed to accept Scott Walker's anti-union rhetoric on public sector workers. The 2010 elections created the political foundation for attacking public sector unions, the growing size and importance of government unions put a target on their back, the 2008 financial crisis helped anti-union opponents legitimize these attacks to the public, and public—especially rural—resentment of government employees fueled the negative portrayals of public sector workers.

With the groundwork set, state legislatures across the country took up the issue of public sector collective bargaining, but, as a consequence of federalized labor law, states considered a variety of measures. Martin Malin found four common elements in the laws that were enacted in 2011. First, several states repealed collective bargaining laws outright (2012, 154). Oklahoma repealed a law protecting the collective bargaining rights of municipal employees in cities with a population of over 35,000, and Tennessee repealed a law granting teachers collective bargaining rights, replacing it with a more limited process called "collaborative conferencing" (154). Several states enacted laws specifying that certain workers were no longer granted collective bargaining rights, including: doctors, lawyers, and some supervisors (Nevada); some university faculty, police, and firefighters (Ohio; voters repealed this law); and "state university faculty, all employees of the University of Wisconsin Hospitals and Clinics, and day care and home health care providers" (Wisconsin) (156).

Second, states limited the scope of public sector bargaining. In Wisconsin, bargaining was limited to "base wages" (Malin 2012, 157). Ohio, Massachusetts, and New Jersey limited employees' ability to bargain over health care (157). Idaho and Indiana prohibited any bargaining by teachers beyond compensation, and Michigan and Illinois added more restrictions on what teachers could bargain over, such as the school calendar (158–160).

Third, states gave employers more power to unilaterally act when negotiations break down between workers and the government (Malin 2012, 160). Wisconsin eliminated arbitration for most public sector workers, which means there is no remedy for an impasse (160). Idaho no longer requires mediation in the event of an impasse; this opens the door for school boards to act unilaterally in such situations (160). The Ohio law, repealed by voters, would have eliminated interest arbitration (161). New Jersey, Nevada, Nebraska, Michigan, Indiana, and Illinois also made changes to the process and/or effectiveness of interest arbitration (161–163). Finally, several states passed statutes granting new powers to employers during a financial emergency. Nevada, Ohio (later repealed), and Michigan all passed laws granting power to employers to void all or part of negotiated contracts in times of financial emergency (164).

Fourth, the "paycheck protection" laws some states passed limited the ability of unions to automatically collect union dues, sometimes money for political purposes, other times all union dues. Existing law already requires unions to keep money for political purposes entirely separate from general union funds, and members donate to political causes on a voluntary basis. However, proponents of the law argue that union members are unable to consent to the actions of their labor leaders, and eliminating automatic dues checkoff would grant them more control. At the extreme, these laws would allow workers who are covered by a union but have chosen not to be members to not pay union dues; proponents argue that all activity performed by a public sector union, including collective bargaining, is inherently political. As will be discussed in the next chapter, this issue was recently taken up by the Supreme Court. In 2011, state legislatures began considering automatic dues checkoff as part of the overall effort to weaken public sector unions; Arizona passed a law placing new restrictions on the procedure (Artz 2012, 134).

Taken together, the various bills proposed and passed during this period represent an extensive, innovative effort to weaken public sector unions across the country. It can be easy to see these most recent attacks as simply the consequence of the Great Recession and the Republican wave in the midterm elections, but there is also a great deal we can learn by looking at these modern events within the broader context of U.S. labor history. Wisconsin in particular can offer a useful frame for situating the last several years within the longer time horizon of American history and thus gaining a deeper understanding of organized labor.

Labor Through the Lens of Wisconsin

The monthlong battle over public sector collective bargaining rights in Wisconsin was a noteworthy moment in organized labor's history of protest.[3] While the massive protests and international media coverage of the events in Wisconsin were unique, the budget repair bill that inspired the protest was not. Instead, Governor Walker's attack on public sector collective bargaining rights should be seen as part of a longer history of contention over government unionism in the United States resulting from the lack of a national-level law that addresses public sector collective bargaining rights. The events in Wisconsin thus offer a lens for understanding the consequences of divided labor law for organized labor in the United States. This section looks at the events in Wisconsin leading up to Act 10 and its aftermath because they encapsulate the conclusions drawn throughout this book about the ramifications of divided labor law for labor's current political weakness. Examining the events in Wisconsin can tell us a great deal about the consequences of divided labor law for organized labor today, both in Wisconsin and nationally, and serves as a reminder that the issues discussed in this project remain a very real, ongoing struggle within the labor movement.

Wisconsin Before Act 10

The metaphor of sleep pervades Wisconsin labor leaders' memories of their movement before Scott Walker took office. Prior to Act 10, they were "asleep at the wheel"; relatively peaceful labor relations in the public sector had "put everybody to sleep, you could pay your monthly dues, know that your contract would improve a bit each year, and not have to do anything for it" (Interviews #16, 18).[4] Wisconsin labor leaders remember a complacent movement that had lost its connection to their communities; it had become a disparate group of unions that were not communicating with each other: "it used to be you could just show up to the [state] AFL-CIO executive board, report on your own issues, then leave" (Interview #16). Looking back, labor leaders felt that they and their unions were just going through the motions rather than leading a vibrant, influential social movement.

Part of the reason labor was "asleep" prior to Act 10 can be traced to the divided history and contentious relationship between public and private sector unions in the United States. The public and private sector unions in Wisconsin were not a fully integrated, cohesive force prior to Governor Walker's attack. Union membership differences were one source of conflict. Beginning in 2011, the creation of a proposed open-pit iron-ore mine split the movement in the state, pitting conservation-minded public sector unions against private sector unions desperate for jobs. Some government unions sided with environmentalists, decrying the potentially devastating environmental impacts of the mining operation as well as the dangers posed to a nearby reservation, its residents, and their groundwater. In contrast, many private sector unions saw the mining venture as desperately needed capital investment and jobs in a depressed economy (Interview #23); for example, the plan included mining equipment to be built in Milwaukee by union labor. The proposed mine created dissension among unions and their members: as one reporter noted, "Randy Bryce, the political coordinator of Milwaukee Iron Workers Local 8 and one of Walker's most tenacious opponents, reluctantly supported the legislation. 'They're trying to divide us,' he told me, 'but my members need work'" (Kaufman 2012). The conflict—environmental protection versus job creation—cut through the labor movement in Wisconsin, pitting public sector unions against private sector unions.

Likewise, in 2006 when a constitutional amendment to ban gay marriage was on the ballot, public sector unions—especially teachers unions—were some of the largest contributors to the campaign to oppose the referendum (Moore 2007). While the state AFL-CIO came out in opposition to the referendum, it was clear that they "aren't part of the big movements like gay marriage and women" (Interview #16). Membership policy differences were not the only source of division prior to Act 10.

Public and private sector union differences also reflect a long-standing lack of shared understanding as private sector union density declined precipitously and public sector union issues received little sympathy from private sector unions. In general, "there was rhetoric but not a lot of behavior of helping each other" (Interview #23). When Governor Walker's budget repair bill was introduced, these differences were emphasized by anti-union forces in an effort to divide the labor movement. For instance, a television advertisement from the Wisconsin Club for Growth, a conservative advocacy group, exclaimed: "But state workers haven't had to sacrifice. They pay next to nothing for their pensions, and a fraction of their health care. It's not fair. Call your state legislator and tell them to vote for Gov. Walker's budget repair bill. It's time state employees paid their fair share, just like the rest of us" (Milwaukee Journal Sentinel 2011). Governor Walker recognized the danger of a unified labor movement and hoped to create inter-union conflict (Interview #20). In an infamous prank phone call, a radio talk show host, impersonating the conservative billionaire David Koch, managed to call and speak to Governor Walker. In the discussion, Walker explained his effort to differentiate public versus private sector unions: "cause I'm trying to keep out the, as many of the private unions as possible, I said this is about the budget, this is about public-sector unions" (Wisconsin State Journal 2011). The conditions in 2011 were ripe for sowing discord between the private and public sector unions.

The private sector industrial unions had been suffering for decades as a result of de-industrialization and automation, which led to the loss of key manufacturing jobs. As one labor leader explained, "It was clear during the campaign that Walker was trying to divide private from public sector workers by emphasizing public sector as the haves being supported by the have nots. The private sector unions have a longstanding frustration over this.... The private sector has been hammered so hard, it's very easy to exploit that" (Interview #20). As discussed in Chapter 6, the effort to divide public and private sector unions was far less successful than in the 1970s thanks to the shared sense of crisis in the movement. However, the "sleeping" labor movement, complacent and lacking cohesion between unions prior to the budget repair bill, helps illustrate the failure of the 1970s to create a unified, vibrant labor movement before the difficulties of the 1980s, a failure that has persisted until today.

Walker's Budget Repair Bill

When Governor Walker proposed his budget repair bill on February 11, 2011, it caught many in the labor movement by surprise and awoke a movement that had been asleep for too long. Walker's attack on public sector collective bargaining rights "gave them a wake-up call" and "the entire labor movement was dunked into freezing Lake Michigan and woken up like never before" (Interviews #19, 28). Labor leaders would likely have been less surprised by Governor Walker's attack if they had taken a longer and more expansive view on public sector labor history. What happened in Wisconsin was not new, nor would it be the last time such retrenchment of public sector collective bargaining rights occurred (e.g., Iowa passed similar legislation in 2017).

The effects of divided labor law were evident in Wisconsin: even in a seemingly "safe" state the rights of public sector workers proved inherently tenuous and subject to the whims of state and local lawmakers. Act 10 scales back government employees' collective bargaining rights by limiting what public sector unions can bargain over to only wage increases at or below inflation, requiring the firing of striking workers, prohibiting automatic payroll deduction of union dues, and requiring unions to recertify every year. Scott Walker's successful effort to curb public sector collective bargaining rights was part of a longer tradition: "In fact, states change their collective bargaining rules frequently, and often without much protest or dissent. . . . In many states, collective bargaining rights have been a fleeting thing that can easily come and go with changes in administration" (Maynard and Goodman 2011). Indiana governor Evan Bayh granted state workers the right to collectively bargain in 1989 through executive order. When Governor Mitch Daniels rescinded the executive order granting public sector collective bargaining rights to state workers in Indiana in 2005, "it was a very quiet transition" (Maynard and Goodman 2011). Wisconsin was unique because of the unprecedented protests to try to protect public sector collective bargaining rights, not because of the legislation itself.

Public sector collective bargaining rights in Wisconsin also remain highly unequal; there is great variation among cities and regions. In progressive areas of the state, like Madison, local elected officials and schools boards continue to negotiate contracts with their unions. In other areas of the state, as one local president somewhat hyperbolically explained, "what was once a seventy-four page contract can now be printed on a sticky note. Decades of developing best practices, agreements and negotiations are just gone. Now all of those decisions are in the hands of the employer" (WI AFL-CIO Convention, October 2, 2012). By eliminating many collective bargaining rights, Act 10 returns Wisconsin to the period prior to the 1960s, when local unions obtained recognition largely through the beneficence of employers and with few protections if that relationship turned sour.

Divided labor law gave Wisconsin lawmakers the opportunity to scale back rights thanks to several features inherent in federal arrangements. First, at any time, a state or locality has abundant examples of policy alternatives in action. There is no single standard for state treatment of public sector employees. States vary tremendously in terms of the generosity of their collective bargaining rights and the uniformity of these rights across employee categories and levels of government. Opponents of Act 10 could not simply look to other states that grant public sector collective bargaining rights to serve as an example in Wisconsin because Governor Walker and his supporters could just as easily point to several states to illustrate that public sector employees do not merit collective bargaining rights. Walker could even justify scaling back public sector rights because the nearby state of Indiana had done just that in 2005.

Second, groups engaged in political conflicts that have become intractable at the national level can find more success at lower levels of government. Anti-union opponents at the national level have proven successful at ossifying private sector labor law but have failed in outright retrenchment of the Wagner Act. One response to the impasse at the national level has been to focus attention on the state and local levels. Right-to-work laws are one such example, and the renewed focus of anti-union opponents on attacking public sector collective bargaining rights is a similar development. While it was not the model used in Wisconsin, the American Legislative Exchange Council (ALEC), a conservative organization that teams with state legislators to draft legislation, has produced numerous draft bills targeting public sector collective bargaining rights that have been introduced and passed in legislatures across the country (McIntire 2012). For example, ALEC's model bill, the Public Employee Paycheck Protection Act, eliminates automatic dues checkoff for union members, making it much harder for unions to collect union dues from their members (ALEC 2017).

Third, national-level rights become reinforced as case law over time creates path-dependent pressures to maintain existing law. While Wisconsin's collective bargaining law had a much longer history than most, when Walker proposed his legislation opponents could not claim that public sector workers had a protected right to collectively bargain because no national statute exists. In contrast, private sector labor law has over eighty years of NLRB case law serving as positive feedback on national-level private sector collective bargaining rights.

Fourth, federalism welcomes and even encourages variation and innovation at the local level. Supreme Court Justice Brandeis first invoked the metaphor of states as policy laboratories in a dissenting opinion in 1932. Brandeis noted that "it is one of the happy incidents of the federal system that a single courageous state may, if its citizens choose, serve as a laboratory; and try novel social and economic experiments without risk to the rest of the country" (Volden 1997, 78–79). Presidents from Reagan to Clinton to Obama have all included the idea of states as sites of experimentation in executive orders and memoranda they have issued regarding federalism.[5] As Reagan noted, it is "the nature of our constitutional system" that "individual States and communities are free to experiment with a variety of approaches to public issues."[6] From Supreme Court justices to presidents, there is a pervading belief that experimentation at the state and local levels is a natural, and laudable, feature of American federalism. Thus Governor Walker's proposal of Act 10 can be seen as part of the long-standing tradition of experimentation states have taken with regard to public sector collective bargaining rights.

Finally, and most fundamentally, states and localities lack the expectations of national standards and equality—in other words, a floor of protection—that have been central to rights protections at the national level. With the issue of public sector collective bargaining rights left unaddressed at the national level, states responded in a variety of ways. Many states deliberately denied their public sector employees collective bargaining rights. As a consequence, states and localities remain sites where the basic tenets of government unionism can be contested, which often leads to volatility surrounding public sector collective bargaining rights.

Federalism provided the opportunity as well as the motive for Walker's budget repair bill. The close ties between organized labor and the Democratic Party often create Republican animosity toward labor and union-friendly policies, as well as the motivation to pursue anti-union policies. Divided labor law, by promoting the growth of the public sector and the decline of the private sector, put a target on the back of the public sector. In public, Governor Walker vigorously maintained that his budget repair bill was strictly about improving Wisconsin's budget situation. In private, he was more candid. Prior to announcing his budget repair bill at a private dinner in the executive residence with his cabinet, "Walker held up a photograph of Ronald Reagan and told his cabinet that what they were about to do recalled Reagan's breaking of the air-traffic-controllers' union strike in 1981. 'This is our time to change the course of history,' Walker said" (Kaufman 2012). Walker understood the significance of his proposed bill; the consequences of Act 10 have set back the union movement in Wisconsin.

The Aftermath of Act 10

The enactment of Act 10 was an emotional and tangible blow to organized labor in Wisconsin. After devoting massive amounts of time and energy to opposing the Act, labor leaders and members saw their efforts fail and then had to witness a severe decline in membership as well as funds. As one labor leader said, "A lot of time, energy, and an awful lot of work [was] decimated with a stroke of the pen" (Interview #20), referring not only to the effort to oppose the bill but also the half century of public sector labor relations that this labor leader and others had devoted their lives to cultivating. Public sector union density in Wisconsin dropped from 50.3 percent in 2011 to 22.7 percent in 2016, a loss of over 100,000 members in just five years in a state with only approximately 350,000 union members in 2011 (Hirsch and Macpherson 2017). The General AFL-CIO state fund lost $100,000 as a result of the loss of membership dues in 2011 (WI State AFL-CIO Convention, October 1, 2012). AFSCME Council 24, representing state employees, estimated that they lost 60 percent of their membership between 2011 and 2014, and their annual budget has declined from $6 million to $2 million since Act 10 became law (Greenhouse 2014a). The Wisconsin Education Association Council dues from membership "are off nearly 50%—$12 million in lost revenue as of 2014" (Umhoefer 2016). The founding local of AFSCME, Local 1, dropped from 1,000 to 122 members in 2014 (Greenhouse 2014a).

Membership losses have been severe because public sector unions must recertify every year and no longer receive automatic dues checkoff. This requires a significant amount of work and resources. Some unions have chosen not to recertify, given the limits on what they can bargain over anyway, and focus instead on servicing members without formal recognition. Other unions have tried to maintain their official status. One AFSCME organizer, who represents maintenance, security, and other low-paid building personnel, described the difficulties in reconnecting with the membership of her local. Because her members are some of the lowest-paid state workers, many do not have email or up-to-date contact information, which means she has to connect with them at the worksite—all one hundred buildings. Many of the members work the third shift, which means showing up at 2:30 AM, often with an interpreter in hand, to convince the members to re-up with the union (WI State AFL-CIO Convention, October 1, 2012). This exercise has to be repeated every year.

While the membership declines in Wisconsin have been particularly steep, such losses are echoed in other states as well. The concerted effort against public sector unions has proven successful and has contributed to the loss of public sector union members. In 2013, private sector union members outnumbered public sector union members for the first time since 2010 (Trottman 2014). There are now 7.4 million private sector union members and 7.1 million public sector union members (Hirsch and Macpherson 2017).

Looking only at the numbers, the situation for public sector unions, and organized labor more broadly, appears dire. However, labor leaders see a major positive outcome of the events in Wisconsin: the labor movement is no longer sleeping. Rhetorically, the movement in Wisconsin is emphasizing solidarity like never before. Common refrains at the Wisconsin State AFL-CIO Convention in October 2012 were: "We're in this together, not just private vs. public," "We've put aside our differences . . . solidarity is the private sector standing with the public sector," and "We've had petty difference and turf battles in the past. All of that was put aside." Leaders emphasized that the experience of protesting Act 10 taught them and their members "what solidarity is supposed to look like" and reified the sacrosanct principle of solidarity: "If you pick a fight with one of our brothers and sisters, this whole family is coming after you." The closer bonds between the two sectors within the movement appear to extend beyond the rhetoric to an intangible sense of shared interests as well.

Wisconsin's labor unions are also trying to forge a more engaged, activist membership with deeper roots in their communities and with other groups. At the October 2012 convention labor leaders spoke hopefully about making their workplaces, like the firehouses, more open to the public and re-creating the union halls as community spaces once again (Interviews #16, 19). Leaders hope to revive the feeling that the unions are part of the community so that the public will want to fight on behalf of the unions because they feel that the unions fight on their behalf. Practically, this translates into fostering better relationships across unions and forging alliances with other like-minded groups. We Are Wisconsin, an organization that emerged to oppose Act 10, is one example of a broader alliance between labor and progressive groups. We Are Wisconsin now engages in voter education and mobilization and includes a PAC and political fund to help elect progressive candidates.

Wisconsin labor unions are also seeking to return to their more activist roots by moving beyond just servicing their members to instead remaking the union movement into a social movement (Interview #16). Labor leaders described the movement prior to Act 10 as having become "much more like an insurance company that you paid into and were provided with services" (Interview #18). In the old model, "you just pay your dues, the union hires staff and lawyers, and bargains and protects contracts" (Interview #20). Before Act 10, leaders and members "defined the union as the contract" (Interview #23). For the public sector unions, centering an organization's identity on a contract was no longer possible after Act 10. Thus, there is a strong emphasis on creating a new identity and stressing that "collective bargaining is a tactic, not the union" (WI State AFL-CIO Convention, October 2, 2012). Many unions in Wisconsin responded to Act 10 by electing new leaders to help usher in this new activist orientation. If unions are to find their identity and strength outside the contract and instead through avenues like political activity, then they need a coordinated effort to do so. All of the labor leaders interviewed stressed much great coordination across unions at the local, state, and national levels was now happening. The labor unity tables, which were discussed in Chapter 6, are one such example of the concrete efforts at inter-union coordination and cooperation.

Efforts to reorient the labor movement in Wisconsin and nationally may have come too late, however. The window of opportunity for a national public sector labor law closed nearly forty years ago, and it remains unclear if it will ever reopen. The labor movement today requires a new approach to organizing and political activity but may lack the ability to adapt to the new reality of a post–Act 10 environment. In particular, "the current [labor] leadership has never experienced an organizing model" (Interview #20). If unions have been operating as insurance agencies, as one labor leader said, this means that union employees have been trained to run the insurance model of handling grievance procedures, not to kick-start a social movement. In other words, "staff that was built to be litigators, now have to be organizers" (Interview #18). The transition has not been easy or wholly successful. One national leader described traveling to union locals across the country to help them "reimagine their reason for being and [help] them to kind of reframe their agenda to their own members and to the public. It really was a wake-up call, for them too. The wake-up call is that you can't just be working with your own members. You really have to consider the broad public as your constituency, not just your dues-paying members. In some ways, the union has to see itself as operating in the public interest" (Interview #33). One local president he worked with had ousted the former president in a bid to revitalize the union after Act 10. The staff of the union local was so entrenched in the old, grievance-based model of doing business that "it took him nine months but the staff all left. All left. It was a really good thing" (Interview #33). While things worked out in the end for this local, it begs the question: What is happening in the countless other unions that are not undergoing such a fundamental leadership shake-up? Another leader described staff retiring early to keep their benefits before Act 10 takes full effect, resulting in a loss of institutional knowledge at the union (Interview #18). It is unclear whether labor is willing and able to transition to an organizing, activist model or whether the talk of change and solidarity is just rhetoric.

Reinventing the labor movement will be even more difficult because all of this renewed energy comes at a time when both public and private sector unions are on the defensive and weakening, their opponents have become highly mobilized, and economic challenges push against increased union strength. In Wisconsin, the labor leaders interviewed in 2012 were gearing up for the presidential election but were "all suffering from emotional and election fatigue" (Interview #21). Many of Wisconsin's local elections do not coincide with the national election, and, on top of that, anti-Walker opponents mounted an ultimately unsuccessful recall campaign against the governor. Counting all of the elections and their primaries individually, one labor leader figured that they had mobilized for seven elections from 2011 to 2012 (Interview #21). While labor leaders try to remain hopeful, after so much effort with only modest payoffs, there were cracks in the façade. Leaders described the monthlong takeover of the state capitol as one of the most remarkable and powerful experiences in their lives, but ultimately they lost. Leah Lipska, president of AFSCME Local 1, thinks the numerous defeats combined with severe financial strains have beaten down public sector workers: "'A lot of people are tired,' she said. 'They're tired of politics'" (quoted in Greenhouse 2014a). As another labor leader explained, "I will never forget. This was personal, especially for those of us who believe in the movement. . . . Thinking and talking about it is like reliving a funeral" (Interview #21). The labor movement has not been beaten, but the retrenchment of public sector collective bargaining rights has significantly damaged labor's strength and resiliency.

The consequences of Act 10 have become even more apparent in the years since its passage. Capitalizing on the weakened labor movement, Wisconsin passed right-to-work legislation in 2015, striking a blow to private sector unions (Taylor 2016). Right-to-work in Wisconsin, combined with Act 10, has weakened labor's strength and reduced its size, which has serious political consequences for turnout in American elections. In the past, organized labor has played a pivotal role nationally in educating their members about politics and mobilizing them to participate in elections. For example, several scholars have shown that union members and union households turn out in higher numbers relative to the rest of the population (Delaney, Masters, and Schwochau 1988; Verba, Schlozman, and Brady 1995; Chang 2001; Radcliff 2001; Masters 2004; Freeman 2010; Kerrissey and Schofer 2013; Rosenfeld 2014).[7] Looking at the American National Election Studies cumulative file, Francia (2012) finds that, controlling for other factors affecting turnout, living in a union household increases one's probability of voting by 4 percentage points. He notes that "in 2011 . . . there were a reported 14.8 million members in the United States with an estimated 28.3 million Americans in union households. When 28.3 million union households are multiplied by the model's estimated impact of .04, the overall aggregate impact is about 1.1 million more votes nationally" (8). The higher rates of participation among union members and households have been recorded over time and across elections. In general, unions have also successfully mobilized members to support Democratic candidates. Compared to non-members, union members have consistently voted more often for union-endorsed candidates than other candidates and thus more Democratic candidates (Juravich and Shergold 1988; Sousa 1993; Delaney, Masters, and Schwochau 1988, 1990; Clark and Masters 2001).[8] Given the powerful role of unions in mobilizing voters, the staggering decline in union members in Wisconsin since Act 10 was enacted likely has affected political outcomes. From 2011 until 2016, Wisconsin lost 136,000 union members (Beck 2017). In 2016, "Exit polls show[ed] that even as union support for the Democratic nominee fell from 2012 to 2016, union households still voted for Clinton over Trump by wider margins than nonunion households" (Rowell and Madland 2016). Given what we know about labor's ability to mobilize its members, especially for Democratic candidates, the fact that Clinton lost Wisconsin only by approximately 22,000 votes suggests that a stronger union movement in the state could have affected the outcome; Wisconsin has lost nearly five times as many union members since Act 10 as decided the 2016 presidential election in the state.

The events in Wisconsin vividly illustrate the vulnerability of public sector collective bargaining rights. Despite all of labor's resources and the significant protests they mounted against Act 10, the labor movement faltered because, absent a national floor of protection, Wisconsin was able to remove public sector collective bargaining rights through state-level legislation. Divided labor law has contributed to an embattled and weakened labor movement in Wisconsin that is struggling to redefine itself in the face of a new legal environment.

While this chapter illustrates the consequences of the divided legal regime, established by the Wagner Act, for organized labor over the last several decades, the consequences for the labor movement cannot be understood simply by moving from decade to decade. In the next chapter, we will look at how these consequences have shaped the size, strength, and effectiveness of organized labor in American politics.

Chapter 8

Conclusion: The Consequences of Labor's Enduring Divide

In October 1953, the "Trade Union and Collective Bargaining Rights of Public Employees" conference was held in Munich, Germany. The conference brought together public sector labor leaders from Austria, Belgium, Denmark, Finland, France, Germany, Great Britain, Holland, Norway, Sweden, Switzerland, Tunisia, and the United States. In his opening remarks at the conference, General Secretary M. C. Bolle of the International Federation of Unions of Employees in Public and Civil Services commented on the state of trade union rights around the world. He noted that in his travels he had discovered that many countries in Asia and Latin America that were members of the International Labor Organization, which affirms collective bargaining rights for employees, continued to deny these basic rights to workers (IFUEPCS 1953, 6). But, he emphasized, disregarding the rights of workers happens "even in countries reckoned the most advanced" (6). As an example, he singled out the United States for the "inclination on the part of the authorities to withhold trade union and bargaining rights from public servants" (6).

At a conference bringing together public sector unionists from many advanced industrial countries, Bolle was right to note that the United States stands out for its approach to public sector employees' collective bargaining rights. As Chapter 1 emphasized, among advanced industrialized countries, the United States continues to be distinctive for the way in which it has separated public sector labor law from private sector labor law and the limited, piecemeal rights that have been granted to government employees. In 1940, David Ziskind noted, "The law pertaining to government labor disputes has been especially inchoate. It cannot be found congealed in court decisions or flaunted in legislative enactments" (231). His assessment is equally appropriate today. The last seven chapters have traced chronologically the consequences of public sector employees' exclusion from the Wagner Act. This chapter examines the consequences of this exclusion for today's labor movement and then addresses the policy implications of these findings.

Consequences for the Modern Labor Movement

What does government employees' exclusion and the separation of American labor law mean for the development, size, and strength of the U.S. labor movement today? The AFL-CIO's Public Employee Department summed up one part of the answer nicely: "one country . . . two different worlds" (Lucak 1987). Absent a national public sector labor law, government unionism was ultimately limited because state- and local-level innovations proved to be imperfect approximations of the Wagner Act. Federalism cannot explain every aspect of labor's development over the last half century, but it is vital for understanding the brief rise and then plateauing of public sector union density at the same time that private sector union density was declining. More broadly, the damage to the public sector labor movement from exclusion has shaped the broader labor movement as well. The institutional split of public and private sector labor law has had important consequences for the movement's size, strength, and effectiveness today.

Labor's Size: The Geographic Concentration of Labor

The absence of an overarching federal law has contributed to the dramatic variation in and regional concentration of state-level public sector union density (see Figure 8).[1] As discussed earlier, states with a strong, existing union movement and Democratic governors and legislatures were more likely to pass pro–public sector collective bargaining laws; the existing union movement and Democratic states were already regionally concentrated in the 1960s and 1970s. As a result, the regional nature of labor has continued unabated with the rise of public sector unionism. States in which more than 40 percent of the public sector workforce is unionized are limited to parts of the West, Midwest, and Northeast, whereas less than 30 percent of the public sector workforce is unionized in the South, Mountain-West, and Central-Midwest (Hirsch and Macpherson 2017). Labor's geographical concentration, both

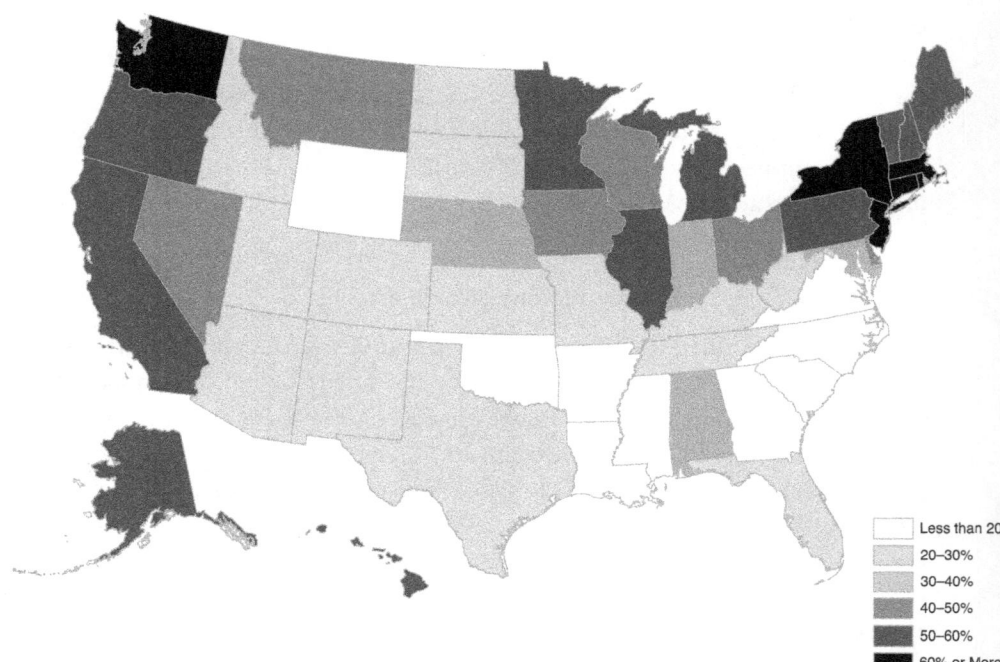

Figure 8. Percentage of public sector workforce that is unionized, 2010. Hirsch and Macpherson 2017.

public *and* private, is remarkable: "fully one-half of all union members lived in only six states by 2000" (McCartin 2008, 123). Thus, while labor represents over 14 million Americans, its electoral clout is limited by its geographical concentration. Continued geographical concentration is particularly problematic for organized labor because it suggests that the possibility of a filibuster-proof supermajority in the Senate to support federal labor law reform is increasingly remote.

If public sector employees had been included in the Wagner Act or had been able to pass their own national public sector law before the closing of the window of opportunity in 1976, public sector employees likely would have had greater success than their private sector counterparts organizing in anti-union states owing to the constraints public sector employers face that prevent serious resistance to unionization. The success public sector employees have had in organizing in anti-union states gives a sense of this possibility. The lowest public sector union density is still over 10 percent in states that have no public sector collective bargaining rights (Hirsch and Macpherson 2017). This union density is certainly due in part to federal employees, but it is also because government unions have successfully gained limited recognition from some school boards and municipalities despite the legal prohibitions in place (Freeman and Han 2012b). Today's public sector union density levels in anti-union states illustrate what public sector unions have been able to achieve despite the lack of collective bargaining rights, which suggests great possibilities for growth if they were given a legal foundation to support their efforts. Instead, government unions have had to pursue collective bargaining rights on a state-by-state basis and have been prevented from making significant inroads in anti-union states, reinforcing the geographic concentration of labor.

Labor's Strength: The Unequal, Vulnerable Rights of Public Sector Employees

Public sector unions found success and expanded their membership at the same time private sector unions were being frustrated at the national level, but the victories made at the state and local levels were not equivalent to what would have been possible had public sector unions been included in the Wagner Act. The multiple points of access at the state and local levels provide opportunities for reformers, but decentralization inevitably results in laws that lack the kind of national standards needed to promote equality (Mettler 1998, 13). Legislative reforms were hard-won and highly variable. In states strongly opposed to unionization, public sector unions had to navigate just as many veto points as private sector unions have faced at the national level. The result for public sector labor law is what AFSCME has declared "a patchwork quilt of conflicting, confusing and often inadequate legislation" (AFSCME 2002). This patchwork quilt includes an estimated "110 separate state statutes governing public sector labor relations, augmented by numerous local ordinances, executive orders, and other legal authority" (Slater 2004, 196). A third of states either explicitly outlaw collective bargaining for public sector employees or have no statute addressing the issue (Freeman and Han 2012b, 17). Other states vary tremendously in how pro-bargaining their collective bargaining laws are and in terms of which groups of public sector employees are included or excluded.

Collective bargaining provisions frequently apply differently for teachers, state employees, police, and other government workers. One of the areas of greatest variation is whether the state or locality permits government employees to strike, but states differ on even the most basic tenets of collective bargaining, including which groups of public sector workers are permitted to unionize and what issues they may bargain over. One consequence of this variation is that an estimated 33 percent of local and state employees (six million workers) did not have collective bargaining rights in 2002 (USGAO 2002, 14; U.S. Census Bureau 2003).[2] Not only is federalism synonymous with variation, but, as Aaron Wildavsky (1984) identified over thirty years ago, "federalism means inequality." Suzanne Mettler notes that "when social and labor policies have been left in the hands of states and localities, standards have been lowered or neglected in more areas than not" (1998, 13). Public sector bargaining law is certainly no exception. Leaving public sector labor law to the states not only lowered standards and created unequal treatment but also left labor law more vulnerable to the vagaries of the states.

The recent conservative turn in state legislatures across the country illustrates the precarious nature of public sector labor law and an important lesson about federalism: "for every liberal state policy 'laboratory,' there are at least as many—or more—conservative policy laboratories" (Robertson 2014). Lou Cannon notes that "as of mid-June [2011], 49 bills had been enacted in 23 states and Puerto Rico that included some form of restriction on collective bargaining in the 2011 session" (2011, 14). Using data from the National Conference of State Legislatures' Collective Bargaining and Labor Union Database, Freeman and Han estimate that, from 2011 to 2012, there were: "733 bills in 42 states relating to public employee unions, 140 bills relating to union dues/agency fees, 55 bills on political activities and contributions, 171 bills for public safety employees, and additional bills in other categories making a total of 1,707 bills in 50 states. . . . The majority of these bills . . . were designed to weaken unions and their collective bargaining rights" (2012a, 393). While the scope of the attacks in 2011–2012 is large, the nature of the attacks is not unique.

Even before the most recent wave of attacks, changes in public sector bargaining laws have been frequent and often regressive (Wasserman 2006). The year 2011 may have seen the most active retrenchment of public sector labor law, but it had started long before. For instance, in 2005 Indiana governor Mitch Daniels rescinded the executive order permitting collective bargaining with state employees, and Missouri governor Matt Blunt also rescinded an executive order recognizing state employee collective bargaining. In 2011, the Indiana legislature passed a law barring future governors from regranting collective bargaining rights to state employees (Freeman and Han 2012a, 390). The attacks in Wisconsin, Ohio, Indiana, and elsewhere demonstrate the mixed blessing of federalism: excluding public sector workers from the Wagner Act allowed them to succeed at the state and local levels while private sector unions struggled to reform federal law, but the flexibility of federalism can go both ways and public sector collective bargaining rights have been retrenched as well.

The 2016 elections illustrate the continued vulnerability of public sector collective bargaining rights and the enduring importance of divided labor law for understanding organized labor today. The elections ushered in single-party Republican rule at the national level and in twenty-five states. Several of these states have sought to remake their state's government employee labor laws. For instance, in Iowa, lawmakers moved swiftly to pass a bill very similar to Act 10 in Wisconsin. The bill limits collective bargaining to wages, eliminates dues checkoff even though workers already opted into the system, and requires recertification elections with a majority of all workers in the bargaining unit—not just those voting—approving the union before negotiating every contract. Also taking a page from Wisconsin, the bill exempts public safety workers, in what opponents saw as a "divide and conquer" strategy (Noble and Pfannenstiel 2017; Rodriguez and Sanders 2017). Without a national public sector Wagner Act, actions like Iowa's are to be expected as the states continue to address the issue of government employee collective bargaining in their own ways.

At the national level, the absence of a public employee Wagner Act has also made federal workers legally vulnerable. The election of Donald Trump to the presidency in 2016 raised the specter that he might take aim at federal employee unions. Harkening the "divide and conquer" strategy, Trump has actively met with and courted private sector unions, particularly construction, mining, and steelworkers unions (Scheiber 2017; Greenhouse 2017). At the same time, Trump has signaled much less sympathy for public sector unions. Governor Scott Walker made headlines when, after visiting the White House, he reported that he had talked with Vice President Mike Pence about "what we've done here in Wisconsin, how they may take bits and pieces of what we did with Act 10 and with civil service reform, and how they could apply that at the national level" (Spicuzza and Marley 2017).

President Trump cannot simply pass an Act 10 for federal employees because many federal workers' rights are bound up in civil service law, but, absent a Wagner Act for federal employees, he can weaken these rights through executive order. In his 2018 State of the Union Address, Trump suggested that he was considering taking on federal collective bargaining rights, albeit through Congress rather than an executive order. He asked Congress "to empower every Cabinet Secretary with the authority to reward good workers and to remove federal employees who undermine the public trust or fail the American people" (Trump 2018). However, Trump ultimately chose to act unilaterally, signing three executive orders in May 2018. The first order "makes it easier to fire and discipline federal employees," including weakening seniority rules and shortening the appeal period (Scheiber 2018). The second order "directs federal agencies to renegotiate contracts with unions representing government employees so as to reduce waste." Finally, the third order limits the amount of "official time" federal employees with positions in the union can use during normal working hours to perform their union roles (Scheiber 2018). As part of the implementation of these executive orders, federal agencies have begun evicting unions from office space within the agencies, making it harder for unions to meet with and thus represent their members (Naylor 2018). The content of Trump's executive orders is being challenged in the courts. To date, however, the Trump administration's efforts have sought to weaken federal workers' collective bargaining rights and make it harder for federal employee unions to do business with their members.

By paving the way for legislation like Act 10, its sister law passed in Iowa in 2017, and Trump's executive orders, divided labor law thus continues to shape the fortunes of organized labor today. For public sector unions, the only legal development at the national level has been a dramatic step backward as a result of the recent Supreme Court decision *Janus v. American Federation of State, County and Municipal Employees* (2018). The case was in some ways the culmination of attacks on public sector unions at the state level begun in 2011. As anti-union opponents achieved legislative success in over a dozen states across the country in the 2010s, they expanded their efforts to the judiciary as well (Scheiber and Vogel 2018). One legal avenue these groups pursued was a "paycheck protection" movement that sought to challenge how and in what ways unions could collect dues. Prior to *Janus*, any government employee who did not join a union but was covered by that union had to pay an agency fee to the union, also known as a "fair share" fee. Labor unions argued that this fee, which is expressly not used for political activity, prevents workers from free riding by enjoying the benefits of the union without joining or paying for the union representation they are receiving. In contrast, opponents argued that all activity by public sector unions, including negotiating contracts, is inherently political and thus non-members should not be forced to subsidize activities that violate their free speech.

In 1977, the Supreme Court in *Abood v. Detroit Board of Education* made a distinction between agency fees that went toward collective bargaining and money that went toward political activities. The Court held that non-members' dues being used for political activities was a violation of their First Amendment free speech but that agency fees were not a violation and helped prevent free riding. In *Janus* (2018), the Court reversed its decision, ruling that "in addition to affecting how public money is spent, union speech in collective bargaining addresses many other important matters" and thus merits First Amendment protection. The *Janus* decision essentially makes public sector employment equivalent to private sector employment in right-to-work states where non-members can opt out of supporting the union that is representing them in collective bargaining. It is unclear at this time how much money public sector unions will lose or how many members they will be expected to represent without financial support. Thus, rather than a floor of protection through a public sector Wagner Act, government employees have instead been dealt a crippling blow that serves as a ceiling, preventing states from passing more union-friendly legislation. National legislation like the Wagner Act that grants a floor of protection provides the most potent, durable, and meaningful rights, but, like Taft-Hartley, decisions at the national level that undermine rights can have the reverse effect, dampening rights across the country.

Labor's Effectiveness: The Lack of a Nationally Cohesive, Geographically Diverse Movement

Whereas the Wagner Act gave private sector workers the fundamental right to unionize, as the preceding examples illustrate, the rights of public sector employees have proven more vulnerable. There is no firm commitment at the national level that government "employees shall have the right to self-organization, to form, join, or assist labor organizations, to bargain collectively through representatives of their own choosing" (NLRA 1935, Sec. 7). Instead, as the AFSCME president Jerry Wurf noted in testimony to Congress in 1974, "No one pattern prevails among the 50 states and 80,000 governmental units, save one: that public employees are no where near the equals of workers in the private industry" (Wurf 1974, 4). Federalism as a governing structure welcomes experimentation and innovation at the state and local levels. Experimentation in public sector labor law might sound appealing because it allows union-friendly states to pass very generous legislation. Indeed, in some states government employees possess greater rights than do their private sector counterparts, such as mandatory card-check certification, a much more manageable means of organizing a union than the traditional NLRB election procedure. But these gains come with serious costs; state- and local-level collective bargaining laws will never be on an equal footing with national-level rights because of the inherent differences between the two: national-level rights create a durable level of uniform protection that state- or local-level laws cannot provide.

In thinking through the consequences of divided labor law, it is helpful to consider the alternative. What if public sector employees had been included in the Wagner Act or received their own national-level law? Public sector unions might have had more success than private sector unions in hostile states if given the chance through a national-level law that protected their collective bargaining rights because of the constraints on public sector employer resistance. Private sector unions have struggled to organize new members as a result of the outdated legal framework that fails to constrain employers' union-avoidance strategies; hostile employer resistance—and the legal framework that permits it—is a significant barrier to union organizing at the federal level. As discussed earlier, public sector employers face pressures that discourage such vehement resistance and lack many of the tools, like employment-at-will, that private sector employers use to resist union organizing. If given national collective bargaining rights, and with a more amicable organizing environment, public sector unions would be able to make inroads into anti-union states. Instead, government unions are limited in their growth by lack of collective bargaining rights in anti-union states and renewed attacks in previously safe states; their geographic concentration and vulnerability mean the entire labor movement is smaller and less secure than it could be and unlikely to change without labor law reform. Thus, while the public sector union density spike in the 1960s–1970s slowed the decline of overall union density, this trend is unlikely to continue because government unions have reached the limits of state-level innovation.

What about private sector unions? Would they benefit from private sector labor law devolving to the state and local levels in order to end the national stalemate, as Richard Freeman (2006) and other have suggested? In the short run, private sector union density might increase as employees' collective bargaining rights would be strengthened in union-friendly states. Ultimately, however, this would leave private sector employees just as vulnerable as their public sector counterparts to retrenchment of their fundamental collective bargaining rights. The example of the one aspect of private sector labor law that has been left up to the states, Section 14(b) of Taft-Hartley, is a sobering reminder. Although Taft-Hartley is a national-level law, Section 14(b) does not mandate or outlaw right-to-work but instead gives states the option to become right-to-work states. In other words, 14(b) is a federalism provision within a national law. Leaving the decision of right-to-work up to the states has resulted in the same variability as seen in public sector labor laws at the state level: Michigan passed a right-to-work law in 2011, Wisconsin in 2015, West Virginia in 2016, and Missouri in 2017 (Missouri voters overturned the law in July 2018). All of this suggests that a national law protecting both public and private sector collective bargaining rights would offer the most protection for American labor unions and the best possibility for expansion.

Organized labor's political success depends on geographically diverse union density. A high-density labor movement translates into economic and political leverage, and if labor is geographically diverse, this leverage can reach a filibuster-proof level in the Senate. While union-friendly states with generous laws have provided a safe haven for union strength, they are not sufficient to create a large, geographically diverse union movement. The extension of collective bargaining rights has been crucial to the growth of union density, both private and public. However, most public sector unions continue to be concentrated in union-friendly states that have passed collective bargaining statutes. These unions have, in turn, responded by focusing a disproportionate share of their political resources at the state and local levels. Until a floor of protection exists for all public sector employees, we are unlikely to see dramatic growth in union density akin to what we saw in the 1930s and 1940s for the private sector and the 1960s and 1970s for the public sector. Thus, the experimentation within federalism does not benefit the labor movement despite the generous public sector provisions in some states, because these union-friendly states do not make up for the states where public sector employees lack few or any collective bargaining rights, nor do they promote a geographically diverse, nationally focused, strong, unified labor movement.

Divided Unions

This project set out to understand organized labor's current political weakness and the seemingly divergent paths of private and public sector unions over time. In doing so, this work has focused on explaining why public sector union density rose dramatically in the 1960s and 1970s and then plateaued at the very time private sector union density began declining precipitously, as well as on the consequences of these separate development paths and the resulting public sector union ascendency for organized labor's political activities. The separate density patterns displayed in Figure 1 are neither natural nor inevitable. Instead, this project has focused our attention on the timing and sequencing of when public and private sector employees gained collective bargaining rights and where they obtained these rights. The United States stands apart for the divided nature of its labor law with private sector labor law firmly entrenched at the national level and public sector labor law relegated to the states and localities. Divided labor law is a crucial link in explaining the weakness of organized labor in American politics today.

The passage of the Wagner Act in 1935 consolidated private sector labor law at the national level, whereas public sector labor law remained unconsolidated, leaving the institutional environment of the public sector unstable. Federalized labor law is problematic because public sector collective bargaining rights remained unresolved and the state and local levels do not offer rights equivalent to those at the national level; public sector unions could never achieve the same rights and results at the state and local levels that they could if they had applied equal organizing effort under a national law.

In the long run, federalism has not done organized labor any favors. Federalism enabled public sector innovation at the state and local levels, but this innovation is also a vulnerability because federalism, as a governing concept, allows and even encourages experimentation at lower levels of government. Absent a floor of protection and pressure for uniform treatment across jurisdictions, public sector collective bargaining rights have been unequal and under continual change, including retrenchment, at the state and local levels. Government unions' legislative successes ultimately have been limited. They have been limited to union-friendly states, reinforcing the geographic concentration of labor. As Jerry Wurf explained, AFSCME preferred "a federal law governing state and local government labor-management relations, than to dribble out our lives trying to convince 50 state legislatures, 5,000 city councils, 10,000 school boards and who knows how many other public bodies to devise an impartial mechanism at the lower level" (quoted in Flynn 1975, 83). Absent a national law, "dribbling out" their time pursuing state- and local-level collective bargaining rights was the only option for public sector employees and unions, and they were doing just that in the 1940s and 1950s at the very moment the private sector labor movement reached its peak of power and influence.

The separation of public sector labor law from private sector labor law prevented a large unified union movement in the aftermath of the Wagner Act that could have pressed for more generous New Deal policies. The exclusion of government employees from the Wagner Act and the lack of their own national statute meant public sector union growth was delayed, fundamentally altering the labor movement as public and private sector unions' development was thrown out of alignment. In other words, the timing and sequencing of when public and private sector employees gained collective bargaining rights discouraged cooperation and a strong, unified labor movement. Private sector unions thrived in the 1940s and 1950s, while public sector unions were only managing handshake agreements with some employers, devoting significant time and resources to fights in every state and locality for basic recognition.

It wasn't until the 1960s that government unions found legislative success at the state level and grew precipitously. Public sector unions' legislative success was limited, however, because economic crises and conservative backlash at the end of the 1970s closed the window of opportunity for public sector union rights legislation at the national level. The brief moment when high private sector union density overlapped with a strong public sector—the 1970s—was one of missed opportunities as the public sector unions, delayed in their growth because of divided labor law, encountered an already entrenched private sector labor leadership rather than an ally. The cultural, economic, and political crises of the decade magnified labor's differences, making a strong public-private labor movement in the 1970s difficult.

Tracing the separate development trajectories of public and private sector unions leaves us with one fundamental question: "What would have happened if the most political unions [the public sector unions] had been larger and more influential in the labor movement's formative years, or when labor was larger and more influential within society as a whole?" (Slater 2004, 200). The conclusions reached in this project emphasize the overwhelmingly negative effects of divided labor law. Public sector union growth came after the peak of private sector union strength, too late to have a significant effect on New Deal politics, assist in the opposition to Taft-Hartley in 1947, or help exert pressure for national labor law overhaul before the window of opportunity closed at the end of the 1970s. Further, public sector unions were forced to fight their way into an already established labor movement, meaning their politicized, social justice outlook was derided instead of welcomed, and labor eschewed rather than joined forces with the New Politics movements that the public sector unions were associated with. The labor movement that emerged at the end of the 1970s was divided, overly complacent, and ill prepared to deal with the challenges of deindustrialization and the growing hostility of employers and the state to unionization. Now that government unions have become such a dominant force in the labor movement, their legal vulnerability has made them ready targets for anti-union forces.

The timing and sequencing of when public sector employees gained their collective bargaining rights compared to their private sector counterparts is also crucial because labor unions' power and influence comes not just from the sum of the individual unions but also through their organization into a larger federation, the AFL-CIO. The timing of public sector union growth meant private sector unions peaked when almost all public sector employees still lacked collective bargaining rights. The delayed growth of public sector unions meant the AFL-CIO was never comprised of a unified union movement representing private and public sector unions, both at their peak of power and membership.

Looking toward the future, the volatility surrounding public sector collective bargaining rights will persist as long as states and localities remain sites where the basic tenets of public sector unionism can be contested. Without major partisan shifts in the United States, government unions are unlikely to dramatically increase their density. In states where public sector unions have had success, their enduring high density has made them glaring targets as private sector union density continues to drop. Absent something drastic that enables an overhaul of private sector labor law or a federal guarantee for public sector collective bargaining rights, the American labor movement must confront an uphill battle to retain existing membership levels and political relevance. Organized labor faces an uncertain future in part because of the constraints placed on it by public policies, which have molded and patterned the labor movement's development. Divided labor law shaped the development trajectory of public sector unions—including their more unequal and vulnerable collective bargaining rights—as well as contributed to today's declining, geographically concentrated labor movement. Ultimately, divided labor law has weakened organized labor as a force in American politics with potentially important ramifications for the representation of the working class in our democracy.

Policy Consequences

This project is a powerful illustration of the potent role public policies—in this case divided labor law—can play in shaping the internal dynamics and external fortunes of a seemingly private organization: organized labor. Policies may play a significant role in shaping other private organizations, including corporations, nonprofits, and PACs. Thus policymakers should be fully aware of the impact policies can have on organizations and the environment they operate within, two things that are often thought of as external to politics. Further, the conclusions drawn in this project about federalism should apply to other cases as well. Rights and privileges relegated to the state and local levels, absent a floor of protection, should display the same vulnerability to retrenchment as have public sector collective bargaining rights. Right-to-work laws, consumer protection laws, and election laws (e.g., voter ID laws and primary election rules) should all exhibit this feature of federalism. Lawmakers' decision to devolve to the state and local levels should not be made without an appreciation of the vulnerability such federalized arrangements entail. The conclusions reached in this project address a larger universe of cases but also contain important lessons for thinking about organized labor's central and threatened place in American politics today.

During an interview I conducted with a local labor leader in Wisconsin in 2012, he was visibly upset and distracted, having just met with a police officer before our meeting. At the end of our conversation, he revealed that he had arrived at the office that morning to find their American flag had been stolen from the flagpole outside. The police officer had told him it was likely just some local vandals, but the labor leader couldn't help but think that it was something more, that it was someone making a statement about unions, and people like him, being unpatriotic (Interview #25). Today's attacks and rhetoric against organized labor should not make this leader or the public doubt the important role labor plays in American politics. Union forces, whether it was the CIO in the 1930s or the public sector unions in the 1960s, have been at the forefront of American progressivism, helping mobilize broad swaths of Americans to become involved in politics and in protecting the interests of working Americans.

In the future, public sector unions, weakened due to their legal vulnerability and the attacks this has allowed, appear unlikely to continue to stave off private sector union decline. Labor's decline poses a significant threat to the representation of working Americans' interests in our political system and the rise of economic inequality and insecurity.[3] As McCartin notes, "With less than 7 percent of nongovernmental workers unionized, private sector unions no longer have the leverage to improve wages and benefits for those beyond their ranks. Thus, by default, public sector unions have become the single most effective social force capable of speaking out for a just economy that lifts the standards of all workers, public and private" (2011a, 50). Thus, the institutional forces that have contributed to private sector union decline and the unequal and vulnerable collective bargaining rights of public sector workers should be of concern to all Americans.

As a consequence, the importance of national labor law reform, which includes both private and public sector union members, should be recognized as crucially important to ensuring representation of working Americans' interests in our political system. National-level rights create a floor of protection that is not present in state- and local-level provisions, and this is fundamental to fostering a vibrant, cohesive labor movement. National-level laws also may institute a ceiling, restricting the bounds of rights provision. Labor scholars have rightly pointed out that the Wagner and Taft-Hartley acts, by creating a ceiling, have limited some of the more radical tools in private sector unions' repertoire like boycotts and wildcat strikes (Tomlins 1985). However, unlike a floor, a rights ceiling is not an inevitable feature of national-level laws and, when we compare national-level rights to state- and local-level rights, national-level rights provide more uniform, stable, durable protections. With decentralized rights, very generous laws in some states are insufficient to make up for the states with no rights provisions.

The content of public sector collective bargaining rights certainly has important ramifications for contract negotiations and other aspects of labor union success, and ceiling provisions can be major stumbling blocks, but the fundamental right to organize must take precedence over the generosity of that right; one must get a foot in the door before negotiations can even begin. After all, once one has a foot in the door with the right to collectively bargain, higher levels of union density foster greater economic and political influence, which public and private sector unions can leverage to lobby for more generous collective bargaining rights. As the "Officers' Report" of the 1950 United Public Workers of America convention put it at the time: "Civil rights are not academic. They are the means by which all other rights are to be obtained. For years we have pointed out that the rights of public workers and their unions must be protected, or the rights of all workers and their unions would be destroyed" (UPWA 1950, 34). A nationally protected right to form and join unions and collectively bargain was as fundamental in 1950 as it is now for creating the foundation of robust union organizing. Absent that protection, this weakness has been exploited as anti-union opponents have targeted public sector union rights as a first step in taking on the entire labor movement.

What could a national Wagner Act for public sector employees look like? In the 1970s, legislation was proposed that would simply delete the section defining "employer" in the Wagner Act as not including federal, state, or municipal governments (Brown 1974). Such a law would then place public sector workers within the framework of the Wagner Act and under the auspices of the NLRB. In the 1930s, this would have been the obvious choice and dramatically altered the course of labor's development. However, now that public sector labor relations are established, state laws exist across the country, and there remain key differences between the public and private sector, this straightforward solution may lead to a great deal of conflict and uncertainty over issues like strikes by public safety workers and what happens in states with more generous collective bargaining rights for government employees than the Wagner Act. The more mainstream legislation in the 1970s, the National Public Employees Relations Act, instead proposed a separate law, analogous to the Wagner Act, but with key differences to conform to the unique nature of public sector labor relations. The bill permitted strikes but only after other mediation procedures had been exhausted and included the exception of "clear and present danger to the public health or safety" (Brown 1974, 715). The bill contained more generous collective bargaining rights than the Wagner Act, including not permitting right-to-work, whereby non-members can freeride by not paying dues, and allowing supervisors to organize. The bill would preempt weaker state laws, all but guaranteeing that every state collective bargaining law would be replaced by the more generous national law (714–715).

The reality today is that Supreme Court decisions, beginning with *National League of Cities* in 1976, have made it less clear that the Court would uphold the constitutionality of a single national law that wipes out existing state laws like those introduced in the 1970s. Thus, new legislation introduced in Congress the day after the Supreme Court's *Janus* decision in 2018 offers more of a hybrid approach. The bill, known as the Public Service Freedom of

Negotiation Act (PSFNA), would guarantee "the rights of public employees to form or join unions, act concertedly for the purpose of collective bargaining or other mutual aid or protection, and bargain collectively with their employers" (PSFNA 2018, Section 2(b)). The bill would create a federal authority that would establish what these basic collective bargaining rights entail and would then assess whether each state meets these minimum standards. States that meet these standards would keep their own laws and procedures. States that do not meet these standards would fall under the authority's regulations and oversight with the authority acting in much the same way as the NLRB in the private sector (Sections 4 and 5). The bill expressly prohibits strikes by public safety workers (Section 6(a)). While still allowing some state autonomy, this new legislation mandates the floor of protection for public sector employees that has been lacking and so consequential for government unions and organized labor since the Wagner Act in 1935. Given the current partisan makeup, this bill will be dead on arrival in the 116th Congress. However, it does offer a concrete policy option for addressing divided labor law and working to revitalize the labor movement in the future.

Absent national labor law reform, private sector union density is unlikely to bounce back without updates to existing law that rein in hostile employer resistance. Likewise, the instability of public sector collective bargaining rights and the large portion of government employees lacking any rights are likely to continue until government unions receive a national-level law of their own. Jerry Wurf's declaration at AFSCME's 1972 convention still holds true today: "The needs of our membership in the fifty states for the rights and protections such as those extended to other workers cannot be met by a law here and a law there" (quoted in Hower 2013, 301). Public sector collective bargaining rights will remain vulnerable; public sector union success will remain limited; and labor will continue to punch below its political weight until a national statute protects public sector employees' collective bargaining rights.

Ultimately, organized labor wants their members to believe that "what separates us is so little compared to what we share," but divided labor law has served as a countervailing force sowing division and discord within labor's ranks (WI AFL-CIO Convention, October 2, 2012). Examining the development of public and private sector unions over the last half century reveals that public policies have influenced the course of organized labor's development. Divided labor law is not an inconsequential division but rather has acted as solidarity's wedge, limiting the cohesion, the effectiveness, and ultimately the strength of organized labor in American politics.

Appendix

Interview Method Description

As I began thinking about how the legal divide between public and private sector unions might matter for labor as a political organization, there was no literature to turn to for help in generating hypotheses. As such, I utilized my initial interviews primarily as theory generating. In the fall of 2012, I interviewed twenty-eight labor leaders in Washington State and Wisconsin about labor's political activities both past and present (see Table 1). I also sat in on several political strategy meetings, attended the Wisconsin AFL-CIO State Labor Convention, and spent time with union members. My thinking was also shaped by learning about the private sector union movement before the Wagner Act and how other differences within labor moved from benign distinctions to salient divisions in the union movement.

I chose Washington State and Wisconsin as sites for my field research for two reasons. First, both states have large public sector union movements and relatively large private sector union movements, which would therefore allow me to make suitable comparisons. Second, Wisconsin is emblematic of the most recent conflicts over public sector collective bargaining rights whereas Washington State has remained relatively conflict free. This enabled me to avoid mistakenly attributing something to a public/private difference when it might have been the most recent attacks that are driving the difference. I visited both states in the buildup to the 2012 president election in order to examine union political activities at a time when they were most salient for organized labor.

I set up interviews through a snowball sampling method. Many of the labor leaders I spoke with, particularly local union presidents, were unaccustomed to dealing with the press, much less researchers. I found that setting up interviews based on personal recommendations from others helped me gain entrance and trust in future interviews. I ended up speaking with a variety of labor leaders including presidents of local public and private sector unions, state union presidents and political directors, central labor council leaders, and state AFL-CIO executives. These interviews helped generate my theory about how the public/private divide matters for organized labor's cohesion: divided labor law, by setting public and private sector unions on different development trajectories, made the public/private division more salient owing to the incongruent timing of public sector union growth during a period—the 1970s—where economic pressures heightened this conflict, and it permanently disrupted the balance of power.

To test this theory, I then used multiple methods to triangulate my findings including examining union electoral spending and public opinion data, analyzing secondary sources, and interviewing national-level labor leaders. I conducted twelve such interviews with union vice presidents, political directors, and legislative directors, as well as AFL-CIO political strategists. Multiple methods were utilized because measuring organizational behavior is difficult and thus using a variety of techniques to try to answer the same question can increase the confidence in the conclusions. Through the interviews and other methods, it became clear that the legal divide between public and private sector labor law still matters in important ways for labor's political activities today.

Table 1. Union Leaders Interview Details

Interview #	Date	Public/Private/ AFL-CIO	Local/State/ National
Washington State			
1	8/13/12	Private	Local
2	8/13/12	Private	Local
3	8/13/12	AFL-CIO	Local
4	8/13/12	Private	Local
5	8/13/12	AFL-CIO	State
6	8/14/12	Private	State
7	8/15/12	Public	State
8	8/16/12	Public	Local
9	8/23/12	Public	State
10	8/23/12	Public	State
11	8/23/12	Public	State
12	8/23/12	Public	State
13	8/27/12	Public	State
14	8/30/12	AFL-CIO	State
15	11/7/12	AFL-CIO	State
Wisconsin			
16	9/18/12	Public	State
17	9/18/12	Public	State
18	9/19/12	Public	Local
19	9/20/12	AFL-CIO	Local
20	9/24/12	AFL-CIO	State
21	9/25/12	AFL-CIO	Local
22	9/25/12	Public	Local
10/1–10/2 Wisconsin AFL-CIO State Labor Convention			
23	10/4/12	Public	Local
24	10/5/13	Public	Local
25	10/8/13	Private	Local
26	10/9/13	Public	Local
27	10/9/13	Public	Local
28	10/9/13	AFL-CIO	State
Washington, DC			
29	5/9/13	Public	National
30	5/10/13	Public	National
31	5/13/13	Public	National
32	5/13/13	Public	National
33	5/14/13	Public	National
34	5/15/13	Public	National
35	5/16/13	AFL-CIO	National
36	5/16/13	AFL-CIO	National
37	5/17/13	Public	National
38	5/28/13	Public	National
39	5/28/13	Public	National

Notes

Chapter 1

1. Governor Walker described this moment when speaking candidly to a prank caller from a radio station posing as billionaire campaign contributor David Koch.

2. The total loss of members was actually over 120,000 when including losses in the private sector as well (Hirsch and Macpherson 2017). Beck (2017) estimates that 136,000 members have been lost since 2011.

3. Data compiled from the NCSL Collective Bargaining and Labor Union Legislation Database by research assistant Devin Sotak.

4. There unfortunately is no uniform data set that measures public and private sector union density over time. All of the available data have issues of comparison over time as the definition of what constituted a union and how membership was measured changed. In addition, public sector unions were not always distinguished from private sector unions, and some public sector unions, like the National Education Association, were not considered a union but a membership association for some time. Taken together, these discrepancies mean we should be cautious in giving too much weight to any specific density level for a given year. Further, we need to recognize that while the trends illustrated in Figure 1 appear to bear out across a variety of different data sets measuring union density, we cannot be totally confident in the comparability of the measurements across time. For a description of these measurement difficulties, see Hirsch and Macpherson 2017.

5. One exception is Joseph Slater's *Public Workers*, but his historical account stops in the 1960s.

6. On the exclusion of public sector unions from labor history, see McCartin 2006 and Shaffer 2002.

7. Canada, Australia, the United Kingdom, Germany, France, Sweden, Norway, Finland, the Netherlands, Spain, and Japan.

8. The rate of public sector unionization may decline given the recent Supreme Court decision, *Janus v. American Federation of State, County and Municipal Employees* (2018), which ruled that unions can no longer collect agency fees from non-members that they represent in collective bargaining.

9. Data compiled from the NCSL Collective Bargaining and Labor Union Legislation Database by research assistant Devin Sotak.

10. Despite the Great Recession, total public sector employment actually increased during this time, so the decline cannot directly be attributed to unemployment.

Chapter 2

1. It was the central disagreement expressed in the minority viewpoint included in the report of the bill from the House Committee on Labor to the floor, and an amendment seeking to strike the exclusion was hotly debated on the House floor (NLRB 1949, 2910, 3200).

2. These documents include (1) a full legislative history of the act compiled by the NLRB (NLRB 1949); (2) the personal papers of Senator Robert F. Wagner and Leon Keyserling (the relevant papers of Leon Keyserling and Senator Wagner are held in the Special Collections of the Georgetown University library); (3) Kenneth M. Casebeer's analyses on the drafting of the Wagner Act, particularly Leon Keyserling's involvement (1987, 1989, 1990); (4) Leon Keyserling's writings about the drafting process (1945, 1975); (5) oral history interviews, conducted in the late 1960s to the mid-1970s, with the major drafters of the Wagner Act, namely Milton Handler, Lloyd Garrison, Philip Levy, Howard Smith, and Lee Pressman (NLRB Oral History Project 1968–1975); and (6) the publications of some of the existing public sector unions of the time as well as the papers of the Wisconsin State Employees Association (WSEA), which became the founding local of the American Federation of State, County and Municipal Employees (AFSCME) in 1935 (the relevant papers of the WSEA and AFSCME are held in the state archives of the Wisconsin State Historical Society).

3. For instance, the United Federal Workers of America 1944 "Officer's Report" calls for wage increases and procedures for layoffs and termination under their discussion of civil service reform (UFWA 1944, 12).

4. Public employee publications consulted were the *Wisconsin State Employee* (1932–1936), the *Federal Employee* (1934–1935), and the *Post Office Clerk* (1934–1935).

5. The Wisconsin legislature was pursuing its own labor disputes bill at the same time that the Wagner Act and the Wisconsin bill also excluded public sector workers (Padway 1935).

6. Also, for elected officials, the prospect of government unionism posed another threat to their power: patronage jobs. Instituting rules governing hiring and promotion, including seniority, through a collective bargaining agreement with a union would undermine the ability of politicians to appoint party loyalists to government jobs, thus endangering a key tool of party politics.

7. This was the conclusion reached by labor attorney Joseph Rosenfarb in his 1940 in-depth study of the Act, which included a glowing preface by Senator Wagner himself. Rosenfarb concluded that "the exception of the political entities of our federal system from the operation of the act is in accordance with the prevailing tradition that labor unionism among government employees is hedged in by limitations on union activities, such as strikes and picketing, not applicable to labor engaged in private industry" (58).

8. President Andrew Jackson would grant the Washington, D.C., naval shipyard workers a ten-hour day in 1836 after a strike and mass demonstration (Kearney and Mareschal 2014, 14).

9. Discussions of organizing public employees began in earnest in 1936 (CIO 2015, Series 1, Box 10, State, County, and Municipal Workers: Folder 9). By 1937, the CIO had hired Abram Flaxer as executive vice president of the Organization of State, County and Municipal Workers and given him funding and leave to begin organizing public sector workers across the country (Series 1, Box 10, State, County, and Municipal Workers: Folder 10).

10. For example, see Ramspeck 1935, 31; Ramspeck 1939.

11. A similar case arose in 1936 when the president of a local of the Federation of Architects, Engineers, Chemists and Technicians, Robert Y. Durand, was fired. The union claimed he was discharged for union activity. His employer, the Federal Power Commission, consented to a hearing before a board composed of members from the NLRB, the Railway Mediation Board, and the Conciliation Division of the Department of Labor. The board determined Durand was fired for union activity and recommended his reinstatement (Ziskind 1940, 22).

Chapter 3

1. These density levels are higher if the sample is restricted to non-agricultural private sector employees. According to Leo Troy (1965), private sector union membership grew from just under 13.3 percent of the American workforce in 1935 to 20.7 percent by 1939. Union density reached nearly 30 percent by 1945.

2. Sterling D. Spero's 1948 book, *Government as Employer*, offers countless examples of local, state, and federal restrictions on public sector collective bargaining rights during this period.

3. The fifteen cities reporting police unions were: Los Angeles, CA; Portland, OR; Charlotte, NC; Duluth, MN; Hartford, CT; Miami, FL; Omaha, NE; Tacoma, WA; Flint, MI; Augusta, GA; New Britain, CT; Springfield, IL; Santa Monica, CA; Portsmouth, VA; and Lincoln, NE (IACP 1944).

4. The board's ruling also applied to other cases, an AFSCME local in Omaha, Nebraska, and the Transit Workers Union (TWU) in New York City. Joseph Slater chronicles the transit workers' case, which is another interesting example of previously private sector, unionized employees coming under the employment of the government. The ruling was a loss for the TWU as well, and Slater illustrates how the union, limited by the letter of the law, used innovative tactics to make measurable gains during this period (2004, 125–57).

5. See Dark 1999 and Johnston 2015.

6. There were 22 Democratic senators from right-to-work states in the 89th Congress. The 17 who voted against cloture (and their state and the year their state passed a right-to-work statute) were: Sparkman and Hill (AL, 1953); Hayden (AZ, 1946); Fullbright (abstentia vote recorded) and McClellan (AR, 1947); Holland and Smathers (FL, 1944); Russell and Talmadge (GA, 1947); Stennis and Eastland (MS, 1960); Ervin and Jordan (NC, 1947); Russell (South Carolina, 1954); McGovern (SD, 1946); and Byrd and Robertson (VA, 1947). The four Democrats from right-to-work states who voted for cloture were Burdick (North Dakota, 1948); Bass (TN, 1947); McGee (WY, 1963); and Moss (UT, 1955). Gore Sr. (TN, 1947) did not vote. Foley 1965; NRTLDF 2012.

Chapter 4

1. Public sector union ties with the civil rights movement, the women's movement, and the antiwar movement grew even stronger into the 1970s. The election of Jerry Wurf as president of AFSCME in particular pushed the union to become a strident activist for these sister movements. Not coincidentally, public sector union strike activity grew in tandem with the rise of social protest more broadly.

2. The agreement between the city and UFT was noted by newspapers across the country, including major markets like Los Angeles and Chicago.

3. The law was extended to state workers in 1967.

4. Governor George Leader of Pennsylvania had extended collective bargaining rights to state workers in 1957 through executive order. Leader's order gained far less attention than Wisconsin's action five years later, perhaps because Wisconsin's law was passed by the majority of the state legislature instead of being issued as an executive order by the governor (Pennsylvania State Employees Council 1957).

5. It is unclear why Valletta and Freeman identify Illinois as unique in 1955. Their data set measures public sector collective bargaining law across the states over time. They look beyond legislation to also include case law and attorney general decisions that created state policy when legislation did not exist. They do not explain why Illinois was coded as the first state to authorize collective bargaining, but it is likely that this coding was a result of case law or an attorney general decision. Wisconsin is widely regarded as the first state to recognize public sector collective bargaining rights through legislation.

6. It is illegal for the majority of public sector workers to strike. The laws vary by state and profession. Public safety workers face the most restrictions with only Hawaii and Ohio allowing strikes by police and firefighters. Twelve states allow teachers to strike: Alaska, California, Colorado, Hawaii, Illinois, Louisiana, Minnesota, Montana, Ohio, Oregon, Pennsylvania, and Vermont (Sanes and Schmitt 2014).

7. A work stoppage is defined as a strike or lockout.

Chapter 5

1. This chapter and those that follow utilize information gained from field research and interviews conducted in the lead-up to and aftermath of the 2012 presidential election. For further details on these interviews, see the Appendix.

2. Arbitration is a common practice in public sector labor disputes that allows for a third party to resolve disputes, such as contract negotiations, between union members and the employer. Sometimes arbitration is binding, whereby employees and the employer have to accept the third party's resolution.

3. Police and firefighters unions also grew during this time but did not display the same activist zeal and connection to the New Left as did many other public sector unions.

4. For a detailed description of the conflict between AFSCME and the AFL-CIO over the McGovern nomination and the fallout within the Democratic Party, see Hower 2013, chap. 8.

5. For a more complete description of the rise of anti–public sector union groups in the 1970s, see Hower 2013, chap. 8.

6. In 1975, the AFL-CIO national convention came out in favor of the right to strike for all workers, including those in the public sector. This may have just been a way for the AFL-CIO to discredit public sector unionism and avoid supporting a national public sector law akin to the Wagner Act (see Goulden 1982, 221). However, at times, private sector unions bristled against the full use of militant strikes by public sector unions. A few examples illustrate this well: (1) "'Nobody ever dreamed that the municipal unions would apply tough trade-union tactics,' recalled the leader of a nonmunicipal union, 'everybody thought that they would understand that they were working for a nonprofit institution'" (Tolchin 1975); (2) "When striking black Memphis laborers, including street cleaners, appealed to the local building trades for help, an AFSCME official said, he was told: 'You owe the people of Memphis an apology. Those niggers didn't work. Someone might have slipped on the ice and gotten hurt'" (Johnson and Kotz 1972); (3) When John Crowley, secretary-treasurer of AFL-CIO's San Francisco Labor Council, threatened a general strike as a way to escalate a strike by the city's craft

workers, he may have been too hasty: "When Mr. Crowley sought support from fellow labor leaders last week, the Marine Cooks and Stewards Union sent a telegram saying it didn't consider the pay issue a cause for a general strike. One knowledgeable source says that Harry Bridges, president of the International Longshoremen's and Warehousemen's Union took the same position. Mr. Bridges has declined to comment. Another of the city's powerful labor leaders said he agreed with Mr. Bridges' position" (Libman 1976).

Chapter 6

1. The Taft-Hartley Act's exclusion of supervisors also left out professional workers whose jobs, in such areas as finance and engineering, placed them in the amorphous category of supervisor. The number of "supervisors" doubled in the fifty years after World War II but has largely been off limits to unions and instead used by employers to oppose union organizing (Lichtenstein 2002, 120). Supervisors who refuse to take part in an employer's anti-union efforts may be fired with no legal recourse (CFWMR 1994b, 23).

2. Despite declining union density, management consultants have thrived (Logan 2002, 2006). Aside from an underenforced requirement that union-avoidance consultants and employers file reports, the NLRB lacks the tools to punish consultants for unfair labor practices (BNA 1985, 16).

3. For an overview of this comparativist literature, see Bruce 1994. Other studies include Chaison and Rose 1994; Godard 2003; Murphy 1988; Riddell 1993; and Rose and Chaison 1985.

4. The Supreme Court reversed much of the decision in *National League* with the 5–4 ruling in *Garcia v. San Antonio Metropolitan Transit Authority* (1985), but other decisions have also reasserted some limits of federal regulation on matters not related to interstate commerce. Regardless, by the time of the ruling in 1985, the conservative backlash and the decline of union influence suggest that "by then the damage had been done" (McCartin 2008b, 146).

5. See the *New York Times* series on local and state business subsidies to see just how much of local spending and policy is geared toward encouraging business in localities (Story, Fehr, and Watkins 2012).

6. The great exception for private sector labor law is right-to-work, which is decided by each state individually. This will be discussed in more detail in the following chapters.

Chapter 7

1. The state passed an even more generous law in 2003, four years after the governor's veto caused the previous law to expire (Malin 2012, 152).

2. For a critical discussion of the pension and benefit arrangements states promised their public sector unions, see Moe 2011 and DiSalvo 2015.

3. Wisconsin was chosen as a case study for this project in part because it was the center of conflict over public sector collective bargaining rights. See the Appendix for a full explanation of why Wisconsin and Washington State were chosen as the sites of field research.

4. See the Appendix for interview details.

5. Exec. Order No. 12612, 1987 (Reagan); Exec. Order No. 13132, 1999 (Clinton); 74 Fed. Reg. 24693, 2009 (Obama).

6. Exec. Order No. 12612, 1987 (Reagan).

7. Other researchers have suggested the effect may be contingent on election-specific circumstances. See Juravich and Shergold 1988 and Sousa 1993.

8. Union households over time have also been found to be more supportive of Democratic candidates relative to the rest of the population (Delaney, Masters, and Schwochau 1990; Francia and Bigelow 2010; Francia 2012).

Chapter 8

1. The standard deviation of public sector union density is nearly six times as large as the standard deviation of private sector union density; this vividly illustrates that whereas private sector union density tends to cluster around one (low) level, public sector union density is marked by states with very high and very low densities. Standard deviations were calculated using union density data from Hirsch and Macpherson 2017. Public sector union density tends to be higher than private sector union density across the board because even in states lacking any public sector collective bargaining statutes, federal workers as well as some municipal workers possess collective bargaining rights.

2. The USGAO report defines collective bargaining rights as "union recognition—permitting individuals to join together and form unions and the requirement that employers recognize employee organizations—and 'good faith bargaining'—bargaining with intent to reach an agreement" (24). The figure of 33 percent was determined using the GAO calculation of the number of state and local employees lacking collective bargaining rights, divided by the total number of state and local employees listed in the U.S. Census table.

3. In his recent book, *What Unions No Longer Do* (2014), Jake Rosenfeld is skeptical of the potential of the public sector to combat income inequality and represent the working class. He even titles a chapter of his book "Government Is Not the Answer." However, Rosenfeld focuses largely on the economic gains public sector unions acquire for their members and finds that they are more limited than what private sector unions provide. While this may be the case, this doesn't address the broader influence public and private unions have on their members through expanding their political mobilization and lobbying on their behalf in government. An expanded public sector union movement would be consequential, not just because of the pocketbooks of their members but because the movement would focus American politics on economic and progressive issues on behalf of American workers and advocate for labor law reform for the private sector.

Bibliography

Abood v. Detroit Board of Education. 1977. 431 U.S. 209.
American Civil Liberties Union (ACLU). 1934. Suggested Changes to the Bill by Organizations. Leon Keyserling Collection. Box 1, Folder 8. Special Collections, Georgetown University, Washington, D.C.
American Federation of State, County and Municipal Employees (AFSCME). 1938. Proceedings of the Third Convention of the American Federation of State, County, and Municipal Employees, Atlanta, GA.
———. 1940. Proceedings of the Fifth Convention of the American Federation of State, County, and Municipal Employees, Duluth, MN.
———. 1976. A Chronology of Unionism in U.S. Public Employment: With Emphasis on State and Local Government. Collection 6046, Box 341, Folder 6. Kheel Center, Catherwood Library, Cornell University School of Industrial and Labor Relations, Ithaca, NY.
———. 2002. Continuing the Fight to Bring Collective Bargaining Rights to All Public Workers. Resolution 20, Thirty-fifth Convention of the American Federation of State, County and Municipal Employees, Las Vegas, NV. https://www.afscme.org/members/conventions/resolutions-and-amendments/2002/resolutions/20-continuing-the-fight-to-bring-collective-bargaining-rights-to-all-public-workers.
American Federation of Teachers (AFT). 1937. The Wagner Act and Teachers. *American Teacher* 21 (May–June): 1.
American Federationist. 1919. American Federation of Labor Reconstruction Program. *American Federationist* 26 (2) (February): 129–133.
American Legislative Exchange Council (ALEC). 2017. Public Employee Paycheck Protection Act (July 12, 2012). https://www.alec.org/model-policy/public-employee-paycheck-protection-act/.
Artz, Michael. 2012. Beyond Wisconsin: Public Employee Union Rights Amidst State Attacks on Public Sector Collective Bargaining. *Employment & Labor Law Forum* 2 (2): 131–143.
Baer, Fred W. 1937. The Editor's Alarm. *International Fire Fighter* 20 (10) (October): 1–2.
Ballotpedia. 2010. State Legislative Election Results, 2010. https://ballotpedia.org/State_legislative_elections_results,_2010#Trifectas.
Baumgartner, Frank R., and Bryan D. Jones. 2009. *Agendas and Instability in American Politics.* 2nd ed. Chicago: University of Chicago Press.
Beck, Molly. 2017. Union Membership Down Nearly 40 Percent Since Act 10. *Wisconsin State Journal* (January 27).

Bernstein, Harry. 1978. Prop. 13 Tests Strength of Public Employee Unions. *Los Angeles Times* (June 25): 1.

Bernstein, Irving. 1950. *The New Deal Collective Bargaining Policy.* Berkeley: University of California Press.

———. 1954. The Growth of American Unions. *American Economic Review* 44 (3) (June): 301–318.

———. 1991. *Promises Kept: John F. Kennedy's New Frontier.* New York: Oxford University Press.

Block, Richard N., Benjamin W. Wolkinson, and James W. Kuhn. 1989. Some Are More Equal than Others: The Relative Status of Employers, Unions and Employees in the Law of Union Organizing. *Industrial Relations Law Journal* 10 (219): 220–240.

The Boss. 2013. [Magazine cover.] *Time* (January 21).

Brewster, Chris, Michael Dempsey, and Ariane Hegewich. 2001. The Unions' Response to Change in the Public Sector. In *Public Sector Reform: An International Perspective*, ed. Brendan Nolan. Houndmills, England: Palgrave.

Broder, David S. 1975a. Washington: New Political Generation. *Washington Post* (June 7): A1.

———. 1975b. Not a Happy Day for Labor. *Washington Post* (August 31): C6.

Bronfenbrenner, Kate. 1994. Employer Behavior in Certification Elections and First-Contract Campaigns: Implications for Labor Law Reform. In *Restoring the Promise of American Labor Law*, ed. Sheldon Friedman, Richard W. Hurd, Rudolph A. Oswald, and Ronald L. Seeber, 75–89. Ithaca, NY: ILR Press.

Bronfenbrenner, Kate, and Tom Juravich. 1994. *The Impact of Employer Opposition on Union Certification Win Rates: A Private-Public Sector Comparison.* Washington, DC: Economic Policy Institute.

Brown, Peter A. 1975. Mayors Say: Fire City Workers Who Strike. *Chicago Defender* (July 7): 2.

Brown, Ronald C. 1974. Federal Legislation for Public Sector Collective Bargaining: A Minimum Standards Approach. *Toledo Law Review* (5): 681–720.

Bruce, Peter G. 1994. On the Status of Workers' Rights to Organize in the United States and Canada. In *Restoring the Promise of American Labor Law*, ed. Sheldon Friedman, Richard W. Hurd, Rudolph A. Oswald, and Ronald L. Seeber, 273–284. Ithaca, NY: ILR Press.

Buder, Leonard. 1962. Report from New York City: The Teachers Revolt. *Phi Delta Kappan* 43 (9) (June): 370–376.

Bureau of Labor Statistics. 1968. *Handbook of Labor Statistics.* U.S. Department of Labor. Washington, DC: U.S. GPO.

———. 1977. *Handbook of Labor Statistics.* U.S. Department of Labor. Washington, DC: U.S. GPO.

———. 1980. *Handbook of Labor Statistics.* U.S. Department of Labor. Washington, DC: U.S. GPO.

———. 1983. *Handbook of Labor Statistics.* U.S. Department of Labor. Washington, DC: U.S. GPO.

Bureau of National Affairs (BNA). 1985. *Labor Relations Consultants: Issues, Trends, and Controversies.* Washington, DC: Bureau of National Affairs, Inc.

Cannon, Lou. 2011. Right Turn: Election Success Gave Republicans the Momentum to Push Key Conservative Issues in Many Statehouses. *State Legislatures* (National Council of State Legislatures) (July/August): 14–18.

Carre, Francoise J., Virginia duRivage, and Chris Till. 1994. Representing the Part-Time and Contingent Workforce: Challenges for Unions and Public Policy. In *Restoring the Promise of American Labor Law*, ed. Sheldon Friedman, Richard W. Hurd, Rudolph A. Oswald, and Ronald L. Seeber, 314–323. Ithaca, NY: ILR Press.

Casale, Giuseppe, and Joseph Tenkorang. 2008. Public Service Labour Relations: A Comparative Overview. Paper No. 17. Social Dialogue, Labour Law and Labour Administration Branch. Geneva: International Labour Office. http://www.ilo.org/wcmsp5/groups/public/---ed_dialogue/---lab_admin/documents/publication/wcms_112942.pdf.

Casebeer, Kenneth M. 1987. Holder of the Pen: An Interview with Leon Keyserling on Drafting the Wagner Act. *University of Miami Law Review* 285 (42): 285–360.

———. 1989. Drafting Wagner's Act: Leon Keyserling and the Pre-Committee Drafts of the Labor Disputes Act and the National Labor Relations Act. *Industrial Relations Law Journal* 73 (11): 73–131.

———. 1990. Clashing Views of the Wagner Act: The Files of Leon Keyserling. *Labor's Heritage* 44 (2) (April).

Center for Responsive Politics (CRP). 2013. Organization Profiles. http://www.opensecrets.org/orgs/.

Central Dispensary and Emergency Hospital and Building Service and Maintenance Workers, Local 120, CIO. 1942. NLRB Case #00-R-003548: 1011–1021.

Chaison, Gary N., and Joseph B. Rose. 1994. The Canadian Perspective on Workers' Rights to Form a Union and Bargain Collectively. In *Restoring the Promise of American Labor Law*, ed. Sheldon Friedman, Richard W. Hurd, Rudolph A. Oswald, and Ronald L. Seeber, 241–249. Ithaca, NY: ILR Press.

Chang, Tracy F. 2001. The Labour Vote in US National Elections, 1948–2000. *Political Quarterly* 72 (3) (July): 375.

Chicago Daily Tribune. 1934. Johnson, NRA Chief, Tried for Firing NRA Man. *Chicago Daily Tribune* (August 11): 2.

Christian Science Monitor. 1980. A Strike Against New York. *Christian Science Monitor* (April 9): 24.

Clark, Paul, and Marick F. Masters. 2001. Competing Interest Groups and Union Members' Voting. *Social Science Quarterly* 82 (1) (03): 105–117.

Clawson, Dan, and Mary Ann Clawson. 1999. What Has Happened to the US Labor Movement? Union Decline and Renewal. *Annual Review of Sociology* 25: 95–119.

Clymer, Adam. 1978. Ethnic Groups Split on Social Questions. *New York Times* (November 23): A10.

Coalition of American Public Employees (CAPE). 1975. Pamphlet. Collection 6046, Box 307, Folder 3. Kheel Center, Catherwood Library, Cornell University School of Industrial and Labor Relations, Ithaca, NY.

Cobble, Dorothy Sue. 1994. Making Postindustrial Unionism Possible. In *Restoring the Promise of American Labor Law*, ed. Sheldon Friedman, Richard W. Hurd, Rudolph A. Oswald, and Ronald L. Seeber, 285–302. Ithaca, NY: ILR Press.

Commission on the Future of Worker-Management Relations (CFWMR). 1994a. *Fact-Finding Report*. Washington, DC: U.S. GPO.

———. 1994b. *Report and Recommendations*. Washington, DC: U.S. GPO.

Congress of Industrial Organizations (CIO). 1955. CIO and Congress. Collection 6026, Box 42, Folder 2. Kheel Center, Catherwood Library, Cornell University School of Industrial and Labor Relations, Ithaca, NY.

———. 2015. *Records of the Congress of Industrial Organizations.* Collection No. ACUA 001. Catholic University of America, American Catholic History Research Center and University Archives.

Cosmopolitan Shipping Company, Inc., and National Marine Engineers' Beneficial Association, Local No. 33. 1937. NLRB Case #00-R-00117: 759–766.

Cowie, Jefferson R. 2001. *Capital Moves: RCA's Seventy-Year Quest for Cheap Labor.* New York: New Press.

———. 2010. *Stayin' Alive: The 1970s and the Last Days of the Working Class.* New York: New Press.

———. 2011. Beyond Ohio: Why Public Sector Unions Need to Show Solidarity for Private Sector Workers. *New Republic* (November 8, 2011). http://www.newrepublic.com/article/97160/ohio-referendum-unions-public-sb-5.

Cramer-Walsh, Katherine. 2012. Putting Inequality in Its Place: Rural Consciousness and the Power of Perspective. *American Political Science Review* 106 (3): 517–532.

Dark, Taylor E. 1999. *The Unions and the Democrats: An Enduring Alliance.* Ithaca, NY: ILR Press.

Delaney, John, Marick F. Masters, and Susan Schwochau. 1988. Unionism and Voter Turnout. *Journal of Labor Research* 9 (3): 221–236.

———. 1990. Union Membership and Voting for COPE-Endorsed Candidates. *Industrial and Labor Relations Review* 43 (5): 621–635.

Dembart. Lee. 1976. Municipal Unions Once Were Strong, but Now Feel Under Attack. *New York Times* (June 27): 127.

DiSalvo, Daniel. 2015. *Government Against Itself: Public Union Power and Its Consequences.* Oxford: Oxford University Press.

Donoian, Harry A. 1967. The AFGE and the AFSCME: Labor's Hope for the Future? *Labor Law Journal* 18 (12): 727–738.

Eaton, William Edward. 1975. *The American Federation of Teachers, 1916–1961.* Carbondale: Southern Illinois University Press.

Estlund, Cynthia L. 2002. The Ossification of American Labor Law. *Columbia Law Review* 102 (6) (10): 1527–1612.

Farber, Henry S. 2005. Union Membership in the United States: The Divergence Between the Public and Private Sectors. Working Paper #503. Princeton University Industrial Relations Section.

Farber, Henry S., and Bruce Western. 2002. Ronald Reagan and the Politics of Declining Union Organization. *British Journal of Industrial Relations* 40 (3): 385–401.

Farhang, Sean, and Ira Katznelson. 2005. The Southern Imposition: Congress and Labor in the New Deal and Fair Deal. *Studies in American Political Development* 19 (1) (Spring): 1–30.

Farnham, David, Annie Hondeghem, and Sylvia Horton. 2005. *Staff Participation and Public Management Reform: Some International Comparisons.* New York: Palgrave Macmillan.

Farrell, Michael, and G. F. Marcil. 2008. Collective Bargaining in Canada. *Journal of Collective Bargaining in the Academy* 3 (0): article 47. http://thekeep.eiu.edu/jcba/vol0/iss3/47.

Federal Union Policy Told. 1937. *Los Angeles Times* (September 6): 1.

Fischl, Richard Michael. 2011. "Running the Government Like a Business": Wisconsin and the Assault on Workplace Democracy. *Yale Law Journal, Online.* https://www.yalelawjournal.org/forum/running-the-government-like-a-business-wisconsin-and-the-assault-on-workplace-democracy.

Flint, Jerry. 1978. Union Leader in Tax Debate. *New York Times* (July 3): 7.
———. 1980. Public Employees Face Problem with Tax Revolt. *New York Times* (June 26): A9.
Flynn, Joan. 2000. A Quiet Revolution at the Labor Board: The Transformation of the NLRB, 1935–2000. *Ohio State Law Journal* 61: 1361–1456.
Flynn, Mark J. 1975. *Public Work, Public Workers*. Washington, DC: New Republic Book.
Foley, Thomas J. 1965. Senate Vote Backs Filibuster. *Los Angeles Times* (October 12): 1.
Francia, Peter L. 2010. Assessing the Labor-Democratic Party Alliance: A One-Sided Relationship? *Polity* 42 (3) (July): 293–303.
———. 2012. Do Unions Still Matter in U.S. Elections? Assessing Labor's Political Power and Significance. *Forum* 10 (1): Article 3.
Francia, Peter, and Nathan S. Bigelow. 2010. Polls and Elections: What's the Matter with the White Working Class? The Effects of Union Membership in the 2004 Presidential Election. *Presidential Studies Quarterly* 40 (1) (March): 140.
Freeman, Joshua B. 1993. Hardhats: Construction Workers, Manliness, and the 1970 Pro-War Demonstrations. *Journal of Social History* 26 (4) (Summer): 725–744.
Freeman, Richard B. 1988. Contraction and Expansion: The Divergence of Private Sector and Public Sector Unionism in the United States. *Journal of Economic Perspectives* 2 (2) (Spring): 63–88.
———. 2006. Will Labor Fare Better Under State Labor Relations Law? *58th Meeting of the Labor and Employment Relations Association Series*. http://lera.press.illinois.edu/proceedings2006/freeman.html.
———. 2010. What Do Unions Do to Voting Turnout? Working Paper. http://www.nber.org/papers/w9992.
Freeman, Richard B., and Eunice Han. 2012a. The War Against Public Sector Collective Bargaining in the US. *Journal of Industrial Relations* 54 (3): 386–408.
———. 2012b. Public Sector Unionism Without Collective Bargaining. Working Paper. http://www.people.fas.harvard.edu/~ehan/AEA_2013_Han.pdf.
Freeman, Richard B., and Casey Ichniowski, eds. 1988. *When Public Sector Workers Unionize*. Chicago: University of Chicago Press.
Freeman, Richard B., and Joel Rogers. 2007. The Promise of Progressive Federalism. In *Remaking America: Democracy and Public Policy in an Age of Inequality*, ed. Joe Soss, Jacob S. Hacker, and Suzanne Mettler, 205–227. New York: Russell Sage Foundation.
Freeman, Richard B., and Robert G. Valletta. 1988. Appendix B: The NBER Public Sector Collective Bargaining Data Set. In *When Public Sector Workers Unionize*, ed. Richard B. Freeman and Casey Ichniowski, 399–419. Chicago: University of Chicago Press.
Friedman, Sheldon, Richard W. Hurd, Rudolph A. Oswald, and Ronald L. Seeber, eds. 1994. *Restoring the Promise of American Labor Law*. Ithaca, NY: ILR Press.
Gallup Organization. 1961. Gallup Poll. June 1961 [survey question]. USGALLUP.61-647.R005A. Gallup Organization [producer]. Cornell University, Ithaca, NY: Roper Center for Public Opinion Research, iPOLL [distributor].
———. 1977. Gallup Poll. May 1977 [survey question]. USGALLUP.976.Q005. Gallup Organization [producer]. Cornell University, Ithaca, NY: Roper Center for Public Opinion Research, iPOLL [distributor].
Garcia v. San Antonio Metropolitan Transit Authority. 469 U.S. 528 (1985).
Gladden, E. N. 1967. *Civil Services of the United Kingdom, 1855–1970*. New York: A. M. Kelley.

Godard, John. 2003. Do Labor Laws Matter? The Density Decline and Convergence Thesis Revisited. *Industrial Relations: A Journal of Economy and Society* 42 (3): 458–492.

Gompers, Samuel. 1920. Boston Police and the A.F. of L. *American Federationist* 27 (2) (February): 134–137.

Goulden, Joseph C. 1982. *Jerry Wurf: Labor's Last Angry Man*. New York: Atheneum.

Governed by Our Servants. 1928. *Wall Street Journal* (August 1): 1.

Greenhouse, Steven. 2010. Most U.S. Union Members Are Working for the Government, New Data Shows. *New York Times* (January 22): B1.

———. 2013. At Labor Group, a Sense of a Broader Movement. *New York Times* (September 14): B3.

———. 2014a. Wisconsin's Legacy for Unions. *New York Times* (February 23): BU1.

———. 2014b. Labor Leaders See Focus on Wages as Key to Union and Democratic Victories. *New York Times* (February 20): A11.

———. 2017. The Unions That Like Trump. *New York Times* (April 8): SR5.

Greenstone, J. David. 1969. *Labor in American Politics*. New York: Vintage Books.

Gross, James A. 1994. The Demise of the National Labor Policy: A Question of Social Justice. In *Restoring the Promise of American Labor Law*, ed. Sheldon Friedman, Richard W. Hurd, Rudolph A. Oswald, and Ronald L. Seeber, 45–74. Ithaca, NY: ILR Press.

———. 2003. *Broken Promise: The Subversion of U.S. Labor Relations Policy, 1947–1994*. Philadelphia: Temple University Press.

Hacker, Jacob S. 1998. The Historical Logic of National Health Insurance: Structure and Sequence in the Development of British, Canadian, and U.S. Medical Policy. *Studies in American Political Development* 12 (1): 57–130.

Hacker, Jacob S., Suzanne Mettler, and Joe Soss. 2007. The New Politics of Inequality: A Policy-Centered Perspective. In *Remaking America: Democracy and Public Policy in an Age of Inequality*, ed. Joe Soss, Jacob S. Hacker, and Suzanne Mettler, 3–24. New York: Russell Sage Foundation.

Hacker, Jacob S., and Paul Pierson. 2010. *Winner-Take-All Politics: How Washington Made the Rich Richer—and Turned Its Back on the Middle Class*. New York: Simon and Schuster.

Hamilton, Randy H. 1967. The New Militancy of Public Employees. *Public Affairs Report* 8 (4). Collection 6047, Box 9, Folder 44. Kheel Center, Catherwood Library, Cornell University School of Industrial and Labor Relations, Ithaca, NY.

Harris Survey. 1972. National Productivity Commission. December 1972 [survey question]. USHARRIS.021973.R2J. Louis Harris & Associates [producer]. Cornell University, Ithaca, NY: Roper Center for Public Opinion Research, iPOLL [distributor].

Hirsch, Barry, and David Macpherson. 2017. Union Membership and Coverage Database from the CPS. http://unionstats.com/.

Hower, Joseph E. 2013. Jerry Wurf, the Rise of AFSCME, and the Fate of Labor Liberalism, 1947–1981. PhD diss., Georgetown University.

Hurd, Richard W., and Joseph B. Uehlein. 1994. Patterned Responses to Organizing: Case Studies of the Union-Busting Convention [Electronic version]. In *Restoring the Promise of American Labor Law*, ed. Sheldon Friedman, Richard W. Hurd, Rudolph A. Oswald, and Ronald L. Seeber, 61–74. Ithaca, NY: ILR Press. http://digitalcommons.ilr.cornell.edu/articles/320/.

Hyatt, James C. 1977. Firms Learn Art of Keeping Unions Out: Figures Indicate They're Passing Course. *Wall Street Journal* (April 19): 3.

International Association of Chiefs of Police (IACP). 1944. Police Unions and Other Policy Organizations. International Association of Chiefs of Police. Bulletin No. 4 (September).

International Association of Firefighters (IAFF). 1933a. Editorial Comment. *International Fire Fighter* 26 (1) (January).

———. 1933b. Union Workers Prepare the Way [Political cartoon]. *International Fire Fighter* 26 (7) (July).

———. 1933c. Fifty-Third Annual Convention of American Federation of Labor. *International Fire Fighter* 26 (11) (November).

———. 1933d. A Code for Firemen Under the NRA? *International Fire Fighter* 26 (11) (November).

———. 1939. Congress Passes Law for Fire Fighters. *International Fire Fighter* 22 (8) (August): 3–14.

International Federation of Unions of Employees in Public and Civil Services (IFUEPCS). 1953. Report of the Special Conference on Trade Union and Collective Bargaining Rights of Public Employees. Collection 5582, Box 34, Folder 2. Kheel Center, Catherwood Library, Cornell University School of Industrial and Labor Relations, Ithaca, NY.

Jamieson, Dave. 2013. Union Membership Rate for U.S. Workers Tumbles to New Low. Union Membership 1948–2012 Table. *Huffington Post* (January 23). http://huff.to/10wzlbz.

Janus v. American Federation of State, County, and Municipal Employees. 2018. 585 U.S. 2018.

Jarvis, Howard (with Robert Pack). 1979. *I'm Mad as Hell: The Exclusive Story of the Tax Revolt and Its Leader*. New York: Times Books.

Johnson, Haynes, and Nick Kotz. 1972. Union Ratio of Workers Falls as Economy Rises. *Washington Post* (April 17): A1.

Johnston, Paul. 1994. *Success While Others Fail: Social Movement Unionism and the Public Workplace*. Ithaca, NY: ILR Press.

Johnston, Travis M. 2015. A Crowded Agenda: Labor Reform and Coalition Politics During the Great Society. *Studies in American Political Development* 29 (1): 89–105.

Juravich, Tom, and Peter R. Shergold. 1988. The Impact of Unions on the Voting Behavior of Their Members. *Industrial and Labor Relations Review* 41 (3) (April): 374–385.

Kahlenberg, Richard D. 2007. *Tough Liberal: Albert Shanker and the Battles over Schools, Unions, Race, and Democracy*. New York: Columbia University Press.

Katz, Ralph. 1961. Federation Wins in Teacher Vote. *New York Times* (December 17): 1.

Kaufman, Dan. 2012. How Did Wisconsin Become the Most Politically Divisive Place in America? *New York Times* (May 27): MM30.

———. 2018. The Fall of Wisconsin and the Rise of Randy Bryce. *New Yorker* (July 9).

Kearney, Richard C., and Patrice M. Mareschal. 2014. *Labor Relations in the Public Sector*. 5th ed. Boca Raton, FL: CRC Press.

Kennedy, David M. 1999. *Freedom from Fear: The American People in Depression and War, 1929–1945*. London: Oxford University Press.

Kerrissey, Jasmine, and Evan Schofer. 2013. Union Membership and Political Participation in the United States. *Social Forces* 91 (3): 895–928.

Keyserling, Leon. 1934. NLRB Series: LK's Drafts of Bills to Establish NLRB. Leon Keyserling Collection. Box 1, Folder 18. Special Collections, Georgetown University, Washington, DC.

———. 1945. Why the Wagner Act? In *The Wagner Act: After Ten Years*, ed. Louis G. Silverberg, 5–33. Washington, DC: Bureau of National Affairs.

———. 1975. *Oral History Interview with Leon H. Keyserling, Washington, D.C., May 3, May 10 and May 19, 1971.* Independence, MO: Harry S. Truman Library.

Kingdon, John W. 1984. *Agendas, Alternatives, and Public Policies.* Boston: Little, Brown.

Klare, Karl E. 1978. Judicial Deradicalization of the Wagner Act and the Origins of Modern Legal Consciousness, 1937–1941. *Minnesota Law Review* 62 (265): 265–339.

Klein, Janice A., and E. David Wanger. 1985. The Legal Setting for the Emergence of the Union Avoidance Strategy. In *Challenges and Choices Facing American Labor*, ed. Thomas A. Kochan, 75–88. Cambridge, MA: MIT Press.

Kleiner, Morris. 1994. What Will It Take?: Establishing the Economic Costs to Management of Noncompliance with the NLRA. In *Restoring the Promise of American Labor Law*, ed. Sheldon Friedman, Richard W. Hurd, Rudolph A. Oswald, and Ronald L. Seeber, 137–146. Ithaca, NY: ILR Press.

———. 2001. Intensity of Management Resistance: Understanding the Decline of Unionization in the Private Sector. *Journal of Labor Research* 22 (3): 519–540.

Korns, William. 1957. Unionization of Public Employees. *Editorial Research Reports.* Vol. 2. Washington, DC: CQ Press. http://library.cqpress.com/cqresearcher/cqresrre1957071000.

Kotz, Nick. 1977. Can Labor's Tired Leaders Deal with a Troubled Movement? *New York Times* (September 4): 146.

Labor: A Plague of Strikes. 1971. *Time* 98 (15): 22–23.

Labor: The Year of Confrontation. 1970. *Time* 95 (15): 89–90.

Labor Comes to a Crossroads. 1978. *Time* 112 (10): 38.

Labor Department. 1934. Suggested Changes to the Bill. Leon Keyserling Collection. Box 1, Folder 9. Special Collections, Georgetown University, Washington, DC.

Levy, Peter B. 1990. The New Left and Labor: The Early Years (1960–1963). *Labor History* 31 (3): 294–321.

Libman, Joan. 1976. A Lonely Struggle: Strike of San Francisco Craft Unions Fails to Win the Support of Public or Labor. *Wall Street Journal* (April 15): 34.

Lichtenstein, Nelson. 2002. *State of the Union: A Century of American Labor.* Princeton, NJ: Princeton University Press.

Ligtenberg, John. 1966. The Right of Teachers' Unions to Bargain Collectively. American Federation of Teachers. Collection 6046, Box 359, Folder 1. Kheel Center, Catherwood Library, Cornell University School of Industrial and Labor Relations, Ithaca, NY.

Lipset, Seymour Martin. 1987. Comparing Canadian and American Unions. *Society* 24 (2): 60–70.

———. 1995. Trade Union Exceptionalism: The United States and Canada. *Annals of the American Academy of Political and Social Science* 538: 115–130.

———. 1996. American Exceptionalism: A Double-Edged Sword. New York: W. W. Norton.

Lipset, Seymour Martin, and Gary Marks. 2000. *It Didn't Happen Here: Why Socialism Failed in the United States.* New York: W. W. Norton.

Lipset, Seymour Martin, and Noah M. Meltz. 2004. *The Paradox of American Unionism: Why Americans Like Unions More than Canadians Do, but Join Much Less.* Ithaca, NY: ILR Press.

Logan, John. 2002. Consultants, Lawyers, and the "Union Free" Movement in the USA Since the 1970s. *Industrial Relations Journal* 33 (3): 197–214.

———. 2006. The Union Avoidance Industry in the United States. *British Journal of Industrial Relations* 44 (4): 651–675.
Los Angeles Times. 1978. Los Angeles Times Poll: California Survey Prop 13/Governor's Race # USLAT1978-005. May 22–25. Available in the iPOLL database of the Roper Center, University of Connecticut.
Lublin, Joann S. 1981. Labor Strikes Back at Consultants That Help Firms Keep Unions Out. *Wall Street Journal* (April 2): 29.
Lucak, Paula D. 1987. One Country . . . Two Different Worlds: How the Absence of Collective Bargaining Laws Limits Public Employee Collective Bargaining Rights. Public Employee Department of the AFL-CIO (February). Collection 6046, Box 478, Folder 2, Kheel Center, Catherwood Library, Cornell University School of Industrial and Labor Relations, Ithaca, NY.
Lynn, Frank. 1979. Public Employees Seek a Better Image. *New York Times* (January 15): B2.
Malin, Martin H. 2012. The Legislative Upheaval in Public Sector Labor Law: A Search for Common Elements. *ABA Journal of Labor & Employment Law* 149 (27): 149–164.
Martin, Douglas. 1979. When the Boss Calls in This Expert, the Union May Be in Real Trouble. *Wall Street Journal* (November 19): 1.
Martin, Steve. 2011. Wisconsin Governor Scott Walker's Strategies for Taking on Public Sector Unions. *Journal of Contemporary Rhetoric* 1 (2): 63–69.
Masters, Marick F. 2004. Unions in the 2000 Election: A Strategic-Choice Perspective. *Journal of Labor Research* 25 (1): 139–182.
Maynard, Melissa, and Josh Goodman. 2011. States Mixed on Union Bargaining: Worker's Rights, Washington and Indiana Have Taken Different Tracks. *Olympian* (March 7). http://www.theolympian.com/2011/03/07/1569092/states-mixed-on-union-bargaining.html.
McAlevey, Jane. 2011. Labor's Last Stand. *The Nation* (February 16). https://www.thenation.com/article/labors-last-stand/.
McCammon, Holly J. 1990. Legal Limits on Labor Militancy: U.S. Labor Law and the Right to Strike Since the New Deal. *Social Problems* 37 (2): 206–229.
McCartin, Joseph A. 2006. Bringing the State's Workers In: Time to Rectify an Imbalanced US Labor Historiography. *Labor History* 47 (1) (02): 73–94.
———. 2008a. Turnabout Years: Public Sector Unionism and the Fiscal Crisis. In *Rightward Bound: Making American Conservative in the 1970s*, ed. Bruce J. Schulman and Julian E. Zelizer, 210–226. Cambridge, MA: Harvard University Press.
———. 2008b. "A Wagner Act for Public Employees": Labor's Deferred Dream and the Rise of Conservatism, 1970–1976. *Journal of American History* 95 (1) (06): 123–148.
———. 2009. Unexpected Convergence: Values, Assumptions, and the Right to Strike in the Public and Private Sectors, 1945–2005. *Buffalo Law Review* 57 (3): 727–767.
———. 2011a. Convenient Scapegoats: Public Workers Under Assault. *Dissent* 58 (2): 45–50.
———. 2011b. *Collision Course: Ronald Reagan, the Air Traffic Controllers, and the Strike That Changed America*. Oxford: Oxford University Press.
McGinty, Tom, and Brody Mullins. 2012. Political Spending by Unions Far Exceeds Direct Donations. *Wall Street Journal* (July 10): 1.
McIntire, Mike. 2012. Conservative Nonprofit Acts as a Stealth Business Lobbyist. *New York Times* (April 22): A1.
Mettler, Suzanne. 1998. *Dividing Citizens: Gender and Federalism in New Deal Public Policy*. Ithaca, NY: Cornell University Press.

Miller, Berkeley, and William Canak. 1988. The Passage of Public Sector Collective Bargaining Laws: Unions, Business, and Political Competition in the American States. *Political Power and Social Theory* 7: 249–292.

Milwaukee Journal Sentinel. 2011. PolitiFact Wisconsin: When It Comes to Taking Cuts in Tough Budget Times, Wisconsin State Workers "Haven't Had to Sacrifice." *Milwaukee Journal Sentinel* (February 18). http://www.politifact.com/wisconsin/statements/2011/feb/18/club-growth/group-says-wisconsin-state-workers-havent-had-sacr/.

Mobile Steamship Association (International Longshoremen and Warehousemen's Union). 1938. NLRB Case #00-R-000391: 1297–1324.

Moe, Terry M. 2011. *Special Interest: Teachers Unions and America's Public Schools.* Washington, DC: Brookings Institution Press.

Moody, Kim. 1988. *An Injury to All: The Decline of American Unionism.* New York: Verso.

Moore, Megan. 2007. The Money Behind the 2006 Marriage Amendments. *National Institute on Money in State Politics* (July 23). http://www.followthemoney.org/press/Reports/200707231.pdf.

Morris, Charles J. 2005. *The Blue Eagle at Work: Reclaiming Democratic Rights in the American Workplace.* Ithaca, NY: Cornell University Press.

Murphy, Sheila. 1988. Comparison of the Selection of Bargaining Representatives in the United States and Canada: Linden Lumber, Gissel, and the Right to Challenge Majority Status. *Comparative Labor Law Journal* 10: 65–97.

National Conference of State Legislatures (NCSL). 2017. Collective Bargaining and Labor Union Legislation Database. http://www.ncsl.org/research/labor-and-employment/collective-bargaining-legislation-database.aspx.

National Institute of Municipal Law Officers (NIMLO). 1946. *Labor Unions and Municipal Employee Law.* Washington, DC: NIMLO.

———. 1968. *Latest Developments on Labor Unions and Municipalities: Transcript of NIMLO Labor Relations Seminar.* Washington, DC: National Institute of Municipal Law Officers.

National Institute on Money in State Politics (NIMSP). 2013. Industry Influence. followthemoney.org.

National Labor Relations Act (NLRA). 1935. U.S. Code. Title 29 § 151–169.

National Labor Relations Board (NLRB). 1935. Decisions of the National Labor Relations Board, July 9, 1934–December 1934. Washington: U.S. GPO.

———. 1949. *Legislative History of the National Labor Relations Act, 1935.* Washington, DC: National Labor Relations Board.

———. 2012. *Charges and Complaints.* http://www.nlrb.gov/graphs-data/charges-and-complaints-0.

National Labor Relations Board Oral History Interviews. 1968–1975. Kheel Center, Catherwood Library, Cornell University School of Industrial and Labor Relations, Ithaca, NY.

National Labor Relations Board v. Jones & Laughlin Steel Corporation. 301 U.S. 1 (1937).

National League of Cities v. Usery. 426 U.S. 833 (1976).

National Right to Work Legal Defense Foundation (NRTLDF). 2012. National Right to Work States. http://www.nrtw.org/rtws.htm.

Naylor, Brian. 2018. Public Employee Unions Evicted from Offices as a Result of Trump's Executive Orders. *NPR* (August 7). https://n.pr/2OM5iOa.

NBC News. 2011. Wisconsin Governor Officially Cuts Collective Bargaining. *NBC News* (March 11). http://www.nbcnews.com/id/41996994/ns/politics-more_politics/t/wis-governor-officially-cuts-collective-bargaining/#.VYbSZmTBzGc.

Negronida, Peter. 1975. The Mayor with the Get-Tough Policy. *Chicago Tribune* (July 20): A2.

New York Times. 1934a. NRA Office Picketed; Placards Hit Johnson. *New York Times* (July 1): 20.

———. 1934b. Asks Curb on Johnson. *New York Times* (July 8): 17.

———. 1934c. Labor Board Rebukes Gen. Johnson, Reinstating NRA Man He Dropped. *New York Times* (August 22): 1, 2.

———. 1942a. Refuse Workers Strike in Newark. *New York Times* (October 2): 26.

———. 1942b. WLB Acts to End Strike in Newark. *New York Times* (October 7): 27.

———. 1942c. Rules WLB Covers Employees of City. *New York Times* (November 14): 16.

———. 1942d. Newark to Fight WLB. *New York Times* (November 14): 20.

———. 1942e. Mayor Challenges WLB's Jurisdiction. *New York Times* (November 20): 25.

———. 1942f. Article 14 [no title]. *New York Times* (November 23): 25.

———. 1942g. Bars Strike Right to Civil Servants. *New York Times* (December 5): 17.

———. 1942h. 79 Cities Tell WLB They Won't Heed It. *New York Times* (December 9): 29.

———. 1942i. Mayor Censured as Ignoring WLB. *New York Times* (December 10): 1, 21.

———. 1942j. WLB Gives Reasons for Transit Ruling. *New York Times* (December 25): 21.

———. 1943. Ends Newark Labor Row. *New York Times* (February 5): 11.

———. 1976. Massachusetts Strike. *New York Times* (June 23): 38.

———. 1981. Will the Air War End Labor War? *New York Times* (August 9): E20.

Nixon Poll. 1972. August 1972 [survey question]. USORC.083172.R17. Opinion Research Corporation [producer]. Cornell University, Ithaca, NY: Roper Center for Public Opinion Research, iPOLL [distributor].

Noble, Jason, and Brianne Pfannenstiel. 2017. Here Are the 5 Key Changes in Iowa's Collective Bargaining Bill. *Des Moines Register* (February 8).

Olson, Mancur. 1968. *The Logic of Collective Action: Public Goods and the Theory of Groups*. Cambridge, MA: Harvard University Press.

Orr, Susan, and Peter L. Francia. 2012. Members as a Resource: Mobilizing the Electorate. In *Guide to Interest Groups and Lobbying in the United States*, ed. Burdett A. Loomis, Peter L. Francia, and Dara Z. Strolovitch, 179–181. Washington, DC: CQ Press, 2011. http://library.cqpress.com.proxy.library.cornell.edu/interestgroupsguide/g2iglus-1276-69688-2367042.

Padway, Joseph A. 1935. Wisconsin Labor Disputes Analysis. Wisconsin State Employees Union Records. Box 43, Folder A.F. of S.C. + M.E. Wisconsin Historical Society, Madison.

Pennsylvania State Employees Council. 1957. Governor's Executive Order: Rights of State Employees to Organize in Labor Unions. Collection 6046, Box 342, Folder 1. Kheel Center, Catherwood Library, Cornell University School of Industrial and Labor Relations, Ithaca, NY.

Petro, Sylvester. 1974. *Sovereignty and Compulsory Public-Sector Bargaining*. Winston-Salem, NC: Wake Forest University School of Law.

Phillips-Fein, Kim. 2009. *Invisible Hands: The Making of the Conservative Movement from the New Deal to Reagan*. New York: W. W. Norton.

Pierson, Paul. 2000. Increasing Returns, Path Dependence, and the Study of Politics. *American Political Science Review* 94 (2) (June): 251–267.

———. 2004. *Politics and Time*. Princeton, NJ: Princeton University Press.

Pizzolato, Nicola. 2009. Strikes in the United States Since World War II. In *The Encyclopedia of Strikes in American History*, ed. Aaron Brenner, Benjamin Day, and Immanuel Ness, 226–238. Armonk, NY: M. E. Sharpe.

Pryor, Larry, and Paul E. Steiger. 1977. AFL-CIO—a Curious Uneasiness: Union Opens L.A. Convention Today with Hopes, Fears. *Los Angeles Times* (December 8): B3.

Public Service Freedom to Negotiate Act (PSFNA). 2018. H.R. 6238, 115th Congress.

Public Service Research Council (PSRC). 1982. *Public Sector Bargaining and Strikes*. Vienna, VA: Public Service Research Council.

———. n.d. The Public Stake in Government Employee Unionism. Pamphlet. Collection 5469, Box 515, Folder 2. Kheel Center, Catherwood Library, Cornell University School of Industrial and Labor Relations, Ithaca, NY.

Public Services International. 1985. Report on Trade Union Rights in the Public Services. [Ferney-Voltaire, France]: Public Services International.

Radcliff, Benjamin. 2001. Organized Labor and Electoral Participation in American National Elections. *Journal of Labor Research* 22 (2) (Spring): 405–415.

Radcliff, Benjamin, and Patricia Davis. 2000. Labor Organization and Electoral Participation in Industrial Democracies. *American Journal of Political Science* 44 (1) (January): 132–141.

Ramspeck, Robert. 1935. Ramspeck Addresses Our Meeting. *Federal Employee* 20 (4) (April): 7–9, 31–32.

———. 1939. Rep. Ramspeck's Address. *Federal Employee* 24 (10) (October): 9–10, 22–25.

Raskin, A. H. 1975. Public-Employee Unions Are No Longer Riding High. *New York Times* (December 21): 180.

Riddell, Craig W. 1993. Unionization in Canada and the United States: A Tale of Two Countries. In *Small Differences That Matter: Labor Markets and Income Maintenance in Canada and the United States*, ed. David E. Card and Richard B. Freeman, 109–148. Chicago: University of Chicago Press.

Robertson, David Brian. 2012. *Federalism and the Making of America*. New York: Routledge.

———. 2013. American Federalism as a Political Weapon. In *New Directions in American Politics*, ed. Raymond J. La Raja, 19–40. New York: Routledge.

———. 2014. Federalism and American Political Development. In *Oxford Handbook on American Political Development*, ed. Robert Lieberman, Suzanne Mettler, and Richard Valelly. Oxford: Oxford University Press. Oxford Handbooks Online. www.oxfordhandbooks.com.

Rodriguez, Barbara, and Linley Sanders. 2017. Iowa Republicans Pass Bill Opponents Say Will Gut Public Unions. *Chicago Tribune* (February 16): 1.

Rogers, Joel. 1990. Divide and Conquer: Further Reflections on the Distinctive Character of American Labor Law. *Wisconsin Law Review* 1: 1–147.

Rose, Joseph B., and Gary N. Chaison. 1985. The State of the Unions: United States and Canada. *Journal of Labor Research* 6 (1) (Winter): 97–111.

Rosenfarb, Joseph. 1940. *The National Labor Policy and How It Works*. New York: Harper.

Rosenfeld, Jake. 2014. *What Unions No Longer Do*. Cambridge, MA: Harvard University Press.

Rowell, Alex, and David Madland. 2016. Republican Anti-Union Efforts Made a Difference on Election Day. *Real Clear Policy* (December 1). http://www.realclearpolicy.com/articles/2016/12/01/republican_anti-union_efforts_made_a_difference_on_election_day.html.

Russell, Francis. 1975. *A City in Terror: 1919, the Boston Police Strike*. New York: Viking Press.

Samuelson, Robert J. 2011. Is Organized Labor Obsolete? *Washington Post* (February 28). http://www.washingtonpost.com/wp-dyn/content/article/2011/02/27/AR2011022702873.html.

Sanes, Milla, and John Schmitt. 2014. Regulation of Public Sector Collective Bargaining in the States. *Center for Economic and Policy Research* (March). http://cepr.net/documents/state-public-cb-2014-03.pdf.

Scheiber, Noam. 2017. Union Leaders Meet with Trump, Construction on Their Minds. *New York Times* (January 23): 1.

———. 2018. Trump Moves to Ease the Firing of Federal Workers. *New York Times* (May 25): 1.

Scheiber, Noam, and Kenneth P. Vogel. 2018. Behind a Key Anti-Labor Case, a Web of Conservative Donors. *New York Times* (February 25): 1.

Schickler, Eric, and Devin Caughey. 2011. Public Opinion, Organized Labor, and the Limits of New Deal Liberalism, 1936–1945. *Studies in American Political Development* 25 (2): 162–189.

Schultze, Steve. 2011. Transcript of Prank Call to Walker. *Milwaukee Journal Sentinel* (February 23). http://www.jsonline.com/blogs/news/116751499.html.

Serrin, William. 1981. A Union Chief Muses on Labor and the Controllers. *New York Times* (September 11): A12.

———. 1999. Lane Kirkland, Who Led Labor in Difficult Times, Is Dead at 77. *New York Times* (August 15): 10.

Service Employees International Union (SEIU). 2014. Fast Facts. http://www.seiu.org/a/ourunion/fast-facts.php.

Shabecoff, Philip. 1972. A.F.L.-C.I.O. Chiefs Vote Neutral Stand on Election. *New York Times* (July 20): 1.

———. 1978. Unions Also Are Split into Rich and Poor. *New York Times* (December 31): E4.

Shaffer, Robert. 2002. Where Are the Organized Public Employees? The Absence of Public Employee Unionism from U.S. History Textbooks, and Why It Matters. *Labor History* 43 (3) (08): 315–334.

Shapiro, Fred C. 1976. How Jerry Wurf Walks on Water. *New York Times* (April 11): 199.

Shefter, Martin. 1992. *Political Crisis/Fiscal Crisis: The Collapse and Revival of New York City*. New York: Columbia University Press.

Sires, Ronald V. 1953. The Repeal of the Trade Disputes and Trade Unions Act of 1927. *Industrial and Labor Relations Review* 6 (2): 227–238.

Skelton, George, and William Endicott. 1974. The Public's Servants—How Big? And How Powerful? *Los Angeles Times* (September 10): A1.

Skocpol, Theda. 1992. *Protecting Soldiers and Mothers: The Political Origins of Social Policy in the United States*. Cambridge, MA: Belknap Press, Harvard University.

Skocpol, Theda, and Alexander Hertel-Fernandez. 2016. The Koch Network and Republican Party Extremism. *Perspectives on Politics* 14 (3): 681–699.

Slater, Joseph E. 2000a. The Court Does Not Know "What a Labor Union Is": How State Structures and Judicial (Mis)Constructions Deformed Public Sector Labor Law. *Oregon Law Review* 79: 981–1032.

———. 2000b. Petting the Infamous Yellow Dog: The Seattle High School Teachers Union and the State, 1928–1931. *Seattle University Law Review* 23 (3): 485–502.

———. 2004. *Public Workers: Government Employee Unions, the Law, and the State, 1900–1962*. Ithaca, NY: ILR Press.

Sloane, Arthur A., and Fred Witney. 2007. Labor Relations. *Labor Relations*. 12th ed. Upper Saddle River, NJ: Prentice-Hall.
Sobel, Robert. 1999. *Coolidge: An American Enigma*. Washington, DC: Regnery Publishing.
Sombart, Werner. 1976. *Why Is There No Socialism in the United States?* White Plains, NY: International Arts and Sciences Press.
Sousa, David J. 1993. Organized Labor in the Electorate, 1960–1988. *Political Research Quarterly* 46 (4) (December): 741–758.
Spero, Sterling D. 1948. *Government as Employer*. New York: Remsen Press.
Spicuzza, Mary, and Clay Barbour. 2011. Capital Shocker: GOP's Quick Maneuvers Push Bill Through Senate. *Wisconsin State Journal* (March 11): A1.
Spicuzza, Mary, and Patrick Marley. 2017. Scott Walker Talks to Trump Team About National Expansion of Act 10 Labor Limits. *Milwaukee Journal Sentinel* (February 1).
State, County and Municipal Workers of America (SCMWA). 1938a. Blazing a Bright Trail. *Civil Service Standard* (July 1).
———. 1938b. A Magna Charta for City Employees. *Civil Service Standard* (May 6): 4.
———. 1938c. CIO Convention Asks Social Security for Government Aids. *Civil Service Standard* (December 12).
———. 1938d. Ask Uniform Code, Right to Organize. *Civil Service Standard* (September 22).
———. 1938e. Civil Employees Attend Rally in Thousands. *Civil Service Standard* (April 15).
———. 1939. The Officers' Report of the State, County and Municipal Workers of America, C.I.O. Delivered at the First National Convention, New York.
———. 1941. The Officers' Report of the State, County and Municipal Workers of America, C.I.O. Delivered at the Second National Convention, Lansing, MI.
———. 1943a. The Officers' Report of the State, County and Municipal Workers of America, C.I.O. Delivered at the Third National Convention, Cleveland, OH.
———. 1943b. Labor for Victory [pamphlet]. Folder 1, Section 3, Box 41, Collection 6046. Kheel Center, Catherwood Library, Cornell University School of Industrial and Labor Relations, Ithaca, NY.
———. 1946. Second Class Citizenship [cartoon]. *News of State, County and Municipal Workers* (April).
Stein, Jason, and Patrick Marley. 2013. *More than They Bargained For: Scott Walker, Unions and the Fight for Wisconsin*. Madison: University of Wisconsin Press.
Stern, Boris. 1946. A Decade of Unionism in State, County and Municipal Service. U.S. Bureau of Labor Statistics, Industrial Relations Branch. Folder 42, Box 9, Collection 6047. Kheel Center, Catherwood Library, Cornell University School of Industrial and Labor Relations, Ithaca, NY.
Story, Louise, Tiff Fehr, and Derek Watkins. 2012. United States of Subsidies. *New York Times*. http://www.nytimes.com/interactive/2012/12/01/us/government-incentives.html#home.
Streeck, Wolfgang, and Kathleen Ann Thelen. 2005. Introduction: Institutional Change in Advanced Political Economies. In *Beyond Continuity: Institutional Change in Advanced Political Economies*, ed. Wolfgang Streeck and Kathleen Ann Thelen, 1–39. Oxford: Oxford University Press.
Taft-Hartley Act. 1947. U.S. Code. Title 29 §141–197.
Tayler, George W. 1966. Letter to David L. Cole. David L. Cole Papers. Box 13, Folder 4, Collection 5588. Kheel Center, Catherwood Library, Cornell University School of Industrial and Labor Relations, Ithaca, NY.

Taylor, Don. 2016. Can Renewal Emerge from Destruction? Crisis and Opportunity in Wisconsin. *Labor Studies Journal* 40 (4): 396–418.

Time. 1979. Time/Yankelovich, Skelly & White Poll. April 1979 [survey question]. USYANK.798181.Q15A. Yankelovich, Skelly & White [producer]. Cornell University, Ithaca, NY: Roper Center for Public Opinion Research, iPOLL [distributor].

Tolchin, Martin. 1975. Union Bargaining Power and Municipal Financial Trouble in Strong Union Town. *New York Times* (June 9): 36.

Toledano, Ralph de. 1975. *Let Our Cities Burn*. New Rochelle, NY: Arlington House.

Tomlins, Christopher L. 1985. *The State and the Unions: Labor Relations, Law, and the Organized Labor Movement in America, 1880–1960*. Cambridge: Cambridge University Press.

Tope, Daniel, and David Jacobs. 2009. The Politics of Union Decline: The Contingent Determinants of Union Recognition Elections and Victories. *American Sociological Review* 74 (5): 842–864.

Trottman, Melanie. 2014. Labor Union Membership Rate Stays Steady in 2013: While Public-Sector Members Fell 1.6%, the Private-Sector Inched Up. *Wall Street Journal* (January 24). http://on.wsj.com/1dB4xvP.

Troy, Leo.1965. Trade Union Membership, 1987–1962. *National Bureau of Economic Research*. http://www.nber.org/chapters/c1707.pdf.

Trump, Donald J. 2018. State of the Union Address. Washington, DC (January 30). https://www.whitehouse.gov/briefings-statements/remarks-president-trump-state-union-address/.

Turner, Lowell, and Richard W. Hurd. 2001. Building Social Movement Unionism: The Transformation of the American Labor Movement. In *Rekindling the Movement: Labor's Quest for Relevance in the 21st Century*, ed. Lowell Turner, Harry C. Katz, and Richard W. Hurd, 9–26. Ithaca, NY: Cornell University Press.

Turpin, Dick. 1962. Report Card: Teacher Union Drive Expected. *Los Angeles Times* (January 6).

Umhoefer, Dave. 2016. For Unions in Wisconsin, A Fast and Hard Fall Since Act 10. *Milwaukee Journal Sentinel* (November 27).

A Union for Teachers. 1961. *New York Times* (December 19): 32.

Union Postal Clerk. 1934a. The NRA and Public Employees: Address of Harvey Walker. 30 (1) (January).

——. 1934b. Labor Board Reinstates Donovan, Discharged President of Government Employees. *Union Postal Clerk* 30 (9) (September).

——. 1934c. The Donovan Decision. *Union Postal Clerk* 30 (10) (October).

——. 1935. Collective Bargaining—Its Duties and Problems. *Union Postal Clerk* 31 (11) (November).

United Federal Workers of America (UFWA). 1939. Does the Post Office Recognize Trade Unions? *Federal Record* (May 3).

——. 1944. Officer's Report: Report of the Officers of the Third Constitutional Convention of the United Federal Works of America—CIO. Collection 5653, Folder 3. Kheel Center, Catherwood Library, Cornell University School of Industrial and Labor Relations, Ithaca, NY.

——. 1948. Does Discrimination Hit You on the Job?. Collection 5653, Folder 2. Kheel Center, Catherwood Library, Cornell University School of Industrial and Labor Relations, Ithaca, NY.

United Public Workers of America (UPWA). 1946a. Summary of Proceedings of the United Public Workers of America Convention, Atlantic City, NJ.
———. 1946b. SCMWA Merge to Advance Collective Bargaining Fight. *Federal Record* (February).
———. 1948. Officers' Report to the 2nd Biennial Convention, Atlantic City, NJ.
———. 1950. Officers' Report to the 1950 Biennial Convention, Chicago.
U.S. Census Bureau. 2003. No. HS-31, Nonfarm Establishments—Employees, Hours, and Earnings by Industry: 1919–2002. *Statistical Abstract of the United States, 2003.* U.S. Bureau of Labor Statistics. https://www.census.gov/statab/hist/HS-31.pdf.
———. 2012. No. HS-46, Government Employment and Payrolls: 1946–2011. *Historical Statistics on Governmental Finances and Employment, and Public Employment, Series GE, No. 1, Annual; 1993–1999.* http://www.census.gov/statab/hist/HS-46.pdf.
U.S. Civil Service Commission. 1944. Important Events Relating to the Federal Government Labor Movement. Collection 6047, Box 9, Folder 41. Kheel Center, Catherwood Library, Cornell University School of Industrial and Labor Relations, Ithaca, NY.
United States General Accounting Office (USGAO). 2002. Collective Bargaining Rights: Information on the Number of Workers With and Without Bargaining Rights. Report to Congressional Requesters, U.S. Senate. September. http://www.gao.gov/assets/240/235562.pdf.
Valletta, Rob, and Richard B. Freeman. 1988. *The NBER Public Sector Collective Bargaining Law Data Set.* Appendix B in *When Public Employees Unionize*, ed. Richard B. Freeman and Casey Ichniowski. Chicago: NBER and University of Chicago Press.
———. 2012. NBER Public Sector Collective Bargaining Law Data Set. *National Bureau of Economic Research.* http://www.nber.org/publaw/.
Verba, Sidney, Kay Lehman Schlozman, and Henry E. Brady. 1995. *Voice and Equality: Civic Voluntarism in American Politics.* Cambridge, MA: Harvard University Press.
Visser, Jelle. 2012. ICTWSS: Database on Institutional Characteristics of Trade Unions, Wage Setting, State Intervention and Social Pacts in 34 Countries Between1960 and 2007. http://www.uva-aias.net/208.
Volden, Craig. 1997. Entrusting the States with Welfare Reform. In *The New Federalism: Can the State Be Trusted*, ed. John Ferejohn and Barry R. Weingast, 65–96. Stanford, CA: Hoover Institute Press.
Warren, Dorian T. 2010. The American Labor Movement in the Age of Obama: The Challenges and Opportunities of a Racialized Political Economy. *Perspectives on Politics* 8 (3) (September): 847–860.
———. 2011. The Unsurprising Failure of Labor Law Reform and the Turn to Administrative Action. In *Reaching for a New Deal: Ambitious Governance, Economic Meltdown, and Polarized Politics in Obama's First Two Years*, ed. Theda Skocpol and Lawrence R. Jacobs, 191–229. New York: Russell Sage Foundation.
Washington Post. 1934a. Progressives Score Ouster of Unionist. *Washington Post* (June 20): 1.
———. 1934b. Board Orders Donovan Put Back on Job; Hits Johnson. *Washington Post* (August 22): 1.
Wasserman, Donald S. 2006. Collective Bargaining Rights in the Public Sector: Promises and Reality. In *Justice on the Job: Perspectives on the Erosion of Collective Bargaining in the United States*, ed. Richard N. Block, Sheldon Friedman, Michelle Kaminski, and Andy Levin, 57–86. Kalamazoo, MI: W. E. Upjohn Institute for Employment Research.

Weir, Margaret. 2005. States, Race, and the Decline of New Deal Liberalism. *Studies in American Political Development* 19 (2): 157–172.
Wellington, Harry H., and Ralph K. Winter. 1971. *The Unions and the Cities*. Washington, DC: Brookings Institute.
Wial, Howard. 1994. New Bargaining Structures for New Forms of Business Organization. In *Restoring the Promise of American Labor Law*, ed. Sheldon Friedman, Richard W. Hurd, Rudolph A. Oswald, and Ronald L. Seeber, 303–313. Ithaca, NY: ILR Press.
Wildavsky, Aaron. 1984. Federalism Means Inequality: Political Geometry, Political Sociology, and Political Culture. In *The Costs of Federalism*, ed. Robert T. Golembiewski and Aaron Wildavsky, 55–72. New Brunswick, NJ: Transaction Books.
Wisconsin State Journal. 2011. Transcript of Prank Koch-Walker Conversation. *Wisconsin State Journal* (February 11). http://host.madison.com/transcript-of-prank-koch-walker-conversation/article_531276b6-3f6a-11e0-b288-001cc4c002e0.html.
Wurf, Jerry. 1974. Association of State County and Municipal Workers, Statement of Jerry Wurf, President, in Support of a Federal Collective Bargaining Statute for Public Employees. Collection 6046, Box 341, Folder 2. Kheel Center, Catherwood Library, Cornell University School of Industrial and Labor Relations, Ithaca, NY.
Zander, Arnold S. 1934a. Letter to Senator F. Ryan Duffy. Wisconsin State Employees Union Records. Box 44, Folder Correspondence Miscellaneous 1934. Wisconsin Historical Society, Madison.
———. 1934b. Letter to Senator Robert M. LaFollette Jr. Wisconsin State Employees Union Records. Box 44, Folder Correspondence Miscellaneous 1934. Wisconsin Historical Society, Madison.
———. 1934c. Letter to Congressmen C. W. Henney. Wisconsin State Employees Union Records. Box 44, Folder Correspondence Miscellaneous 1934. Wisconsin Historical Society, Madison.
———. 1934d. Letter to J. F. Emme, Secretary Minnesota State Employees Association. Wisconsin State Employees Union Records. Box 44, Folder Correspondence Miscellaneous 1934.Wisconsin Historical Society, Madison.
Zieger, Robert H., and Gilbert J. Gall. 2002. *American Workers, American Unions*. 3rd ed. Baltimore: Johns Hopkins University Press.
Ziskind, David. 1940. *One Thousand Strikes of Government Employees*. New York: Columbia University Press.

Index

Abood v. Detroit Board of Education (1977), 137
ACLU. *See* American Civil Liberties Union
Act 10 (Wisconsin, 2011), 2–3, 65, 114, 116, 120–29, 135
Affiliation Bill, 41
AFGE. *See* American Federation of Government Employees
AFL. *See* American Federation of Labor
AFL-CIO, 14, 55, 66, 69–71, 75–76, 78–82, 102–3, 107, 112, 119, 124, 125, 142, 154n6; Executive Council, 78–82
African Americans: attitudes of, toward public unions, 87; in public sector employment, 54; public unions' support for, 80–81; in racialized labor system, 18, 48
AFSCME. *See* American Federation of State, County and Municipal Employees
AFT. *See* American Federation of Teachers
agricultural laborers, exclusion from Wagner Act, 18
air traffic controllers, 1–2, 93, 101–2, 123
Alabama, 34–35
Alaska Railway, 40
Alioto, Joseph, 92
American Civil Liberties Union (ACLU), 21–22, 26
American Federationist (magazine), 19
American Federation of Government Employees (AFGE), 25, 27, 54
American Federation of Labor (AFL), 19–20, 24, 28, 35, 40, 55, 65–66, 77–78. *See also* AFL-CIO

American Federation of State, County and Municipal Employees (AFSCME), 19, 35, 49, 54–55, 57–58, 63, 79–82, 85, 89, 100, 112, 133, 140, 153n1; Council 24, 124; District 37, 85, 89; Local 1, 124
American Federation of Teachers (AFT), 24, 34, 54, 81
American Legislative Exchange Council, 115, 122
Americans Against Union Control of Government, 86
Americans for Prosperity, 115
anticommunism, 48, 71, 78
antiwar movement, 76, 79–82, 153n1
A. Philip Randolph Institute, 81
arbitration, 75, 104, 154n2
Arizona, 118
at-will employment, 62, 98, 138
automatic dues checkoff, 11, 117–18, 122, 124, 135. *See also* "paycheck protection" legislation

Babcock, E. Claude, 27
Baer, Fred, 33–34
Baltimore, 86
Barca, Peter, 2
Baumgartner, Frank R., 32–33
Bayh, Evan, 121
Bernstein, Irving, 53
Biddle, Francis, 22
blue-collar workers, 74–75
Blunt, Matt, 134
Bolle, M. C., 130

176 Index

Bonneville Power Administration, 40
Boston police strike (1919), 19–20, 24, 37, 40, 86
Bradley Foundation, 115
Brandeis, Louis, 123
Brewster, Chris, 8
Bronfenbrenner, Kate, 61–62, 96, 98
Bryce, Randy, 119
budget relief bill. *See* Act 10 (Wisconsin, 2011)
Building and Construction Trades Council of Greater New York, 76
Building Service Employees International Union, 41
business activist movement, 100–101
Business Roundtable, 92, 100
business unionism, 70, 82
Byrd, Joseph M., 42–44

California, 85, 88, 90
Canada, 9, 98
Canak, William, 56
Cannon, Lou, 134
Carter, Jimmy, 49, 92
Caughey, Devin, 29
certification elections, 3, 62, 124, 135
Change to Win, 14, 70, 107
Christian Science Monitor (newspaper), 86
Christie, Chris, 105
CIO. *See* Congress of Industrial Organizations
Civil Rights Act, Equal Employment Opportunity Commission, 98
civil rights movement, 54, 76, 81, 153n1
civil service, 18–19, 35–36, 62, 135
Clark, Joseph F., Jr., 54
Clinton, Bill, 49, 103, 123, 128
closed shops, 48. *See also* right-to-work laws
Coalition of American Public Employees (CAPE), 82
Cold War, 71, 76
Cole, David L., 64, 78
collaborative conferencing, 117
collective bargaining rights: defined, 156n2; legal foundation of, 5–6; legislation against, 1–4, 114, 116–24; private-sector, 5–6, 20–21; public-sector, 5–6, 8, 20–21, 25, 27–28, 35–38, 57–61, 74, 114, 116–17, 120–23, 128–29, 134; state-granted, 59–61, 120, 122; variation in, 11, 59, 64, 133–34; vulnerability of, 6, 40, 133–37
Collective Bargaining Rights of Public Employees conference (1953), 130
Communism. *See* anticommunism
Condon-Wadlin Act (New York, 1947), 39
Congress of Industrial Organizations (CIO), 20, 24, 35–36, 40, 48, 55, 65–66, 78, 152n9. *See also* AFL-CIO
Connery, William, 22
conservative organizations, 115
consultants. *See* management consultants
contingent workforce, 96, 99
Coolidge, Calvin, 19–20
Cowie, Jefferson R., 79, 82, 83, 88
Cramer-Walsh, Katherine, 116
cultural factors, in private-public union relations, 76–77

Daniels, Mitch, 3, 121, 134
Davis, Joe, 89
Democratic Party: and labor reform, 50, 55, 92; union support for, 13, 31, 55, 58, 78, 82, 128; union support from, 100, 104; in Wisconsin labor controversies, 2, 58. *See also* southern Democrats
Dilworth, Richardson, 54
discrimination, workplace, 80–81
District of Columbia, 35; firefighters, 40–41
divided labor law: and inter-union relations, 65–94, 105–6; negative consequences of, 5, 11, 12, 131–37, 141, 142–43; persistence of, 101, 108–13; policy consequences of, 143–46; political activities affected by, 108–12; public and private sector labor development affected by, 66–69; Wagner Act as origin of, 5–6, 11–13, 30; and Wisconsin anti-labor legislation, 121–23, 129
domestic servants, exclusion from Wagner Act, 18
Donovan, John L., 25–27, 38

Index   177

dues. *See* automatic dues checkoff; "paycheck protection" legislation
Dunn, Aubert, 22
Durand, Robert Y., 153n11

Eastlund, Cynthia L., 51
economic crises of 1970s, 83–89
economic inequality and insecurity, 14–15
Edison, Charles, 42–43
elections, union, 97, 98, 104. *See also* certification elections
Employee Free Choice Act (EFCA), 104
employee rights, 17–18. *See also* collective bargaining rights
employers: anti-union resistance of, 61–62, 96–99, 102, 138; free speech rights of, 48, 97; public vs. private, 61–62, 75; states' empowerment of, 117
employment-at-will, 62, 98, 138
environmental protections, 119
Executive Order 49 (New York City, 1958), 56
Executive Order 10988 (U.S., 1962), 57

fact-finding, 75
Fair Labor Standards Act, 101
"fair share" fee, 136
Farber, Henry S., 59
Federal Aviation Administration, 102
federalism: effect of, on labor development/effectiveness, 8, 131, 135, 140; experimentation as feature of, 123, 134, 137, 139; general political and social effects of, 143; inequality as feature of, 134; and labor law, 11–13; lack of national-level protections as feature of, 6, 9, 11, 12, 137–38, 140–41; negative assessment of, 12; positive assessment of, 12, 32–33; public sector labor law affected by, 6, 32, 59; variation in laws as feature of, 12–13, 64, 134
federal workers, 24–25, 49, 57, 88–89, 102, 110, 135
firefighters unions, 19, 27–28, 40–41, 105
Flaxer, Abram, 152n9
floor of protection, legislative: lack of, in states and localities, 123, 129, 140–41, 143, 144; union vulnerability without, 6, 9, 11, 12, 129, 139, 140, 146; Wagner Act as, 5, 137. *See also* national-level rights and protections
Florida, 39, 112
Francia, Peter, 14, 128
Fraser, Douglas, 88
Fraternal Order of Police, 76
Freeman, Richard, 59, 134, 138

gag rule, instituted by T. Roosevelt, 24
Garcia v. San Antonio Metropolitan Transit Authority (1985), 155n4
gay marriage, 119
Gompers, Samuel, 20, 24
Government Printing Office, 23, 24
Government Union Critique (newsletter), 86
Government Union Review (journal), 86
government unions. *See* public sector unions and labor law
Great Britain, 28
Great Recession (2008), 104, 116

Hacker, Jacob, 30, 68
Han, Eunice, 134
Hard Hat Riot (1970), 76
Hatch, Orrin, 92
Herndon, Terry, 79
House Civil Service Committee, 22
House Committee on Labor, 22
House Committee on the District of Columbia, 41
Hurd, Richard W., 71

IAFF. *See* International Association of Fire Fighters
Idaho, 117
Illinois, 3, 117
Indiana, 3, 111, 114, 117, 134–35
Inland Waterways Corporation, 40
International Association of Chiefs of Police (IACP), 41
International Association of Fire Fighters (IAFF), 24, 27–28, 40–41, 106
International Fire Fighter (newsletter), 27–28, 33

International Labor Organization, 130
International Longshoremen and Warehousemen's Union, 34
Iowa, 3, 135

Jackson, Maynard, 92
Jackson, Mississippi, 41–42
Janus v. American Federation of State, County and Municipal Employees (2018), 136–37, 145
Jarvis, Howard, 85, 90
Jauch, Bob, 2
job creation, 119
Johnson, Hugh S., 25–26
Johnson, Lyndon, 49, 50
Jones, Brian D., 32–33
Juravitch, Tom, 61–62
"just cause" standard for firing employees, 62

Kennedy, David M., 65–66
Kennedy, John F., 57
Keyserling, Leon, 17–18, 22, 23
Kiess Act (1924), 24
King, Martin Luther, Jr., 58, 63, 79, 81
Kirkland, Lane, 103
Klare, Karl E., 51
Kleiner, Morris, 96, 98
Koch, David, 120
Koch brothers, 115

labor. *See* unions
Labor Coalition Clearinghouse, 82
labor law: federalism's effects on, 11–13, 64; ossification of, 50–52, 97–98, 122; union membership decline linked to, 99. *See also* divided labor law; floor of protection, legislative; labor law reform; private sector unions and labor law; public sector unions and labor law
labor law reform: absence/failure of, 8, 49–51, 96–103; business opposition to, 100–101; Democratic support of, 50, 55, 92; need for, 144–46; popular opposition to, 52; for private sector, 99; for public sector, 100–102; in states, 39, 55–61, 99

Labor Management Reporting and Disclosure Act (1959), 49
La Guardia, Fiorello, 42
Landrum-Griffin Act (1959), 49
Leader, George, 154n4
leadership, union, 70–72, 77–79, 81, 83, 126–27
Lewis, John L., 65
Lichtenstein, Nelson, 103
Ligtenberg, John, 64
Lipska, Leah, 127
Lloyd-LaFollette Act (1912), 24
Local 277 (SCMWA), 42–44

MacGregor, Clark, 78
Malin, Martin, 116
management consultants, 96–97, 98, 155n2
Mandel, Marvin, 86
March on Washington, 78, 79
Maryland, 39
Massachusetts, 86, 117
Maybury Sanatorium, Northville, Michigan, 45
McCartin, Joseph A., 87, 100, 144
McClellan, Howie, 85
McGovern, George, 78, 80, 81
Meany, George, 77–82, 102–3
mediation, 75
Mettler, Suzanne, 134
Michigan, 39, 112, 117, 139
Miller, Berkeley, 56
Miller, Mark, 2
Milwaukee Iron Workers Local 8, 119
Minnesota, 105
Minnesota State Employees Association, 21
Mississippi, 39
Missouri, 134, 139
Moe, Terry, 9–11, 13
Morris, Dick, 115–16
municipalities: opposition to public unions by, 37, 41, 92; as sites for public union organizing, 54; support for public unions by, 58

National Association of Manufacturers, 100
National Education Association (NEA), 75, 79, 82, 89

National Federation of Federal Employees, 20, 24, 25, 75–76
National Federation of Postal Clerks, 25, 28
National Industrial Recovery Act (NIRA), 25–29
National Institute of Municipal Law Officers (NIMLO), 37, 58
National Labor Board (NLB), 17, 25–27
National Labor Relations Act (1935). *See* Wagner Act (1935)
National Labor Relations Board (NLRB), 17, 34–36, 40, 42, 51, 53, 62, 96, 98, 122, 145
National Labor Relations Board v. Jones & Laughlin Steel Corporation (1937), 101
National League of Cities v. Usery (1976), 93, 101, 145, 155n4
national-level rights and protections: lack of, in federal systems, 6, 9, 11, 12, 137–38, 140–41, 143, 144; for private unions, 6, 9, 11, 12, 122; public unions' desire for, 47–48, 100–101; reinforcement of, over time, 12, 122; vulnerability of unions without, 6, 12, 42, 45–47, 59, 122, 129. *See also* floor of protection, legislative
National Public Employees Relations Act, 145
National Recovery Administration (NRA), 25–27
National Right to Work Committee, 86
NEA. *See* National Education Association
Nebraska, 117
Nelson, Gaylord, 55, 58
Nevada, 117
Newark, New Jersey, 42–44
New Deal, 18, 29, 39, 48, 53, 91, 101, 141
New Jersey, 105, 117
New Jersey Civil Service Commission, 42–43
New Left, 70–72, 76–78, 80, 93, 103
New Mexico, 114
New Politics, 142
New York, 39, 64, 89
New York City, 55, 56–57, 84–85; New York City Department of Welfare, 45
New York Times (newspaper), 86, 102
NIRA. *See* National Industrial Recovery Act
Nixon, Richard, 80, 96
NLB. *See* National Labor Board

NLRA. *See* Wagner Act (1935)
NLRB. *See* National Labor Relations Board
NRA. *See* National Recovery Administration

Obama, Barack, 49, 104, 123
Ohio, 39, 40, 112, 117, 135
Oklahoma, 116
open-pit iron-ore mines, 119
organized labor. *See* unions

patronage, political, 152n6
Pawlenty, Tim, 105
"paycheck protection" legislation, 115, 117–18, 122, 134–36. *See also* automatic dues checkoff
Pence, Mike, 135–36
Pennsylvania, 45, 112
Philadelphia, 54
Phillips-Fein, Kim, 100
Pierson, Paul, 30
police unions, 19–20, 41–42
postal workers, 23–25, 28, 44–45
private sector unions and labor law: certification elections in, 62; collective bargaining rights for, 5–6, 20–21; decline of, 83–84, 104–6, 120, 144; and economic crises of 1970s, 83–85, 88–91; employer attitudes toward, 61–62, 75; growth patterns of, 31; identities of, 73–75, 93; labor law reform in, 95–99; membership density in, 4, 31, 54–55, 67, 79–80, 119, 140, 156n1; national-level protections of, 6, 9, 11, 12, 122; organizing environment for, 96–98, 108; political activities of, 108–12; public sector overlapping with, 40, 72–73; public unions compared to, 7, 20–21, 66–94, 104–6, 108–12, 125; public unions supported by, 24, 55, 65; public unions' tensions with, 73–94, 104–6, 119–20; states and localities as venues for, 138–39; status quo attitude of, 71, 76, 79–80, 82; Wagner Act and, 5–6, 8, 17. *See also* divided labor law; unions
Professional Air Traffic Controllers Organization (PATCO), 101–2

Proposition 13 (California), 90, 91
Public Employee Labor Relations Act (1999), 114
Public Employee Paycheck Protection Act, 122
Public Employee Relations Committee (New York), 64
public sector employment: growth of, 53; public attitudes toward, 85–90
public sector unions and labor law: antagonism/fear directed at, 19–21, 24, 37–38, 47–49, 85–88, 100; Canadian, 9; certification elections in, 62; CIO and, 24, 152n9; civil service regulations and, 18–19; collective bargaining rights for, 5–6, 8, 20–21, 25, 27–28, 35–38, 57–61, 74, 114, 116–17, 120–23, 128–29, 134; and economic crises of 1970s, 83–91; employer attitudes toward, 61–62, 75; firing of employees for union activities, 1–2, 25–27, 39, 62, 92–93; growth patterns of, 5, 8, 10, 12, 61, 79–80; historical support for, 23–29; identities of, 73–75, 93, 126; informal agreements made by, 41, 44–45; institutional recognition sought by, 32, 38–47, 52, 55–56, 77; international comparisons of, 8–10, 130; labor law reform in, 100–102; legislation aimed at, 1–4, 11, 134; membership density in, 4, 7–11, 61, 67, 124–25, 132–33, 140, 156n1 (*see also* growth patterns of); missed opportunities for, 10, 29–30, 32, 47–49, 52, 92–94, 100, 126, 141; modern assault on, 1–4, 105–7, 114–29, 134–37; municipal opposition to, 37, 41–42; national-level protections sought by, 34, 47–48, 100–101; and New Left social movements, 71, 77, 81; organizing environment for, 37–39, 53–54, 57, 61–62, 109, 124–26; origins of, 23; outsider status of, 73, 75, 79–82, 93; patronage threatened by, 152n6; political activities of, 109–12; private sector overlapping with, 40, 72–73; private unions compared to, 7, 20–21, 66–94, 104–6, 108–12, 125; private unions' support for, 24, 55, 65; private unions' tensions with, 73–94, 104–6, 119–20; public attitudes toward, 88–89, 100, 102, 116; public support of, 54–55; scholarship on, 7; states and localities as venues for, 5, 6, 8, 32–47, 53–64, 108–12; strength of, 9–11; strikes as weapon of, 83–84, 87, 100, 145–46; successes for, 40, 44–45, 53–64, 83–84, 141; Taft-Hartley Act and, 49; timing and sequencing as factors in development of, 5, 10, 29–30, 52, 66–73, 93–94, 107–8, 140–42; U.S.-specific features of, 7–9, 130, 140; vulnerability of, 1–4, 15, 128–29, 133–37, 146; Wagner Act's exclusion of, 5–6, 11–13, 18–23, 29–30, 33–37, 43, 46, 53, 59, 67, 112, 141; in Wisconsin, 1–3. *See also* divided labor law; federal workers; unions
Public Service Freedom of Negotiation Act, 145–46
Public Service Research Foundation, 86
Purdum, Smith W., 44

Ramspeck, Robert, 22, 25
Rauner, Bruce, 3
Reagan, Ronald, 1–2, 93, 96, 102, 103, 123
recertification elections. *See* certification elections
reform. *See* labor law reform
Republican Party: anti-labor sentiment of, 103, 115–16, 123; single-party rule of, 135; 2010 midterm election gains by, 114–15
Reuther, Walter, 78–79
rights. *See* collective bargaining rights; employee rights
right-to-work laws, 48, 50, 98, 116, 122, 128, 137, 139
Robertson, David Brian, 32–33, 134
Roosevelt, Franklin Delano, 20–21, 26, 33–34, 39, 101
Roosevelt, Theodore, 24
Rosenfarb, Joseph, 152n7
Rosenfeld, Jake, 156n3

sanitation workers, 42–44, 63
Saunders, Lee, 106–7
Scanlon, Larry, 112
Schickler, Eric, 29

Index 181

SCMWA. *See* State, County and Municipal Workers of America
Seattle Department of Social Security, 45
Section 7(a), of National Industrial Recovery Act, 25–27, 38
Section 14(b), of Taft-Hartley Act, 48, 50
Service Employees International Union, 103
Shanker, Albert, 81
Slater, Joseph, 20, 23, 39, 41, 55–56, 67
social movements, 70–72, 76–77, 93. *See also* civil rights movement; women's movement
Sombart, Werner, 6
Sothorn, L. Harold, 27
southern Democrats, 18, 48
Spero, Sterling, 39
stagflation, 84, 87
State and Local Fiscal Assistance Act, 82
State, County and Municipal Workers of America (SCMWA), 35–37, 41, 42, 45–48
states: anti-union legislation in, 99; collective bargaining rights in, 59–61, 120, 122; labor law reform in, 39, 55–61, 99; New Deal ideology eschewed by, 39; private unions and, 138–39; public unions' political activities concentrated on, 109–12; variation in laws of, 12–13, 64, 133–34
Streeck, Wolfgang, 50
strikes: air traffic controllers, 1–2, 101–2, 123; Boston police officers, 19–20, 24, 37, 40, 86; as labor weapon, 23–24, 51, 54, 63, 72, 102, 145–46, 153n1; in 1970s, 72; opposition to public-sector, 19–21, 37, 39, 86, 145–46, 154n6; postwar strike wave, 19, 39; public unions' use of, 83–84, 87, 100; regulations against, 3, 40–41, 48–49, 54, 63, 87, 102, 154n6; teachers, 56
supervisors, unionization role of, 155n1
Sweeney, John, 103–4

Taft-Hartley Act (1947), 8, 48–52, 96, 137, 139, 141, 144, 155n1
taxes, as reason for antagonism toward public employees, 85, 88, 90–91
Tayler, George W., 64
teachers unions, 9–11, 56–57

Tennessee, 116
Tennessee Valley Authority (TVA), 25, 40, 45
Texas, 39
Thelen, Kathleen Ann, 50
Transit Board (Cleveland), 40
Truman, Harry, 48, 80–81
Trump, Donald, 128, 135–36
Turner, Lowell, 71

UAW. *See* United Automobile Workers
UFWA. *See* United Federal Workers of America
Uhlman, Wes, 89, 92
unfair labor practices, 61, 62, 96, 98
unions: decline of, 95–113, 128; "divide and conquer" strategy against, 65, 105, 135; federalism's influence on development of, 11–13; firing of employees for union activities, 96, 98; future of, 142–46; geographic concentration of, 6, 7, 50, 131–33, 139; incongruent development of, 66–69, 73; leadership of, 70–72, 77–79, 81, 83, 126–27; membership density in, 4, 7, 13, 95–99, 103, 106, 140, 151n4; organizing environment for, 48–49, 103–4; political backlash against, 92–94, 105; political impact of, 13–15, 31, 55, 58, 78, 82, 108–12, 128, 132, 139; private vs. public, 7, 20–21, 65–94, 104–6, 108–12, 125; public attitudes toward, 92; relevance of, 13–15; renewal attempts by, 102–4; solidarity and divisions among, 65–66, 68–94, 104–8, 119–20, 125–26, 146; weakness of, 4–9, 15, 68–69, 91, 96, 127–28, 137–39, 142, 144. *See also* private sector unions and labor law; public sector unions and labor law
United Automobile Workers (UAW), 78–79, 104
United Federal Workers of America (UFWA), 36, 44, 46–47, 80–81
United Federation of Teachers (UFT), 56, 81
United Mine Workers of America (UMWA), 104
United Public Workers of America (UPWA), 36, 44–47, 144–45
United States Conference of Mayors, 42

UPWA. *See* United Public Workers of America
U.S. Chamber of Commerce, 100
U.S. Senate, 49–50
U.S. Supreme Court, 23, 39, 51, 101, 117, 136–37, 145

Valletta, Robert G., 59
venue shopping, 32–33, 46–47
Vietnam War, 76, 78–81. *See also* antiwar movement
Villani, Ralph A., 44
Virginia, 39

Wagner, Robert F., 17–18, 21, 23, 27, 55, 56
Wagner, Robert F., Jr., 56
Wagner Act (1935), 17–30; amendments considered for, 29–30, 48, 104 (*see also* outdated provisions of); attempts to overturn, 122; and collective bargaining rights, 5; counterfactual speculation concerning, 23–29, 138; exclusion of agricultural laborers and domestic servants from, 18; exclusion of public sector employees from, 5–6, 11–13, 18–23, 29–30, 33–37, 43, 46, 53, 59, 67, 112, 141; floor of protection provided by, 137; as foundation of private labor law, 5–6, 8, 17; limitations of, 144; as model for subsequent legislation, 56, 57, 100–101, 104, 145; outdated provisions of, 95, 96, 99 (*see also* amendments considered for); precursor to, 25–27; Supreme Court and, 23, 51; Taft-Hartley Act and, 48
Walker, Scott, 1–2, 65, 105, 115, 116, 118–24, 135
War Labor Board (WLB), 40, 42–44
Warren, Dorian, 13, 99
Washington (state), 89, 114

Washington, D.C. *See* District of Columbia
We Are Wisconsin, 125
Weir, Margaret, 39
Wellington, Harry H., *The Unions and the Cities*, 86
West Virginia, 139
white-collar workers, 74–75
Whitley Committee, 28
Wildavsky, Aaron, 134
Winter, Ralph K., *The Unions and the Cities*, 86
Wisconsin: Act 10 in, 1–3, 120–24; before Act 10, 118–20; aftermath of Act 10 in, 124–29; anti-union legislation and sentiment in, 1–3, 65, 105–6, 111, 112, 114–29, 135; collective bargaining rights in, 121; pro-union legislation and sentiment in, 55, 57–58; right-to-work legislation in, 116, 128, 139; union attitudes and activities in, 119–21, 125–26; union density in, 3, 128
Wisconsin Club for Growth, 120
Wisconsin Education Association Council, 124
Wisconsin Labor Relations Act, 35
Wisconsin State Employees Association (WSEA), 19, 21, 57–58
WLB. *See* War Labor Board
women's movement, 153n1
World War II, 7, 31, 40–44, 48, 53
WSEA. *See* Wisconsin State Employees Association
Wurf, Jerry, 74, 79–82, 85–88, 93, 100, 137, 140, 146, 153n1

yellow-dog contracts, 38, 39, 75

Zander, Arnold S., 19, 21, 35, 38–39
Ziskind, David, 24, 130–31

Acknowledgments

I received crucial support at every stage from conception to completion of this book. Cornell University, Stetson University, and Saint Martin's University provided essential research grants and travel funds to facilitate my research and writing. I accessed important archival material in the Kheel Center of the Catherwood Library at Cornell University's School of Industrial and Labor Relations; the Archives of the Wisconsin State Historical Society in Madison, Wisconsin; and the Georgetown University Archives. The Horowitz Foundation for Social Policy generously funded my field research trips to Washington State, Wisconsin, and Washington, D.C.

I am so grateful to the labor leaders in Wisconsin, Washington State, and Washington, D.C., who kindly offered their time; scoured their memories to answer my long list of questions; and opened their doors and welcomed me into their union headquarters and meetings. Their experiences and insights were crucial to this project.

Numerous colleagues provided feedback at various stages of this book. Thank you to Chris Anderson, Sammy Basu, David Bateman, Richard Bensel, Seth Cotlar, Jefferson Cowie, Michael Dichio, Peter Enns, David Gutterman, Jason Hecht, Rick Hurd, Travis Johnston, Michael Jones-Correa, Andrew Kelly, Adam Seth Levine, Michael Marks, Melissa Buis Michaux, Zein Murib, Phil Rocco, Adam Sheingate, Joseph Slater, Mallory SoRelle, Chris Way, and Martha Wilfahrt for their comments, criticisms, and suggestions on this work. An earlier version of Chapter 2 appeared in *Studies in American Political Development*. I am grateful to Eric Schickler and the anonymous reviewers for helping develop this chapter. Peter Agree and Rick Valelly at the University of Pennsylvania Press have been wonderful to collaborate with, both working diligently to facilitate publication. I am indebted to the anonymous reviewers whose detailed, constructive feedback helped strengthen this work. My thanks also to David Luljak for his skillful indexing.

I am grateful to Suzanne Mettler for helping to spark my passion for studying organized labor. She proved invaluable in pushing me to stay true to my vision for this work. Her model of writing historical research with modern-day policy implications is one I have sought to emulate, and this work is a testament to her inspiration. Suzanne has been steadfast in her guidance, including connecting me with the wonderful press publishing this book. Suzanne, thank you for helping see this project through to fruition.

Richard Ellis has been my mentor and friend since my first day of college at Willamette University. Academically, Richard has been a sounding board and source of endless, invaluable advice. Richard and his wife, Juli, have been like a second family, providing friendship and support throughout this process.

My own family has been wonderful cheerleaders. Thank you to Steve, Julian, Grace, Kathleen, Pam, and my extended clan for their support. I lost my mother, Elizabeth, before beginning this process. She was my greatest source of comfort and unconditional love for my first two decades, and her imprint on my life has carried me through many challenges including this project.

Finally, when I began this research, I was just starting to know the wonderful man who would become my husband. I cannot imagine undertaking this journey without you, Casey. You are my best friend and pillar of strength. The completion of this book coincided with the birth of our daughter, Rory. As this chapter closes, and this new one begins, I feel an overwhelming sense of gratitude for the path I have traveled over the course of this project. In a few years, I look forward to showing Rory this work and telling her all about how Mom birthed a book and a baby in the span of a few months and how she and her dad made all the work worthwhile. This book is dedicated to Casey and Rory.

www.ingramcontent.com/pod-product-compliance
Lightning Source LLC
Chambersburg PA
CBHW031439160426

43195CB00010BB/787